PRAISE F~~[barcode: D0776187]~~REEDOM

"Unexpectedly wry and winning memoir... A rare book equally likely to appeal to fans of *Project Runway* and students of contemporary Middle Eastern cultural history."

—*Kirkus Reviews*

"Though her story is unique, all women can be inspired by her bravery and her perseverance. *Fashion Is Freedom* is a great testament to the power of hard work, regardless of where you come from."

—Joanna Coles, editor in chief of *Cosmopolitan*

"I was so moved with Tala's undying determination! I love that she fought back against oppression by moving from Iran to the U.S., launching her fashion line, creating super sexy styles for all, and embracing the bikini as a symbol of freedom!"

—Monica Wise, L*Space founder,
designer, and creative director

"Tala is a beautiful example of empowerment and strength. *Fashion Is Freedom* shows us not only an incredible woman on the rise, but additionally, a woman who did not allow the difficult hardships she faced on her journey to deter her from chasing her dreams and creating change in the world. I am inspired by her bravery and fearless nature."

—Jenna Ushkowitz, actress, producer,
and author of *Choosing Glee*

"When Tala Raassi received an unthinkable childhood punishment—40 lashes for wearing a miniskirt—she didn't hide in shame. She did the opposite, launching a fashion line to celebrate women's bodies. Her story is extraordinary."

—Abigail Pesta, award-winning journalist and vice president of the Overseas Press Club of America

"A truly inspiring story of perseverance and passion. Tala's honest account of the real trials and frustrations facing any fashion entrepreneur proves that hard work and an optimistic spirit pave the way to success."

—Mary Gehlhar, author of *The Fashion Designer Survival Guide* and faculty at Parsons School of Design

"Inspirational and very relevant for young entrepreneurs and creative types, providing plenty of insight into the dos and don'ts of running a small business."

—*Publishers Weekly*

"Tala can serve as an inspiration to young women everywhere for shedding a dark and difficult past to become successful in business, but the most amazing part of her story isn't her achievement. It's that in spite of what she went through as a kid and aside from the incredible things she's accomplished, she is still an incredibly kind, open person—someone from whom we can all learn."

—Josh Ellis, editor in chief of *SUCCESS* magazine

FASHION IS FREEDOM

HOW A GIRL FROM TEHRAN BROKE THE RULES TO CHANGE HER WORLD

TALA RAASSI

This publication is designed to provide accurate and authoritative information in
regard to the subject matter covered. It is sold with the understanding that the pub-
lisher is not engaged in rendering legal, accounting, or other professional service. If
legal advice or other expert assistance is required, the services of a competent professional person should be sought.—*From a Declaration of Principles Jointly Adopted by a
Committee of the American Bar Association and a Committee of Publishers and Associations*

This book is a memoir. It reflects the author's present recollections of experiences over
a period of time. Some names and characteristics have been changed, some events have
been compressed, and some dialogue has been re-created.

All brand names and product names used in this book are trademarks, registered trademarks, or trade names of their respective holders. Sourcebooks, Inc., is not associated
with any product or vendor in this book.

Published by Sourcebooks, Inc.
P.O. Box 4410, Naperville, Illinois 60567-4410
(630) 961-3900
Fax: (630) 961-2168
www.sourcebooks.com

Library of Congress Cataloging-in-Publication Data

Names: Raassi, Tala, author.
Title: Fashion is freedom : how a girl from Tehran broke the rules to change her world /
    Tala Raassi.
Description: Naperville, Illinois : Sourcebooks, [2016]
Identifiers: LCCN 2016005709 | (pbk. : alk. paper)
Subjects: LCSH: Raassi, Tala. | Fashion designers--United States--Biography.
    | Women fashion designers--United States--Biography. | Iranian
    Americans--Biography. | Iranian American women--Biography.
Classification: LCC TT505.R32 A3 2016 | DDC 746.9/2092 [B] --dc23 LC record
available at https://lccn.loc.gov/2016005709

Printed and bound in the United States of America.
VP 10 9 8 7 6 5 4 3 2 1

You taught me to walk, then showed me the courage to sprint.
To the most magnificent soul I know—this is for you, Mom.

TABLE OF CONTENTS

MY MAGICAL IRAN

CHAPTER 1

THE CRIME OF THE MINISKIRT

Should I run or should I surrender to the armed men?

I had no time to ponder the impact that question would have on the rest of my life. My adrenaline kicked in, and I made the split-second decision to bolt, with the armed men just seconds behind me. I ran with fear pulsing in my heart behind Neda, who was a few paces behind Maryam. We navigated our way around the traditional two-level house and dashed through the dark, grassy yard, past the covered pool and the neatly lined and stacked yard chairs, then made a break for it out the large white garage door that opened onto a side street.

We only managed to run half a block before Neda started banging on a neighbor's door, crying and begging for help. Was this how my life was going to end? Even though I was petrified, I was prepared to make my escape. It was my do-or-die moment. I yelled to Neda at the top of my lungs, "Keep running!"

I was sprinting through the streets of Tehran in a miniskirt and high heels, which was, in 1998—and is still today—deemed a criminal act in Iran. It would be equivalent to running across Times Square screaming, "I have a bomb." I had never been on the streets of Tehran in a miniskirt before. It was so liberating, despite the danger, to feel the crisp December air embrace my legs and arms. I felt invincible, empowered, and equal.

"Stop, or I will shoot!"

It was too late—they had caught up with us. That fleeting moment of empowerment vanished as quickly as a bolt of lightning when I saw the three men, dressed in khaki pants and long-sleeved, button-down shirts, standing only a few feet away with their long rifles aimed in our direction. We had no choice but to surrender. In that moment, I felt as though I had left my body and was watching this absurd scene from above, two girls standing in the street, with nothing to arm themselves but their high heels. It looked like a revolutionary battle scene—three armed men versus two female warriors, shining under the streetlight, fighting for gender equality. Except it wasn't a fair fight. We already knew who the victors would be.

We raised the white flag. Neda and I slowly walked toward them in silence, our heads down, defeated. Our heels clicking down the street shattered the quiet of the neighborhood in the Alborz Mountains. My lungs and feet were throbbing from my attempted getaway, but I didn't have the option of dwelling on the pain.

A large rifle was pointed at the back of my head. Had I been transported to the set of some action movie? My imagination ran wild with all the possible scenarios that could play out in the next few seconds. In a flash I saw the man shooting me point-blank in the head and had to shake away the mental images of me lying on the ground, bleeding to death, and my parents grieving over my dead body, their faces ashamed at the sight of my miniskirt. I tried to maintain my composure, but my whole body trembled in fear. I felt like all the oxygen had been sucked out of me, and I couldn't catch my breath.

The men stared at us in disgust and, muttering malicious words under their breath, directed Neda and me back to Maryam's house. One of them screamed louder and louder in my face, "Don't you have any shame? Walk faster." Then, with the butt of his rifle, he struck me so hard in the middle of my back that the button of my skirt flew off. I was launched onto the stacked white metal chairs as a bowling ball splitting the pins, fierce and chaotic. He demanded that I stand up. I struggled to rise, like a newborn fawn with wobbly legs. As I made it onto my feet, I looked at Neda in a state of shock. She was shaking, and beads of sweat streamed down her terrified face.

He ordered us to follow him inside the house. I garnered enough strength to walk while holding onto my skirt, so it wouldn't fall to my feet. I immediately spotted my brother, Aria, who was sitting in the living room that just moments before I had considered warm and cozy. I quietly sat down next to him. He sat stiffly, staring down at the ground, and didn't utter a word. Looking around the room, I saw fifteen boys from the party seated on the antique-looking furniture and realized they had already separated the boys from the girls. Before we could say anything, the armed men shouted at Neda and me to move to the other room. I didn't want to be separated from my brother. I wanted him to protect me!

Aria and I locked eyes. His didn't reveal anything. I looked around at my other friends for comfort, but they all shot me the same exact helpless look. Aria nodded his head indicating that I should listen to the men. I had no choice but to obey. Slowly, I walked away from the living room, shaking in my heels, still holding tightly onto my skirt. The maniacal look in the eyes of the intimidating men frightened me. I quickly turned my gaze to the ground, not wanting to make eye contact with any of them.

In the other room, Maryam's bedroom, it was piercingly silent. This was the same room I had been in just an hour earlier, where my girlfriends and I had happily chatted and taken off our *hijabs* (head-scarves) and *manteaus* (long coats), revealing our party attire. But as I looked around the room at that moment, all of the girls were pale with fear. Most of them sat in groups on the cream-carpeted floor; a few others huddled on the bed.

The door of Maryam's closet was wide open, and her clothes had been yanked off the hangers and scattered all over the floor. I noticed that the girls had already attempted to cover themselves with her clothing. Her *Beverly Hills, 90210* posters had been torn off the walls and ripped into shreds. Pieces of Tori Spelling's detached eyes stared up at me.

The only spot left in the room was next to the door. I knelt on my lower legs, with my feet under my buttocks. I pulled down my skirt as far as possible when I sat down, but it was too short. My thighs showed. The men stared at me as I awkwardly attempt to cover myself, and one shouted, "It's too late to cover yourself! What kind of a woman dresses like this? You are a disgrace." I was undeni-ably humiliated by his repugnance toward me. I wanted to hide my skin as much as I could.

I should've listened to Maman. Her motherly intuition knew that something wasn't right, and she had pleaded with me earlier that day to stay home with the family. My parents had grounded me a few weeks earlier for drinking alcohol and attending a coed party. But this was my sixteenth birthday! I wanted to be with my friends. I hadn't seen them since being grounded. After much insisting, I was granted permission to attend the party, but only if my brother accompanied me. I'd left my house eagerly that evening, donned all in black, wearing a miniskirt with a formfitting T-shirt and round-toed high heels—such a simple, unexceptional outfit.

How ironic that on our way to the party that night, my friends, brother, and I had joked about what we would do if the Komiteh, an armed Islamic Revolutionary group, raided the party. Neda said she would run away, to which her boyfriend replied, "In those heels, I don't think you would get too far!"

She quickly replied, "I guess you will have to bribe them, because these heels are staying on." Aria and I just sat there without a worry in the world and laughed at the couple poking fun at each other. We grew up seeing and hearing these kinds of stories all the time. But you never think bad things could happen to you. They're just sad stories from other people's lives, until they become your own devastating destiny.

Bribing government officials was a common occurrence in Iran; the Komiteh routinely busted parties and took payoffs from citizens who wanted to stay out of trouble. This was the norm. But the men who busted our party weren't the Komiteh—they were the Basij. The Basij organization was created by Ayatollah Khomeini to fight in the Iran-Iraq War that followed the 1979 Revolution. It is a volunteer paramilitary force of young men and women who participate in exchange for governmental benefits, although the participation of many members is often forced.

After the Iran-Iraq War, the Basij began to take charge of internal security and the enforcement of the Islamic Republic's newly established laws, which took away many of the Iranian people's freedoms. The Basijis consider themselves defenders of Islam and believe they have been given permission by God to punish those who commit sins. But which God gave them this authorization?

The God I believe in doesn't punish the innocent. Most Iranians I know don't even consider this group to be Iranian because of the cruel and inhumane acts they have been known to commit against their fellow countrymen and women.

The Basijis started searching Maryam's house for alcohol, drugs, posters, musical instruments, and any other items that they deemed illegal. They didn't find any drugs or alcohol. The only items they found were foreign VHS tapes, satellite TV, Mariah Carey and Ace of Base cassette tapes, and *90210* posters.

While the men searched the house like dogs on a hunt, they caught some of the girls trying to call their parents and confiscated everyone's cell phones. Next they searched our bags. I carried my favorite little black leather purse that was made in my father's factory. Opening the small zipper on the side, they found my pocket-size Quran. Maman always taught me to carry a Quran; she said it would keep me safe. The government official shoved it in my face and hissed, "Do you even know the meaning of the Quran, being dressed this way?" In his mind, it wasn't possible for me to have faith if I "defiantly" wore a miniskirt. He poked me in the head with his pen and said, "You are a sinner, and you will go to hell for your sins." In that moment, my fear grew. No one had ever looked at me with such repulsion before. How could a man be so disgusted by the sight of me? I felt so incredibly dirty and small.

After waiting in silence and uncertainty for at least twenty minutes, we heard our parents outside the window. Some were panicked, but others were calm. We heard them apologizing and reassuring the Basijis: "We are very sorry." "This will never happen again." "We will punish the children, don't worry." The usual things.

I exchanged a confident smile with Neda; our parents had

arrived on this unexpected battlefield, and victory was surely ours. We were so thrilled to hear their voices, knowing that they were there to save us and we could finally go home. However, as we listened through the windows, we began to hear arguing back and forth. It slowly became more and more apparent that the Basijis were not going to compromise. Our parents tried to pay them off. But the religious police ordered us to exit the house and board two separate buses—one for the girls and the other for the boys.

Two guards stood like watchdogs in the doorway facing the corridor. I was reluctant to stand up, only to have them stare at my legs and judge me, so I quickly grabbed a pair of pants while they were distracted and pulled them on. I found my scarf and tugged it down over my eyebrows and up over my chin. I wanted to cover myself as much as possible. Other girls wore sports socks pulled up to their knees with high-heeled shoes or put on pants under their skirts. Looking disastrously mismatched, we exited the room. Despite my state of panic, a part of me realized how ludicrous the entire situation was.

A Basiji told me to put my hand next to Neda's, and he slapped a pair of handcuffs on us. He tightened the metal teeth around my wrist, and they pinched my skin, but I was too scared to complain. Neda and I glanced at each other, alarmed and degraded, and quickly looked down as we made our way out of the house. I had never seen handcuffs in real life before, only in movies. It never crossed my mind that one day I was going to be wearing them.

Two government buses awaited us in the narrow alley outside Maryam's house. They were white and army green—the colors of the religious police uniforms. Seeing my male friends loading into the bus wearing the same outfits they had attended the party in reminded me just how little freedom women had. By law, Iranian men were much less restricted than women in their dress code, but they still didn't have free rein to wear whatever they pleased. Men were allowed to wear short-sleeved shirts, but not shorts, and name-brand T-shirts, but not ones with slogans on them. Ponytails and certain beard styles were also forbidden. The guys at the party were all dressed like any young, trendy European man—jeans, button-down shirts or sweaters, and nice shoes. Some of them had even illegally styled their hair and had funky beards. They definitely didn't adhere to the official list of approved "non-Western" styles. But nevertheless, the Basijis were going easier on the boys. As humans, we weren't being treated equally.

I passed by my parents as they continued to apologize and beg the officials to let us go. My friends and I were much calmer by this point than our families, so we quietly filed into the bus. I tried to catch my parents' eyes, but they were busy arguing for our release. No matter how much they tried, the Basijis had already made up their minds. We would be taken away.

Through the bus window, I saw angry mothers being held back by the guards. In the distance, some of Maryam's neighbors and their children stood outside their homes watching us, while others peeked through their windows to find out what the ruckus was about. As the buses pulled out of Maryam's sheltered street, about seven other vehicles filled with our parents trailed us. It was comforting to know that they were only a car length away. It gave us a glimmer of hope and turned our fear to anger; in a way, we felt safe enough to get angry about what was happening to us.

Girls began speculating about how we would be punished. I tried to block out the horrific stories I'd heard about people who'd been taken away by the Basij and raped, lashed, and tortured. Hoda confidently reassured us that her parents would bribe the officials and we would all be released immediately. Leila disagreed and said that only those of us whose parents were present to bribe the officials would be freed. Either way, we all agreed that this would be over in no more than a couple of hours, and we were already thinking about how we would boast about our arrest at school the next day. So many of our friends had been busted and let go on the spot, or sometimes even arrested and taken to jail, and whenever a situation like that arose, they would become the center of attention. Now that we were experiencing it firsthand, we felt like we were in the trenches with the enemy.

The two Basijis sitting in the front of the bus kept a close eye on us the entire ride. They turned around and glared at us every so often, to make sure we knew who was in charge. They chatted amongst themselves, probably saying things about how we were disgraces to Iran. The bus ride was very noisy, and it almost felt like we were going on a normal school field trip. But our paranoia and fear of the unknown hovered thickly above us. I couldn't help thinking that this was a field trip to hell.

The bus finally passed through a large army-green door and stopped near a relatively small brick building, about two levels tall. The sign said "Vozara Prison." All noise in the bus came to a sudden halt. I couldn't believe where we were.

They ordered us to get off the bus, stand in line next to the girl we were handcuffed to, and stay still. My teeth started to chatter, and I suddenly noticed how cold the rest of my body had become. I looked at Neda and said, "At least I know we are stuck together." As uncomfortable as it was to be handcuffed, it was reassuring to have my best friend next to me. Neda grabbed my hand and squeezed it firmly. I squeezed hers back.

It was already past midnight. The dark yard was semi-lit by lights shining from outside the building. Throngs of people of all ages sat and stood everywhere in the vast open space, amongst the government buses and cars. I couldn't hear myself think as a cacophony of sounds echoed around me—people cried, laughed, and argued. Some cursed the government and the supreme leader, shouting *"Marg bar Khamenei"* ("Death to Khamenei"), which was very common to hear among antigovernment protesters.

Peripherally, I could see Aria and some of the guys with their hands behind their heads, sitting along the side of the brick building. They looked more distraught than scared. Over the sounds of cars honking and zooming past the prison, I could hear some of the parents arguing with the guards. They were trying to access the building, but the door closed with a giant clank in their faces, and they were banned from entering.

The government officials ordered us to file into the building. Inside, the walls and floors were stark white. We walked through the glass doors, which slammed loudly behind us, leaving the ounce of hope I had left on the other side. Before we had time to process where we were headed, the guards told us to walk down a dimly lit white-spiraled staircase. The narrow staircase seemed endless—round and round we went. I don't know how many floors we descended, but the facility was shockingly deep.

When we finally reached the bottom of the stairs, I looked around curiously. Only two wooden desks and a cluster of black plastic chairs filled the empty space. Photos of President Mohammad Khatami and some of his associates, whom I didn't recognize, lined the wall. The men looked like carbon copies of the president. Arabic writing that must have been a *surah* (chapter) from the Holy Quran covered the vacant spaces of the walls.

We were told to get into groups of four, find a spot on the dank concrete floor, and sit down. I settled uneasily next to three of my closest friends. When you are with people you love, it makes you feel safe from the things that scare you the most. Now we were in the bowels of this infamous prison, at the bottom of a terrible pit, and I had never felt more removed from my family and the reality where I belonged.

Women dressed in black *chadors*, traditional cloaks that covered them from head to toe, handed us three-page stapled questionnaires to fill out. We were surprised that they wanted not only our full names, but our nicknames as well. We tried to explain to the officials that we didn't have any nicknames. I guess they assumed we were prostitutes from the way we were dressed. They insisted that we write one down.

I came up with "Tala Bala." *Bala* in Farsi refers to someone who is loud, funny, and flirty. My father used to call me that, but I quickly realized that it wasn't the best exercise of judgment on my part to use it here. Irate-looking government officials stared down at me as I huddled on a cold prison floor in Tehran. This was serious. They viewed me as a sinner, a criminal, and an infidel.

Another section of the form required us to describe how we were dressed. I wrote down the way I was dressed now, after putting on Maryam's clothing. The official didn't accept my answer and demanded that I be truthful "…or else." I knew from the severity of her voice that I had to comply.

They also asked us to write down the amount of makeup we

were wearing and the color of our nail polish. Wearing makeup and nail polish in public are both forbidden, but despite this prohibition, I used to buy the most fabulous cosmetics in Tehran's boutiques. This wasn't the first time I'd worn makeup and nail polish, but it was the first time I was questioned for it.

After completing the form, we were told to take off our belts, shoelaces, and any pieces of jewelry or clothing that could potentially be used as a weapon in jail. We were being treated like terrorists caught plotting to overthrow the government. I was so angry, and I resented the female officials. I wanted to know what made them believe that they were more faithful than we were. I was taught to trust in the power of graciousness and kindness, not acts of force and oppression. A female official directed us to follow her through a small metal-barred door. When I walked in, I wasn't scared, but I was shocked by my surroundings and taken aback by the vacant stares and ghastly silence of the women already inside. I had heard many stories of people who'd been arrested and sent to Vozara Prison. This was going to be my chance, however grim, to witness what happens in one of the most notorious prisons in Iran.

$$\infty$$

As I lay disillusioned on the soiled, bloodied bed, I questioned my faith in humanity. I had just been brutally punished by the Iranian religious police. Some say I deserved it; others say I should have been stoned to death. My crime? Attending a coed party wearing a miniskirt when I was sixteen years old.

My name is Tala Raassi; I am an Iranian American fashion designer, today living in the United States.

In a 2012 issue of *Newsweek* magazine, I was honored with the title of "One of the Most Fearless Women in the World," alongside Oprah Winfrey, Hillary Clinton, Angelina Jolie, and many other influential women.

Many fashion designers pursue their careers because of their love for rich kaleidoscopes of textures, patterns, colors, and shapes. Others, like myself, are also inspired by an event or a specific purpose that brings meaning to their designs. I seek to spread a broader message—"Fashion is Freedom." My clothing line represents much more than fashion. My provocative designs celebrate a woman's choice to wear whatever she desires without the fear of being judged or punished.

This book will take you on my unforgettable journey, from my growing up in Iran—a nation infamous for using brutal methods to maintain strict Islamic values and for eliminating any opposition to its rule—to becoming a respected swimwear designer in America, the "land of the free." I write candidly about how events in my childhood and the searing pain of failed businesses and relationships scarred me, and about what drives me now.

Some people go through life and learn to cope with difficult experiences they have faced, like acts of insensitivity and discrimination. I needed to comprehend and change them. I couldn't continue to be complacent and watch my world crumble. I needed to transform my experiences into something positive.

One life-changing tragedy has propelled me to begin an internal revolution, one that allowed me to discover my independence, strengthen my faith, fight for gender equality, and ultimately follow my dreams. It kick-started my transformational and incredible expedition that continues to this day.

My life has been one hell of a ride, and I invite you to take a seat. I hope that when this roller coaster reaches its final destination, you will be left reevaluating your life goals.

This isn't a story about my being punished for wearing a mini-skirt. This is the story of all my friends and countrywomen who walked that dark path alongside me and beat it, and of every girl in the world who is victimized by senseless acts and restrictions. This is a story of finding a voice and standing up, of using that strength to build, grow, and thrive in living color.

This is a story of becoming fearless enough to follow your dreams.

CHAPTER 2

WITH LOVE THERE IS NO FEAR

I was born in Silver Spring, Maryland, on December 17, 1982. That makes me a Sagittarius, which means I was born fearless... Thank God.

My parents had come to the United States urgently in the fall of 1982. Eight months earlier, Maman had pulled back the bedding covering Aria's little body one morning and screamed in horror at the sight of him. My three-year-old brother was lying in bed unconscious and barely breathing, his face entirely blue. My parents rushed him to the hospital. The diagnosis? He had a serious heart condition and had to undergo open-heart surgery immediately. My parents sought out a top surgeon in the United States. It wasn't easy for them to get a visa, given the strained diplomatic relations between America and Iran following the 1979 Revolution, but somehow they managed.

Maman was eight months pregnant with me when she flew to Washington, DC, which was explicitly forbidden by the airline. She hid her pregnancy by wearing loose-fitted clothing, which she had to wear anyway when she left Iran, so it didn't raise any suspicion. Aria was in bad shape, and my mother wasn't going to let an airline policy stop her from saving her child. My parents stayed in the States for as long as they could to ensure that my brother's health would be in the best condition possible. As a result of this traumatic event, I was lucky enough to be born on U.S. soil and possess an American passport. We relocated back to Iran two years later.

I grew up in a unique family. Most of my family members—men and women alike—were business owners. It wasn't common for women to work in Iran back then, let alone be entrepreneurs, but my family was open-minded. My mother's father owned one of the biggest bakery manufacturers in Tehran. He sent my aunts and uncles to colleges in Washington, DC. But Maman's wish was to open the first chocolate factory in Tehran. She studied German in school and planned to attend an artisan chocolate-making program in Germany. Of course, that dream changed after she met Baba.

Baba, just like his father, was an entrepreneur. Throughout the years, he had been involved in real estate, imports and exports, as well as manufacturing goods such as handbags, leather, and pasta. When people asked me what my parents did for a living, I never knew how to give a clear answer. There wasn't one. I mastered my answer much later in life: "I am the daughter of a bunch of crazy, risk-taking entrepreneurs."

On a pleasant spring day, Maman, her sister, and their mother were strolling around the bustling streets of Shemiran when Baba drove by in his electric-blue Ford GT convertible. He immediately spotted her. She was easy to pick out of a crowd. Her shiny, thick black hair reached the middle of her back, and her big brown eyes attracted attention. She had a perfect nose that no one believed was real. Her love for fashion was visible in the way she presented herself; she was always dressed to perfection. She was feisty and poised—even I'm taken aback by her confidence at times. Years and many life-changing experiences later, she still carries that legendary confidence wherever she goes.

My parents had met a few times before through mutual friends, but their cordial relationship changed quickly after she ran into him that day. He cracked a joke about how tall and beautiful she was. Baba had an indescribable way with words. If smooth talking were a profession, he would be its Bill Gates. They briefly exchanged pleasantries, and that certainly wouldn't be the last time. Their love story blossomed from there.

Baba courted Maman before the 1979 Revolution, so he was able to take her to the movies, discotheques, and parties. Iran was a radically different country back then from what it is today. There was freedom. Women didn't have to cover themselves. Alcohol was legal, and the culture was secular. Unfortunately, my generation didn't get to experience that same kind of environment.

After a few short months of seeing each other, Baba asked Maman to marry him. The Iranian wedding tradition is for the *khastegar*, the suitor, and his family to visit the potential bride's family and ask for her hand in marriage. The bride's family usually hosts a welcome party for the suitor and his family to get better acquainted. Maman's family hosted an intimate *khastegari*, serving fine Iranian cuisine, with only their immediate family members in attendance. In an effort to impress each other, everyone wore posh clothing and their finest jewelry. Appearance was everything in a society where every single detail was noted and analyzed—down to what color nail polish the women chose to wear.

In the Iranian culture, the potential groom and bride's families come together to talk about why their children are best suited for each other. Typically, "good" families pursue "good" families. To put it more bluntly, it all depends on how wealthy the families are. If the woman and her family accept the proposal, the parties jointly agree on an engagement date. I can't even begin to imagine my engagement happening this way. Today, I would go to my parents and say, "I love this guy. We are getting married. Help me plan. Thank you!" No negotiation necessary!

Maman's father, however, attempted to put a stop to her engagement; he wanted her to attend the German artisan chocolate-making program, and he especially wanted her to get an education. It was such a rarity for a father to not only allow, but actually encourage, his daughter to pursue her career goals versus a husband. It didn't help that Baba had a reputation for being a "player" around town. What did it take for my grandfather to finally bless their marriage? Maman's relentless persistence, a solid quality that I inherited from her.

After their wedding, Maman and Baba started their lives in Shemiran, a wealthy northern suburb of Tehran that's probably comparable to Beverly Hills. This mysterious place has charmed Iranians for generations. Narrow roads and back alleys weave through the natural beauty of the village. Regal palace complexes and villas built by shahs adorn the mountain range, and foreign ambassadors reside in lavish embassies. The warm people and the cool climate make it a welcoming place. Once you've lived in this magical suburb, you won't want to live anywhere else.

I grew up in a beautiful four-level home constructed of marble. We lived on the same street as my immediate family members on Baba's side, so I had plenty of cousins and friends to play with. Having so much family around was like having lots of moms and lots of dads. Love wasn't just coming from my parents, but from my aunts and uncles and their friends and extended family. Hugs and kisses were never-ending, but if I did something wrong I had to answer not only to my parents, but also to the entire community. The air was always filled with the delicious aromas of Persian food and the sounds of children playing around the gardens and streets.

Our backyard had a sizable swimming pool set in a luscious garden filled with *yas* (jasmine) flowers, fruit trees, and vegetables. We spent hours upon hours playing hide-and-seek around the pool, in the water, and amongst the trees. There was no shortage of places to hide in the vast property. I would veil myself beneath mulberry trees and feast on the delicious berries while waiting to be found. Aria and my cousin Payam would pull many unfair pranks on us girls. During one particularly frustrating game of hide-and-seek, they snuck back inside the house and watched TV, leaving us searching for them in the yard for hours, defeated. How rude!

The boys also thought it was funny to grab us, throw us into the pool, and jokingly try to drown us. Luckily for me, Baba had already thrown me into the pool when I was two years old to make me learn how to swim. I loved swimming so much that my family nicknamed me the "Little Mermaid."

Learning to do new things was never too frightening or complex for my parents. "What's the problem? Just do it!" Baba would always say. Many of the things I was forced to learn as a child scared the hell out of me at the beginning. But sometimes you do your best when you're scared and off balance; the mystery of the unknown keeps you on your toes. As a result, I grew up going after things that I often didn't know much about. I still face every challenge head on, and after all these years it *still scares* me, but it's better to be afraid and try something in spite of it than it is not to do it at all.

Maman was our interior decorator. She was constantly

revamping the entire house. I would flip out whenever I came home
from school and couldn't recognize my room. She would move my
furniture around, hang new curtains, switch my bed comforter, and
anything else she needed to do to change the look and theme. I wish
I could go back in time and be more grateful and appreciative of her
exceptional talent. Instead, every change meant war between us.

One time my poor mother wanted to surprise me and made
the most elegant black-and-white bedsheets and curtains for my
room. She wanted to redo my bedroom to make it more appropriate for my age. When I left for school that morning, my room was
exactly the way I liked it. When I arrived home in the afternoon,
everything had changed, and I did *not* like the alteration. Maman
and I got into a heated argument, which resulted in me destroying
my entire room. I mixed colored paint with water and splattered it
all over the walls and ceiling using a spray bottle. Maman actually
cried, and she didn't touch my room for a really long time after that.
I felt horrible for acting so insane (even though the combination of
bright, colorful paint and the black-and-white theme came out to
be quite the work of art).

Our district was a tight-knit community where regular visits
to each other's homes were the norm. It was very family-oriented,
which made me feel loved and safe. My parents wouldn't worry at
all if I played in the street with the other kids. The same groups of
students walked home from school in matching uniforms, as the
melody of the *adhan* (the Muslim call to prayer) played in the background. Aria and the boys played soccer in the street after school.
The people working in the local supermarket waved to all the familiar faces walking by.

The heavy, sweet scent of *yas* flowers swept through the air of Shemiran's streets. Gorgeous people dressed to the nines flocked from near and far to shop and dine in the ritzy neighborhood. Lush trees, bushes, and flowers lined every garden. Foreign retail chains didn't exist, since they were forbidden after the Revolution, but almost every boutique in the district was bustling and brimming with stylish, expensive goods. Montblanc pens and Cartier watches were typical storefront displays. And I would be remiss not to mention the prevalence of plastic surgery.

People always wanted to outdo each other, which was bound to happen in the upper crust of society. Almost every garage had a fancy car (or two, or three), making each home seem even more luxurious. Most had swimming pools in their backyards—the bigger the pool, the bigger the house. Your next-door neighbor bought a fancy car? The neighbor down the block bought an even fancier one. Traveling to an exotic location? Big deal. Your neighbor across the street went to an even more exotic location. Think you're going to throw a killer party? Nope, someone will have you beat. And that person would be Maman. When it came to throwing fantastic parties, no one else could compete.

Everything was like a contest growing up, and that couldn't have been more exasperating for me. I didn't want to take tennis lessons like Elaheh; or English classes like Nassim. And if I had one bad grade, I wouldn't hear the end of it. Maman would say, "Do you know that Nahid's daughter got a perfect score?" My parents always thought there was some other kid out there who would do better than I did, and that's why they wanted me to push myself harder. And because of that, I have always been on an up-and-down roller-coaster ride in search of my Iranian perfection.

Most weekends, my parents sought escape from their busy

lives in Shemiran. We had a weekend home just two hours away in Karaj—a sanctuary of greenery and fresh air. We called our garden there the Rose Garden. Rows of colorful roses in hues of pinks, reds, and whites filled the whole place, from the entrance all the way to the end of the property. I spent a great deal of time throughout my childhood in the lush surroundings of the Rose Garden.

Baba grew the most succulent fruits and crisp vegetables on the property. The cherry, wild apricot, walnut, and green cherry-plum trees gave the garden a magical, lively feel. When rich, ripe fruit fell to the ground, I always wanted to be the first to collect it. I would bring my big straw basket to the garden and gather as much as I could. (I know—cue the Disney music.)

I would regularly climb a rickety old wooden ladder up the tall walnut tree to reach the roof of a small storage room. My friends, cousins, Aria, and I would sit on the roof for hours playing games and eating fruit we had collected from the garden. The cuts and bruises we acquired in the process didn't bother us. Whenever Baba found us there, he would be furious. He always worried too much about our safety. Everyone was already scared of him to begin with, so when we heard him screaming, we would climb down the ladder and sprint back to the villa.

Inside the villa, our favorite hobby was sharing creepy stories. One rainy night, a group of us gathered around a long white-stemmed candle that Aria had snatched from the kitchen. Payam ordered us to place our fingers above the flame, hold them there for about a minute, and then touch our foreheads. He pretended to read "witchcraft" from a book and then, suddenly, he closed his eyes and monkey-like noises came out of him—"OO-OO AAA-AA OO-OO." Abruptly, he opened his eyes and, staring straight in our direction, told us to go look in the mirror. Our foreheads had black marks on them. Our fingers had been stained from the smoke rising up from the candle, but we didn't know that. Payam and Aria made us believe that the ghost in the room had marked us. Boys will be boys!

Once, Aria and Payam surprised us with the movie *The Exorcist*. They were beyond excited and set the mood just right to get our blood pumping. Lights off, candles on. Aria told us that every girl who watched the movie ended up like its main character—evilly possessed. I couldn't sleep in the dark for many years after that. And by "many years," I mean up until a year or two ago!

That was one of my first peeks into American culture: an eerie, shadowy family drama with a young girl who turned her head 360 degrees. This could possibly be why I never wanted to leave Iran—my first exposure to what it was like to live in a foreign country was absolutely traumatizing. No thanks. The girl's evil laugh still rings in my ears. My parents thought it was "cute" that I was so scared by the movie and joked about it. I'm pretty sure that if I'd grown up in the United States, I would have been taken to see a psychiatrist. I had problems sleeping alone in the dark for a *decade*. In my culture, you "deal"—you learn to get over your fears.

Watching *The Exorcist* made me see America as a dark, mysterious place where the devil walked the streets. It was nothing like the magical Iran I was so used to. All I knew of my home was safety, beauty, and love. In my head, the cartoons I watched were happening in Iran—Cinderella was dancing at the Rose Garden and Ariel, the Little Mermaid, was swimming in the Caspian Sea. I was living my fairy-tale life, oblivious to what was happening just minutes away from me. The devil didn't walk the streets of Iran—or did he?

CHAPTER 3

THEATER OF WAR

Even though I had an amazing childhood surrounded by beauty, culture, and the love of my family and friends, there was always a dark shadow that hung over us: the oppressive weight of the government, religious differences, and a war that left a mark on everyone's life in one way or another.

On April 1, 1979, the Shah (king) was overthrown. Ayatollah Khomeini won the popular vote by a landslide, and Iran became an Islamic Republic. The Ayatollah became Iran's spiritual and supreme leader, single-handedly changing the future of many generations to come. He implemented a new constitution reflecting his principles of Islamic government, which included extreme regulations like the dress code for women. Alcohol was banned, clubs were shut down, coed parties were forbidden, listening to Western music became illegal, and many other limitations were placed on the Iranian people. Practically overnight, we became a drastically more conservative culture.

My parents grew up experiencing a different Iran than my generation did. They grew up with freedom and the ability to experiment and grow. Before Mohammad Reza Pahlavi, the Shah of Iran, was overthrown by the Islamic Revolution, Iran was establishing itself as a modern nation. The Shah began westernizing Iran, initiating reforms that the United States and United Kingdom supported. Women made great strides in the fight for gender equality. They were discouraged from veiling and encouraged to participate in various public gatherings, attend school, and enter the workforce. The Shah granted women the right to vote in 1962. Iranian women were advancing much faster than women in other regions in the Middle East—but that progress was short-lived.

When the Islamic State won the Revolution, women lost their battle for gender equality, and their status shifted drastically. Exposing hair and skin was viewed as too Western for the Islamic Republic of Iran. Women could no longer appear in public without being covered. The government viewed the *hijab* as a way to protest the West and its ideals. Iranian women had been among the most fashionable people in the world; their style was striking and set trends across the globe. It was a travesty to take that away from them.

Wearing the *hijab* ultimately comes down to religious affiliation and, for some women, personal beliefs. There are many Muslim women who wear the veil, even when they aren't forced to, because that's how they choose to express their faith—and more power to them, I say, for standing up for what they truly believe in. I have a lot of respect for women who cover, especially those who do it of their own free will. However, after the Revolution in Iran, the veil developed into a symbol of Iranian women's limited freedom, and eventually it affected their identity as a whole. It marked the beginning of the subordination of Iranian women.

Most Iranians I know, like everyone else in the world, love to dance, listen to music, and socialize. The young generation in particular loves to party, dress fashionably, and live freely. Therefore, after the ban of alcohol and coed parties, a generation of secret rock stars was born, but only behind closed doors. People started building elaborate bars and dance floors in their homes to keep their parties private. They vary in size and location—from ski resorts and villas in distant mountainous areas of Tehran to beach houses by the Caspian Sea. The normal protocol is for girls to arrive covered, as though they are going out in public, and then take off their *hijabs* and *manteaus* once the party has started. Underneath their coverings, they wear their most fashionable party attire. These parties offer illegal alcohol and usually a variety of drugs, and the partygoers dance the night away to the top hits from around the world.

If people are caught by Iranian officials breaking these laws, they could be subject to very cruel and harsh punishments, but this young, freedom-hungry generation will always aspire for change. They will never stop conflicting with the government until it alters its laws and its cultural mentality. The more someone's freedom is limited, the more motivated he or she will be to bend or even break the rules. The danger of getting caught elicits a sort of curiosity and excitement, despite the fear of consequences.

The Islamic Republic shaped a generation that experienced a substantial overnight change from modernization to limited liberty. It resulted in a culture clash between the people and the government. It created confusion between familial, cultural, and political values; the distinctions between religious beliefs and the freshly enforced Islamic rules were ambiguous at best. The internal war of differences that the Revolution spawned continues to go on today.

Growing up in that milieu was very confusing for me. I couldn't separate our traditional cultural values from the newly created regulations. Everyone had a point of view: their very own point of view! People hated the new government, blamed the old kingdom, argued about what Islam did or did not require, and ultimately everyone was angry with someone. We were a dazed generation that was trying to find its independence, and we still are.

In addition to this cultural war, there was another war that affected the nation. In September 1980, Saddam Hussein, the leader of Iraq, formally declared war on Iran and invaded western Iran by land and air. The protracted military conflict between Iran and Iraq lasted a lengthy eight years and was the longest and bloodiest war of the twentieth century. During this period, Iran was massively disorganized from the 1979 Revolution. Hussein believed that he could easily take advantage of the turmoil in Iran and quickly conquer the regions he sought to invade.

At the war's peak, missiles bombed our neighborhood regularly. No one was safe anymore, not even those huddled in the mountains or in wealthy suburbs away from the chaos. As a very young, confused kindergartner, I never fully comprehended the severity of what was happening around me, but I sometimes still felt sad and empty. From time to time the windows shook in our house, and I heard the sounds of bombs detonating around us. The destruction was only blocks away. Shrieking screams could be heard all over the city, at all hours. The loud, horrendous sound of sirens and alarms constantly blared through the TV and radio and from the neighborhood mosques.

Some nights, my family and I sought refuge in our murky, dimly lit basement until the attacks passed. At times, there would be up to twenty people in one room. Having a crowd made it less scary, especially when Maman and my aunts would tell us stories and make up games to distract us. Whenever the lights flickered during the bombings, I would run into Maman's arms and hold on tightly.

I still played outside with my friends amid the destroyed buildings around us. One day, while I played with my Barbies and Aria played Nintendo, we suddenly heard a bomb detonate. The entire house rocked back and forth. Then the windows shattered, and pieces of glass rained down around us. Houses next to ours were hit with a round of explosions. Aria and I looked at each other, paralyzed with fear. Our parents were nowhere in sight. I thought they had died in the bombing. We heard loud screams, followed by sirens in the streets—the same loud sirens I dreaded so much. Baba finally ran into the room. The moment I saw him I began to scream and cry, and he picked me up immediately. I kicked and punched him because I was angry with him. My father was the most powerful person in my world—I was upset that he couldn't stop the mayhem.

After a while, people became desensitized to living in the middle of a war zone. Troublesome and horrifying things seemed normal—like the military checkpoints and snipers on top of buildings. The people of Iran have been through so much throughout history that chaos has come to seem ordinary. But that doesn't mean they aren't searching for ways to overcome adversity and thrive. Iranians have learned how to live and look forward to tomorrow without dwelling on yesterday's pain.

That is true even of young children in Iran, including me. I've always felt artistic from a very young age, and although I didn't realize it at the time, drawing helped me work through the effects the war had on me. When I was just five years old, I drew a picture of a little girl playing with her toys in her bedroom. The sun shined inside her bedroom through her shattered window. I drew reflections of trees onto the shattered glass on the floor. Maman framed the drawing, saying that it had a special meaning—peace during a time of war.

In 1986 my family left Tehran for the summer. The bombings around us had become more frequent, and our extended family overseas was concerned. They didn't understand how we could live in a war-torn country. Maman's side of the family had a beautiful villa in Shomal, the northern region of Iran, by the Caspian Sea. The older, three-bedroom villa had a massive garden that was a maze of colors from the diverse flowers and trees that thrived there. The area was a fun, flirtatious place, with the Caspian Sea luring people from near and far looking for a quick getaway from the urban bustle. The moist air from the sea merged with the dryness of the mountains, creating a perfect climate, one devoid of suffocating dust and broken glass. It seemed like the perfect place to escape the war.

However, the atmosphere by the sea had become significantly different since the Revolution. Gone were the days when people could sunbathe and splash around in the water in swimsuits with the opposite sex. Being with family didn't matter. Women still had to wear full Islamic attire when men were present. Walls of canvas divided the beaches—one for the men and another for the women. Or, more accurately, the entire beach was reserved for the men, leaving a small, curtained portion for the women. In these curtained areas, women could swap their *hijabs* for swimwear.

During that summer we spent by the Caspian Sea, the war was never far away. It was difficult to maintain contact with our relatives who had stayed in Tehran because all the phone lines at the villa were disconnected. Every day, Baba would wait in line for hours with hundreds of others to use a public phone to speak with his family.

One day, while Baba waited in line, he heard on the radio that bombs had gone off on our street in Shemiran. He was so afraid that he would hear the horrifying news that his family had died that he actually peed his pants. When it was finally his turn to make the phone call, he was relieved to discover they were still alive. But it turned out that the bombing had devastated an area that was only a block away from our house. Weeks later, when we returned to Tehran, we saw all the damaged homes in our neighborhood and discovered that the windows on the left side of our house had been shattered. We were lucky. Many people across the country lost their entire homes and loved ones during the war.

By July 1988, Iran was exhausted and isolated and had no choice but to finally accept a cease-fire mandated by the United Nations: UN Resolution 598. Khomeini compared his acceptance of the cease-fire to drinking a cup of poison.

The war devastated the population and economies of both countries. Ultimately, neither Iraq nor Iran achieved what they intended by entering into the war. Khomeini didn't overthrow Saddam Hussein, and Saddam Hussein didn't overthrow Khomeini or force him to redraw borders to Iraq's benefit. Despite Hussein claiming victory over Iran, in reality, he only managed to avoid defeat, and only because other countries came to his aid.

For Iran, the war inflicted a heavy human and material cost, but it also dissipated much of the enthusiasm over the new Islamic Revolution. Iranians began to question the capabilities of their clerical leadership. The Iran-Iraq War left the country in painful condition. Few modern conflicts have been as lengthy, bloody, and futile. Shortly after the war, Khomeini died, and Iran entered into a new era of recovery.

My family, just like everyone else's, was heartbroken over the war. They witnessed their beautiful country endure a massive revolution followed by a devastating war. One and a half million lives were lost, and people were left saddened and helpless.

I still remember the image of a wrecked house in our neighborhood, as though I were looking at a photo of it today, with its items scattered in the street: picture frames shattered to pieces, clothing and furniture peeking out of the dust and rocks that remained of the building. I recall squeezing Maman's hand because I was horrified. People shouldn't have to go through such misfortune. Deep scars—emotional, physical, and economic—were left in the country. In America, living inside our comfortable bubble, we get enraged by heavy traffic, our Starbucks order not being correct, rainy weather, and other trivial matters, while people all over the world are living through what I witnessed in my childhood—and worse—every single day. It's important to know that things can always be worse and to cherish every little bit of bliss that we are given.

War changes you. Civilians who shouldn't have been touched by the conflict were devastated by loss. Even more than thirty years later, the Revolution and the war still profoundly affect the younger generations of Iran. Seeing things like that as a child changed me. Today, I try not to dwell on small, petty things.

CHAPTER 4

BEHIND CLOSED DOORS

In that theater of war, I still witnessed people who were full of life and culture, people who wanted to hold on to their traditions, beliefs, and personal values. About seventy million people live in Iran, all with diverse lifestyles and outlooks. But I grew up in a modern society with few boundaries.

My parents hosted lavish parties almost every Thursday night. The guest list usually included friends, family, business partners, and ambassadors. The ambassadors made it much easier to get away with hosting parties. Police stood guard outside, so the Komiteh wouldn't interfere.

Maman would spend the whole week preparing. There was always some delicacy in the oven or on the stove that filled the house with rich aromas of herbs and spices, from *zaferan* (saffron) to fluffy, white Persian rice. She cooked an abundant variety of food, ranging from delicious appetizers, such as *mast-o-khiar* (cucumber and mint yogurt), *kashk-e-bademjan* (eggplant and walnut dip), and *salad olivieh* (potato salad), to traditional Iranian dishes like *fesenjoon* (chicken stew with pomegranate syrup and walnuts), *ghormeh sabzi* (herb stew), and *gheymeh* (beef and split-pea stew). Every intricate dish was full of zesty flavor. It was unthinkable for her to have a party without cooking the countless dishes in her repertoire. She would spend hours preparing and decorating them, to the point that you would feel guilty for even touching the food—they belonged on display in a cookbook.

My parents didn't need to hire a band. Throughout the festivities, many of their friends played instruments and sang a mix of Iranian and Western music. My favorite was the *santoor*, a stringed instrument played with a pair of wood-curved mallets, whose whimsical, hypnotic melodies always gave me joy. The beats of the *tabl* (drum) livened the party. Guests moved to the rhythms of each pulse of the hand hitting it. Iranians know how to move their bodies in ways that can be very sensual yet elegant. Think Shakira. The style is influenced by a blend of Persian traditions and belly dancing. Sometimes you can even see dashes of Western influence in the way they move.

Because music played and women took off their *hijabs* in the presence of men, to stay hidden from government officials, the parties were hosted in our large drawing room. Every curtain in the room was drawn, so no one had to worry about outsiders looking in. The room was furnished with antique furniture that my parents had collected over the years. Decadent Persian rugs and beautiful, unique artwork decorated the space. Each table was filled with perfectly ripe, in-season fruit that usually came from the Rose Garden, along with nuts and sweets from my grandfather's factory. "A guest should always have something to nibble on," Maman would say.

The drawing room was the one room in the house that was reserved for our guests, and off limits to Aria and me. My parents' friends were loud and entertaining, and there was never any shortage of jokes—many of which I wish I hadn't heard because they weren't appropriate for my young ears. They laughed for hours upon hours. I couldn't wait until the day I could join them. I would sit cross-legged on the floor and peek into the room to catch the men discussing politics and business and to watch the women dancing and gossiping. Every time I felt someone was about to look in my direction, I quickly dodged them. Often Baba would catch me and embarrass me in front of everyone. He said I was nosy, but that didn't stop me from peeping into that new, luxurious adult world.

Baba intimidated everyone who met him, but if you gave him an hour he could win over anyone with his charm and wit. Every woman fell for him. He was very manly, stylish, and charismatic. His wealth didn't hurt either. His sense of humor was dry, but in two sentences, he could make an entire room buckle with laughter. His comebacks were like nothing you had ever heard before.

I always found my father rather mysterious and felt like I couldn't truly understand him. Nothing was ever a big deal to him except his reputation. He had a straightforward attitude toward life, which included not taking people's feelings into account. Even if he knew he was in the wrong, he didn't know how to apologize, and his way of showing love and affection was to insult. Instead of saying how beautiful I was, he would jokingly tell me how ugly I looked. Don't try to understand it—it was his term of endearment. He would hug me, bite me, and pinch my cheeks until I wanted to cry from the pain. So watch out! If you tell me I'm ugly, I'll probably think you find me attractive.

People often say I have his presence. I don't see it. Or maybe I don't want to see it. Apparently, we speak the same way, we have the same mannerisms, and we are both straight shooters and natural-born leaders (or we both pretend that we are). We also walk the same way—backs straight with our feet pointing outward. Maman always told us to remember to look down, or else we would trip. This is probably the reason I'm always tripping over things.

My parents had an interesting relationship. They shared a certain love that is rare and hard to explain. It wasn't the kind of love where they held hands all the time or said "I love you" all day. It was the kind of love that spoke through action. You could tell just how much Baba admired Maman, but it was hard for him to put it in words. For her part, Maman was always surprising Baba with something. Every year for his birthday she would throw him a crazy surprise party, which would piss my father off every single time, and he wouldn't hide the fact that he hated it. She would always dress up and put on lipstick before Baba came home, dim the lights, and make sure the house was spotless. She would do things without ever speaking of them. I grew up perceiving that, and I wondered if my father ever noticed.

Maman always tried to be the perfect hostess, and I admired how welcome she made her guests feel. She was always so glamorous too. Every Thursday morning before her big soiree Maman went to the beauty salon, and as a little girl I accompanied her to watch the women, in awe of their beauty and elegance. Occasionally Maman would let me get dolled up too, but more often she gave me short mushroom haircuts that I hated. Looking like Lloyd Christmas from *Dumb and Dumber* wasn't exactly what I was hoping for.

Private women-only beauty salons were social scenes. The women shed their *hijabs*, exposing their most fashionable outfits underneath. Their makeup and hair was done to perfection, as though they were already heading to the party. They arrived hours before their appointments and stayed much longer after their hair, nails, makeup, and eyebrows were done to gossip, chain-smoke, and sip Turkish coffee.

One of the main reasons I loved going to the salon was to lose myself in their most recent international magazines about hair and fashion. The ones at my house were no longer exciting. I had already memorized all the images. I daydreamed about living in a society where women wore Saint Laurent, Chanel, Dior, and other high-end designers openly in public—right where they belonged.

These designers made their grand entrances behind closed doors in Iran. Maman's friends only revealed head-to-toe designer clothing and their most luxurious gold and diamond jewelry at house parties and hair salons. The bigger the hair and the heavier the makeup, the more compliments they received. Maman doesn't get dressed up like that anymore. I always wonder what happened to her passion for entertaining.

One woman in particular from Maman's group of friends always stood out to me because of her sex appeal. Her name was Homaira. She was a divorcée who split her time between Iran and Germany. She was different from my mother and her other friends. I found Maman beautiful, elegant, and very classy. But Homaira was sexy, energetic, and super flirty. It was like she had a certain power that she used from her appearance. She was tall and had fire-red hair, and she entered every soiree flamboyantly with a very short, form-fitting dress, exposing her long legs and curvy body. She was always outgoing and very pleasant to Maman and me—and even had us over for tea a few times.

When I was twelve years old, Maman left for two months to attend her sister's wedding in the United States. Aria and I stayed behind with Baba and Ehteram Khanoom, the maid we grew up with. We had never been without Maman for that long before!

One night, while she was still in the States, I woke up to Baba walking into my room. He delicately pulled my blanket over me to tuck me in. On his way out toward the kitchen, I heard him talking quietly on the phone. He was almost whispering. The clock struck 1:00 a.m. I assumed he was talking to Maman since there was a big time difference.

The next day, on my daily call with Maman, I asked what she and Baba had been talking about so late at night, and she said, "I wasn't talking to Baba last night, honey." Women have an inexplicable intuition. We know instantly when something doesn't feel right. Maybe Maman suppressed hers, because the discussion ended without any further questioning.

Even at a young age, I knew something didn't add up. I was curious to find out who my father was speaking to at night. The following day, I called Maman and told her, "I think you should stay in the States and never return." It was a shocking request, but I was so worried about her well-being that I didn't want her to come back and face the person on the other end of the line. I decided to play detective and find out the identity of the 1:00 a.m. caller.

Back then, neither caller ID nor address books in phones existed. But a feature on this particular white Panasonic phone allowed you to redial the last number. So the next night, when I overheard Baba on the phone again, I devised a plan. Before leaving for school the following morning, I would redial the last number that appeared on the small screen and write it down. I guess this way of thinking was why my parents believed I would make a great lawyer. I consulted Aria, who seemed disinterested in my detective work, but agreed to look through the phone book with me nonetheless.

When I anxiously returned home from school, I sprinted to the large brown leather phone book in the hallway, which rested on the antique wooden phone table. I sat on the bloodred velvet chair with the book in my lap, waiting impatiently for Aria to come home. I have no idea why I felt the need to go through every single phone number in the book, but my gut told me that I had to. I quickly flipped through page after page without blinking. As, Bs…Fs…and *bam*!

Found the match! Thank God for technology; these days, it's much easier to hunt people down. The phone number belonged to Homaira, the flirty, sexy, redheaded woman from my parents' parties. Why was Baba talking to her so late at night? When I found out he was talking to someone I knew, I felt at ease. I wanted to believe their friendship was purely by association, so I didn't ask my father any questions.

Maman finally came back home bearing many gifts. Opening marvelous gifts that came from overseas was one of the best things that ever happened in my childhood. The gifts were special because I couldn't find them in Iran back then. I sat in her bedroom and collected each present one by one, like a little kid on Christmas day. She brought back the trendiest clothing, along with other goodies from toys to candy. The collection of Barbies and their clothing, as well as all the M&M's and bubble gum I ever wanted—it was like heaven to me. As I stuffed my face with the unnecessarily large piece of bubble gum, I casually told Maman about Homaira, not knowing that I was about to destroy her entire world. Her reaction to the news was something I will never forget. The sweet taste of bubble gum quickly turned sour.

She started shaking and asked me a million questions with a quivering voice—"When did the calls take place?" and "How long did they speak for?" and "Did Homaira ever come to visit the house?" *Oh*

God! I thought, *what have I done?* I was so scared that something was wrong, and my parents weren't going to be okay.

After answering all her questions doubtfully, she grabbed the same Panasonic phone Baba had used to call Homaira and hurried out to the balcony. I knew something was really wrong when my uncle, grandfather, and grandmother all came over to the house. I was told to stay in my room and not come out.

Later that evening, from inside my room, I heard my parents and family members screaming at the top of their lungs for hours. I sat on the edge of my bed, with my feet dangling down, and just stared at the white door. I couldn't make out what they were saying, and I didn't want to. I was afraid I would hear information that would tear me apart. I thought I was responsible for Maman's pain.

When Maman finally came to my room, I could tell she had been crying. She told me to pack because we were going to stay at my grandfather's house for a while. I packed up all the new gems that Maman had brought back, along with my school stuff. On the way out, my mother didn't even glance at Baba as she exited the house with her father in tow. Baba looked at me, and I said, "Love you, Baba, see you tomorrow." I could tell he was devastated, but I wasn't fazed by it. I was on Team Maman.

I tried to block out my parents' troubles and focus my energy on how excited I was to visit my grandfather. I loved his house, and he spoiled the hell out of me since I was his only granddaughter left in Iran. His house was located in Darband, a much quieter suburb of Tehran. The word *darband* literally translates to "the door of a mountain," which makes sense since the village is built into the mountain. Its natural beauty is undeniable, and it was very popular among people seeking a change of scenery from hectic city life. It always gave me tranquility, despite what was happening around me.

I still didn't understand what was going on between my parents, but Baba visited us almost every night. He wasn't allowed inside the house because Maman didn't want to see or talk to him, so Aria and I would hang out with him in the yard or outside the house.

Yes, Baba cheated on Maman with Homaira—what a bitch! Maman didn't let my father off the hook easily, and it took many apologetic pleas to get us to return home. Although Maman eventually forgave him for the sake of their reputation, family, and children, I know she never forgot his betrayal. It aged her and completely changed her. Their relationship was also never the same. All the trust was lost. I don't know for sure whether my father stopped cheating on my mother, but I'm pretty damn sure my grandfather put an end to his affair with Homaira.

"A woman must always look her best, always please her man, always dress nicely for him no matter how long they have been together, always surprise him, and always make him wonder what's next." These were the wise words of the most inspiring woman in my life, Maman. Despite their incessant arguing, Maman made sure the house was filled with love. She was always pretending to be unbreakable. She was like a superhero to me.

What did my mother do to deserve a broken heart? She is an absolutely stunning woman, from a great family, and had so much love for her husband and children. I have come to realize that people cheat and that *anyone* could cheat under the right, or perhaps the wrong, circumstances.

Everyone deals with emotional pain differently, but it is part of my family's culture not to talk about it. My way of dealing with the pain was to project it onto Baba. He was an easy target, and the energy between him and me only got worse when we returned home and I fully understood what had happened. I never looked at him the same way again. I resented him and couldn't forget the pain that he caused Maman—the center of my world. I didn't even dare share the news with my friends because of my family's reputation.

My father and I never spoke about the affair. I think he had too much pride to explain himself. Maman didn't share her thoughts with me until I told her I was writing about it, but I'm still not sure she divulged everything. She still wants to protect Baba from me—a daughter who keeps piling on anger for what he did. Although I hope to never experience a cheating partner, I want to be the kind of woman my mother is.

My father's mistake cast a long, dark shadow across my life. When I got old enough to stop idolizing love stories, I analyzed the closest fairy tale in my life, which was my parents' love story. I was convinced that cartoons were lies and fairy tales didn't work in real life. Even though Baba cheated on Maman, he had also cheated us, his children, of trust, love, and commitment. Even now, as a strong and outgoing woman, it's been an ongoing struggle for me to trust men, and I always assume they will cheat on me.

As humans, we are challenged to trust each other. Trust pervades nearly every aspect of our daily lives from personal to business relationships. It is fundamentally important in the healthy functioning of all of our relationships with others, and our life experiences may affect the way we trust in the future. One of the people I had trusted the most in my life took that power of trust away from me, and it has been haunting me for the past twenty years.

CHAPTER 5

THE POWER OF MONEY

Our society loves to glorify billionaire entrepreneurs like Mark Cuban and Elon Musk, but in reality, there are millions of others out there who have accumulated substantial debt from their failed businesses. Entrepreneurs pay a steep price—financially and mentally—when they flop.

We learned to live with the huge elephant in the room. We ignored the pain and suffering each of us felt, until a few months later when I came home from school and found my parents troubled and uneasy. I instantly knew something was wrong again, and I would later become very familiar with their anxious faces.

Baba stroked my hair and told me everything was going to be fine, that I shouldn't worry. I had lost all trust in him, but I could still see the burden in his eyes. Later that night, I overheard Baba telling Maman that we needed to downsize. I couldn't fathom living anywhere other than the Elahieh district of Shemiran. Our entire family lived there, and I grew up in that house. I didn't want to leave my magical life for anything else.

When my father followed up his failed marriage with a failed business, I had little sympathy. But today I can understand and relate to his struggles. They played an integral part in helping me cope with building my own destiny. And he had it much worse than I did. I didn't have children, a spouse, and a family to support. You can never truly understand what someone is going through unless you experience it yourself. And once you do, you'll withdraw your prior judgment. I spent my time blaming Baba instead of trying to understand him. If I could go back in time, I would show him more empathy. One of Baba's business partners had bailed out of the country, leaving Baba to deal with the aftermath of a variety of bad business decisions that ultimately jeopardized everything he had worked for. My family's financial situation became very fragile, but I was oblivious to the extent of the damage at the time. To put it simply, my father had lost an absurd amount of money.

There was no way to blame anyone else for our family's financial demise. Not only did my father choose to put us in commercially risky situations, he also spent money frivolously, without thinking twice. He would spend thousands of dollars hosting gatherings for his friends. Baba was the kind of man who would buy my cousin a car because his parents couldn't afford it. No one actually needed the things he was buying, but his desire to please everyone was a major factor in his fiscal irresponsibility.

Baba was never the same. Everyone goes through periods in their lifetime where they feel sad, frustrated, and less motivated, and they get less pleasure out of life. But Baba didn't know how to deal with this hit, and he couldn't find the strength to adjust to a new lifestyle. He became sick—sick from depression and desperation. His symptoms were severe, and his feelings became extreme—so extreme that he couldn't get out of bed.

This charismatic man seemed to shrivel up overnight. He spent his days and nights sleeping his life away and seldom left his room.

Baba's depression not only affected him, but everyone around him. Maman quickly took over Baba's role in the family. I admired her for that. She worked at her father's factory and did everything in her power to try to ameliorate our financial situation.

It wasn't long before my parents' relationship began to deteriorate even more. It felt like no matter how much everyone tried to support him, Baba couldn't dig himself out of his black hole. He was hit so hard by the reality of what had happened that all of his willpower vanished. Eventually, Maman moved Baba out of their room so his negativity wouldn't rub off on her. It was sad to watch him psychologically crumble. I always thought of Baba as a powerful man, and now he was helpless. He was unexpectedly dethroned and hurled into a life of slavery to his failure.

After a while, our house in Shemiran was no longer filled with extravagant people, the Rose Garden started to feel isolated, and arguments between my family members became a never-ending ordeal. Where were all the people who used to play music, dance to the beat of the *tabl*, or tell ghost stories in the garden? When my parents could no longer throw those lavish parties, half our "friends" slowly vanished. People want to be around you when your life glistens, but the moment your shine begins to fade, so do they.

Baba slept his life away for nearly two years, and then he finally got out of bed. He would occasionally join us for dinner, and a few times a week his brother and lawyer would come over to the house for meetings. Sometimes he would even crack jokes. My father had found the strength to get himself back up and create a plan for a better future. He wanted to start another business—a pasta factory!

Baba didn't have any background in pasta-making, or the food industry for that matter, but he believed that there was a major need for pasta in the Iranian market, and he wanted to capitalize on that demand. This is a perfect example of why I said my family members are a bunch of crazy risk-taking entrepreneurs. They do what they think feels right at the time.

Baba and his brother sold property to finance the new business venture and opened a massive pasta factory in Karaj, near the Rose Garden. I think Baba intended the factory to be a big "fuck you" to everyone who cut ties with our family. That was his way of saying, "Look at me now, I went from being powerless to powerful again." The factory itself was lovely, and I can assure you, there was never a shortage of pasta in our house. Boxes and boxes of pasta. It was out of control, to a point that anyone leaving our house would leave with a box of pasta. I felt hopeful, seeing their pasta commercials on TV and seeing my father walk with purpose again. He always needed a certain level of power to make him stand strong.

Sadly, Baba was either cursed or simply made horrible business decisions. The pasta factory went bankrupt soon after, and Baba and his brother were forced to get rid of it. As it turned out, the key ingredient my father didn't understand in business was that you have to start small and let your business grow organically. They spent all of their money creating a beautiful, gigantic factory without first understanding what it really took to run it. It was a characteristic mistake for him to make; it had much to do with the over-the-top lifestyle he was accustomed to.

History repeated itself, and Baba fell into another state of deep depression. But this time around, it was much darker than his first. This was the third time he had failed his family and himself. I still didn't feel sorry for him. I was waiting for a miracle, for things to go back to being magical again. But as his failures piled up, his depression deepened. It was hard to be around someone whose attitude and personality depended on how much money was in his bank account.

There will always come a time in your life where no matter how positive and strong you are, things will go from bad to worse, and from worse to unbearable. Life is hard, and whoever told you the contrary was lying. My father can attest to that. Knowing how to adapt after you've lost everything is one of the most difficult struggles. How you garner the strength to bounce back is what will help make you a wiser person. Baba couldn't get used to living more modestly because of his ego. He would find quick fixes, instead of long-term solutions, to financing his extravagant lifestyle. Not so wise. He approached business deals based on how the outside world perceived him. He couldn't face the prospect of failure.

But I came to realize something important: If everything was always perfect, then we would never grow, and we would stay weak. A failure is not just a failure, it's an opportunity. Besides, who sets the bar for failure? It's not the end, it's the beginning. So get hurt, cry it out, and walk right through the mud until you find that light again.

Fail every day! Get knocked down. Get back up. You become more when you do more.

CHAPTER 6

FINDING BRILLIANCE IN CREATION

You learn how strong you are when you have no other choice but to *be* strong. Even though I was young, I learned that I have thick skin and will do anything to reach my goals. Nothing was given to me anymore; I had to work for it, and I worked hard. Sometimes you have to do things you've never done before, but the outcome makes the struggle worth it. You'll be amazed at how capable you are when you take risks.

I'm loquacious, and somehow I always get what I want. The "getting what I want" part was a lot easier when I was younger. Nowadays, it requires much more than just charming adults. I always negotiated my grades with teachers. In the Iranian educational system, grades were marked out of twenty, and I always managed to get a perfect mark. The art of persuasion really came in handy. If I felt something wasn't fair, I voiced my opinion. It didn't matter if it pertained to me or to someone else.

My parents were convinced that I was going to become a lawyer because of my strong character. And even though I spent most of my time reading fashion magazines, not legal books, I still wanted to have the ability to bring justice where justice was due. Maman made business cards when I was twelve years old that said "Tala Raassi,

Attorney at Law." She put them in a cardholder on my desk. At least I felt important when I did my homework. But entering the legal profession especially appealed to me when I met Baba's lawyer.

Baba was an overly serious man. He was the oldest among his siblings, and the wealthiest, so everyone respected and feared him at the same time. His lawyer was a woman, and Baba actually listened to her. Seeing a woman with that commanding power really provoked me. There was something very influential about it, and I envied her. I wanted to have her superpowers, but when I daydreamed about my career in the justice system, I would find myself daydreaming more about the fashionable suits and outfits I would wear, instead of the courtroom. That should have been a clue.

If I really think about it, my designing destiny began with Barbies when I was eight years old. Even though children around the world have been playing with Barbies since the 1960s, they had become illegal in Iran after the 1979 Revolution. The government viewed them as a symbol of Western materialism and destructive to the country's social and cultural values, and it banned them. As a result, store owners were forced to unlawfully stash them in the back of their stores, and customers could only buy them upon request. Their selection was always outdated, so I waited for opportunities to purchase them abroad or receive them as gifts when my family visited from overseas. I also never seemed to have enough clothes for my Barbies. And who wants to wait for the latest styles when you can make them yourself? I know I didn't. I was way too impatient.

Maman owned a gorgeous, long black mink coat that she never seemed to wear. I didn't know why at the time, but now I realize that she must not have felt comfortable wearing it in public after the Revolution. It risked drawing too much attention. One day, I decided that Maman's mink would make a wonderful new outfit for my favorite blond Malibu Barbie. She came with a one-piece pink ruffled swimsuit, and I wished to make her a coat so she wouldn't catch a cold. I thought Maman would appreciate sharing her fur. I cut about eight inches off the bottom to sew the coat together with Maman's needle and thread. I had no idea what the value of fur was at the time. I thought it was just a random piece of clothing that was in storage and had no worth.

I spent hours sitting on my bedroom floor assembling my masterpiece. My fingertips were bloody from all the sharp needle pricks. Even though one sleeve was longer than the other, and the coat turned out only big enough to cover Barbie's shoulders, I was still pumped about the glamour I had crafted. I couldn't wait to present my ill-fitted tiny fur to Maman. When I heard her car pull into the garage, I sprinted down the stairs from the third floor, Barbie in hand, as fast as I could.

"Maman…Maman!" I screamed. She got out of the car and froze, a shaken look on her face. I thought someone had died and she was about to deliver the bad news. The next thing I knew, I was greeted with a slap to my cheek followed by yelling and screaming. Suddenly my glamour was anything but glamorous.

I think Maman considered killing me that day. I learned that the coat had been handed down to her from her mother, who passed away in a car accident at a very young age. It was one of her most precious memories of her mother that she held onto with love.

I was dragged by my arm up to my room and grounded. Eventually, Maman came around and actually helped me fix the Barbie's fur coat since sewing wasn't my forte. As Maman lectured me about how wrong I had been for ruining her coat, I couldn't peel my eyes away from her talented fingers sticking the needle in and out of the fur. I felt like the little coat was getting a professional do-over from an expert. My mother could sew anything. She even made her own engagement dress—an elegant, long, form-fitting red dress with a long train. You could easily see this Saint Laurent-type gown on a celebrity walking the red carpet today. She made clothing, curtains, and other household items, so her materials, patterns, sewing machine, and fashion and home decor magazines were always left around the house. I observed her sewing from a very young age.

Dreaming up and making that fur coat truly sparked my desire to create. I didn't know anything at that young age about being a fashion designer or what it actually entailed. As a child growing up in Iran, I never watched fashion shows on TV. Mainstream designer boutiques didn't exist back then, and women in the streets were always covered. Also, Iranian schools only prepared students for "traditional" careers. When you're raised in a place where independence and individuality aren't really options, your dreams become limited.

My first introduction to the fashion industry was, surprisingly, from my father. One of Baba's biggest business ventures when I was growing up was an awesome leather factory. He exported high-quality Iranian leather out of the country and imported Italian leather to Iran. He then manufactured all sorts of leather goods from it. Maman and I often visited Baba at the factory. I always looked forward to seeing which new project he was working on next.

The manufacturing area was where the magic happened and the place where I begged to spend most of my time. It was filled with workers cutting and sewing the leather into beautiful handbags and suitcases. I played with razor-sharp cutters and cut leftover leather into my own version of art. Of course, Baba always yelled at me and kicked me out of this "dangerous area." At those times when Baba wouldn't allow me in the production area, I would spend my hours sitting behind his desk, pretending to answer phone calls in my school uniform. I wanted to be a businessperson just like him. I envied the independence he had to create things that he wanted. He was producing things that he wished existed on his own terms, and I found a brilliant magic in that combination.

One afternoon, Maman and I visited the factory together. She brought Baba sweets and insisted that I go with her. She enticed me by saying that Baba had a surprise for me: he had a new hand-bag line for me to salivate over! His bag of tricks seemed endless. I waited in the cutting room to catch a glimpse of his masterpiece—the purse that would grace my shoulders for years to come. The workers sat at their workstations meticulously sewing the pieces of leather together. I monitored the factory worker, cigarette perched between his lips, as he cut and flipped the leather around using all sorts of strange and cool tools. His companion would then glue the pieces together. The smell of the glue combined with leather was exotic and invigorating to my curious nose. One piece at a time, it was all coming together.

I fell in love with the small, black clutch made out of Italian leather with a striking gold buckle on the side. With a thin, removable strap, it doubled as a shoulder bag. This would be the bag with the Quran in the side pocket that I wore when I was arrested at my sixteenth birthday celebration. Who knew something so ordinary and unassuming would become part of my forthcoming drama.

I left the factory with five purses in hand—one in each color. Obviously, one of anything in fashion is never enough. I carried all of them out of the factory myself because I didn't want to let them out of my sight. Baba ended up calling the style "Tala" for all their trade shows in the region because he knew how much I loved that bag. Maman tells me that my current fashion career makes sense because I'm "following in Baba's footsteps."

A few months after the fur coat incident, I found myself home alone with Ehteram Khanoom when an idea dawned on me—my fashionable city girl Barbie needed a leather skirt. I had seen a striking leather skirt on a model in one of Maman's fashion magazines, and Baba's imported leather chairs were the perfect material for it. They were his favorite, and he could often be seen reclining on the one by the window reading the newspaper. I guess I hadn't learned my lesson after all. I found a cutter from Baba's factory in one of the kitchen drawers and tiptoed to the chair, so Ehteram wouldn't catch me. I carefully cut a small piece from the side—could I be the next Karl Lagerfeld prodigy?

I bolted the second I heard Ehteram Khanoom approaching the living room. Her voice was panicked as she shouted, "*Ay Khoda, ay Khoda!*" (Oh my God, oh my God!). I immediately hid—not because I was ashamed about what I had done, but because I didn't want to get caught. In my head, no one was going to notice the missing piece from the side.

Baba gave me a good, fatherly slapping around later that day. Then he dragged me to my grandmother's house as Maman pleaded with him to stop. Aria couldn't even defend me anymore. At this point, he just didn't know how to help. I was always getting in trouble with one of my parents for the stupid stuff I would pull. But, of course, I was angry with my father for years for doing this, which I believed was a cruel and undeserved punishment.

Baba ended up gluing the piece of leather back to the chair, but it never looked the same. But what I was most disappointed about was the fact that Barbie never got her cool leather skirt.

A few years later, as I entered my teenage years, my sole focus was to look fabulous at parties. My family was still struggling financially, so my first option was to attend these parties in outdated clothing, and my second option was to find a way to get the trendiest fashions. It was a no-brainer. But I could no longer ask my parents for money and throw tantrums. The thought of poverty was always at the back of my mind, and I learned from a young age that I couldn't rely on anyone for money. In order to maintain the lifestyle I'd had growing up, I had to work hard on my own. But I was only thirteen years old, so getting a job in Iran was out of the question. I chose a third option and did the only thing I knew how to do well—create. If Baba wasn't going to get his life back in order, I was going to construct my own.

Back then braided friendship bracelets were the "it" thing to wear. As teenage girls we used them to accessorize our school uniforms; we would make wishes and promises to each other and tie them on our wrists. At any given time I wore a dozen of them. Clearly, I had way too many wishes. I made them in every style and color you could imagine, and I was good at it too! What better way to make money than doing something that you love? I turned my hobby into a small business and started charging girls at school for the bracelets. I also created beaded necklaces and other jewelry with fishing line for my edgier and fancier styles. Some of these items required thousands and thousands of tiny little beads that I had to pull through the strings, one by one. But I was determined!

My shopping sprees in the heart of northern Tehran's Tajrish district were escapes offering an endless supply of treasures to discover. Nuts, fruits, gold, shoes, clothes, makeup, painted birds, live fish—you name it, they had it. But I was not to be distracted. I had one mission and one mission only at the bazaar: to hunt for material. It was my liberation. Then, when I finally made it home with bags of beads, stones, sequins, and other goodies, I would execute my designs until my eyes grew too heavy, like the sands of time, to stay awake. Slowly, my craft became more refined.

Iranian girls are generally very creative. Whether my friends were rich or not, they were all doing their own pop-up shops. Some made candles and cakes, while others created holiday cards and hand-painted T-shirts. Our trunk shows became a hobby we had fun with, but for me, they were much more. I needed the money!

Luckily, my creations were selling fast. At first I sold them to my friends, and over time everyone in high school wanted one. People hosted parties to sell my products, and organizing house parties to sell our merchandise became a trend among my friends. It was a way for us to make money, and a reason to host parties. We were lighting two candles with one flame! Every week my friends and I would make a list of the invitees, which usually consisted of our friends and the boys we wanted to see. But there were also times when we invited our parents, knowing that they would buy our merchandise to support us. Guilt-tripping them into buying products was my operation.

The money didn't go directly into my piggy bank, but toward the next hot item I was eyeing. It felt good making enough money to finally buy all the merchandise I wanted. Believe it or not, I made enough to shop at nice boutiques around town.

Those were my formative years, when fashion never seemed to escape my mind. Maman had a bookshelf in the library room filled with American fashion magazines. Every day after school, I examined and pretended to read them. I couldn't read English, but I pored over the pages and visualized myself in the outfits. Of course, they were much simpler and more conservative then, as the magazines were from the early eighties and nineties. This made them perfect for any fashionable attorney, but by now my passion for creating and designing had really started to blossom. I wondered if my parents could ever consider this a possible career choice for me. Whenever I brought up fashion, Baba would always say, "You might as well become a tailor."

My creative juices started flowing from a very young age, and no one could stop them. When something comes so innately from within you, it's hard to subdue it from radiating out of you. Follow what you love, and take the slapping, because some people aren't lucky enough to feel that kind of fire.

CHAPTER 7

ROCK-STAR EDUCATION

No one likes to be controlled, and as I got older and ready for high school education, I also developed an unrealistic expectation about freedom. I thought that everyone around me should accept everything I did, no matter how wild I got; but as I got more reckless, my parents and school officials suffocated me even more. I was rejecting their restrictions left and right; they were only authorizing me a moderate amount of fun at any given time, which ultimately made me an excellent liar.

Education in Iran has been a high priority since the early centuries of Islam. It's no longer only available to the wealthy or those who devote their lives to the Muslim religion. Public education is free for all Iranians and required until the eighth grade under the Constitution. Despite the harsh criticism the country receives, at least they make education a high priority, resulting in more than seventy percent of Iranians being literate.

Although Iran's Constitution guarantees the right to education for all its citizens, men and women are not given the same access. One thing is clear: women have surpassed men in enrollment and graduation rates, which really shouldn't come as a surprise. But this imbalance has worried clerics about the social side effects of more educated women, including declining marriage and birth rates. As a result, women are discouraged from majoring in certain areas—for example, engineering, nuclear physics, and hotel management, which are careers considered to be only appropriate for men. It's unfair and disturbing. If a woman is allowed to work in certain other "masculine" professions—taxi driver, soccer player, or firefighter—then why shouldn't she be allowed to become a nuclear physicist?

Since the Revolution, gender segregation has been required in primary and secondary schools. In universities, men and women are allowed to attend classes together, but must sit in different rows. Ayatollah Khomeini and his new regime prioritized the Islamization of the Iranian education system. Proponents argued that mixing genders in classrooms causes moral corruption and distracts students from their studies. I was more distracted by trying to figure out how to escape to hang out with boys. I probably would've been less rebellious if I had attended a coed school. Haven't they ever heard of the saying, "You want what you can't have?"

I attended three different high schools because of my propensity to break school rules. Let's just say that they were too absurd to follow. But despite my "teenage rebel" label, I maintained outstanding academic credentials. At this time in my life, I was also looking for ways to separate myself from my family's issues and shape myself into a different, more exciting social identity.

I made my high school debut with Liana and hundreds of others at a school close to my house. Liana was a stunning Armenian girl who spoke about six different languages. She was the leader of our group and had a lot of impact on my constant quest for more freedom. Our influences over one another were powerful and at times contagious.

Money bought us temporary freedom. I would steal cash from my father's jacket that he hung by the front door, and during school hours, the Armenian badass and I would skip class by telling the doorman we were going home and slipping him cash. It was pretty much a routine every Thursday. We were involved in many different activities and happily volunteered for the majority of school programs to cover our tracks. It was easier to skip class and trick the teachers when we could excuse ourselves for volunteer work or a soccer game. Don't judge—I was resourceful!

But instead of volunteering or attending sporting events, our group would put on bright-colored lipstick and walk around the popular streets of Tehran. We spent hours in the trendiest cafés, sipping hot chocolate and Turkish coffee while smoking cigarettes like they were candy.

Tehran had an impressive café scene, which ranged from modern to traditionally Iranian. From outside, they smelled of sweets, brewed coffee, and Nescafé. Inside, young people would congregate to flirt with the opposite sex and seek refuge without drawing attention or being stopped by the Komiteh.

The most exclusive cafés served the educated youth, who were influenced more by Europe than the Middle East, and in many cases, they were among the few places where women visibly showed their modernity. A misconception exists in the West about Iranian women's dress. Women don't only wear the black *chador*, which is usually worn by the very religious or the most traditional families and government officials. In the safety and support of these cafés, women dressed in their most fashionable outfits, but still respected Islamic customs by covering themselves with fancy headscarves and *manteaus*. Women managed to make *manteaus* stylish by pairing them with belts, unique jewelry, and fashionable shoes and bags. I can only imagine how Iranians would dress if there weren't any limitations. They already looked like they could walk the runway at New York Fashion Week, which may come as a surprise to some.

Aria, like my parents, wouldn't let me smoke cigarettes or flirt with boys. Only occasionally was my brother easygoing, and that was usually only when he was interested in one of my girlfriends. In exchange for him helping me lie to my parents, I would introduce him to my friend he had a crush on. It seemed like a fair trade to me.

Parties were a favorite excuse for Aria and me to sneak out. The undercover mission usually went something like this: we told our parents we were going to the same party, when in reality we went our separate ways and met up right before walking into the house. From time to time my brother would run late, which would force me to hide in the alley waiting for him. I would get so scared that he had gotten arrested and I would have to explain to my parents why I wasn't with him.

In fact, one time my brother and I were stopped by the Komiteh and forced to prove that we were siblings. They moved us apart to different sides of the street and asked us both the same questions: What color is the furniture in your house? What is your grandmother's name? What does your uncle do for work?

But it didn't matter, because we had caught up with the government officials. We had back-up plans at all times and tried to stay one step ahead of them. Even if I wasn't with my brother and had been stopped with a guy friend, we would have had practiced our answers in advance.

Our second favorite pastime was to "cruise" around town blasting music in fancy cars. My girlfriends and I got dressed up and drove around the Elahieh district of Shemiran and Jordan Street, a famous hip street in Tehran. We flirted and exchanged information with those who interested us. We weren't looking for husbands. Some of my friends would eventually date the men they met, but "cruising" was more about socializing and being seen. We felt normal and spontaneous. For a few minutes, we had the luxury of living in a democratic society. We ignored the government checkpoints where officials waited to confiscate cars and arrest socialites. When you feel invincible, jail never crosses your mind.

If you had looked at me at this time, you wouldn't have seen the stereotypical teenage emo rule-breaker. But as with all strong and mysterious women, looks can be deceiving. After getting suspended for skipping school, I was eventually expelled. The principal made it clear that the only way to put my "bad behavior" to rest was to enroll me in a different school than my sidekick, Liana.

The transitional period to the next school was tough, but Liana and I didn't let it interfere with our friendship. My relationship with my parents, on the other hand, suffered. Like most teenagers around the world, I didn't think they had my best interest at heart. Of course, now that I am older and wiser, I can see why they were so strict: they were simply trying to protect me. But at that age, sometimes our hormones get the best of us.

With literally hundreds of students, the new school's campus was so large that it needed its own area code. The change didn't throw me off-kilter since I already knew some of the students from around town. The workload was intense and deadlines were very short. Instruction was content-centered, memorization was emphasized, and students were expected to learn a great deal of factual information. A teacher could ask us to study a three-hundred-page

history book, published by the Ministry of Education, for the following day. Then we were tested on the minute details of what we
had read.

Every female student in Iran wore the same uniform, which
consisted of pants, a *manteau*, and a scarf that covered the hair and
neck. Imagine a throng of one thousand teenagers in the same color
uniform only showing their face and hands. We looked like replicas
of one another. Depending on which school I attended, the colors
of the uniform changed, which is how someone could differentiate
where I went. The *manteau* and pants were usually navy, gray, or blue,
and the headscarf was usually black or navy.

I hated blending in with the rest of the crowd, and most of my
friends felt the same way. This meant that our shoes, backpacks, and
jewelry really mattered. They were the only way to showcase our fashion sense and individuality, and they allowed us to differentiate which
social group we belonged in. My friends and I usually wore matching
colorful friendship bracelets, trendy backpacks, and funky shoelaces;
we rolled up our sleeves and opened our *manteaus* to reveal our shirts
underneath. Being fashionable trumped any other responsibility.

Just like in any part of the world, different cliques in high
school formed—the stoners, geeks, outcasts, and so forth. If I had
to box myself into one clique, it would be the "mean girls." We had
our own area in the schoolyard, sat next to each other in the last
rows of the classroom, played on the same sports team, and walked
to and from school together. We were that obnoxiously close clique
you loathed in American high school movies. But we left the being
mean part to the tomboys. They were the ones who sold drugs and
alcohol in the schoolyard and constantly chastised, beat up, and stole
things from other girls.

The whole point of getting an education is to develop knowledge and skills, to contribute to the future and further your community. Limiting my ability to find independence as a teenager only twisted me into a more reckless Tala. I excelled in school, played sports well (specifically soccer, basketball, and badminton), and was always punctual. What more could you expect from a teenager? The focus was always negative. Don't wear this! Don't do that! I was constantly surrounded by clouds of "don'ts." Looking back at high school, I mostly remember the things that were forbidden, which I didn't agree with then and still don't now. None of that prepared me for what I have been confronted with in life.

Every morning at school, all the students would line up in the schoolyard facing the principal. If the members of the faculty weren't wearing uniforms like ours, they would be dressed in the black *chador*. The principal, teachers, or a student would read a *surah* from the Holy Quran, and all the students would repeat after them. Occasionally, faculty members would select a student at random to stand at the podium to read a *surah* or verse to everyone. This was especially nerve-racking for us, because Arabic wasn't our mother tongue. Despite being taught Arabic, Islam, and how to read the Quran in school, my friends and I never truly understood what we were reading. I always wondered why they couldn't just let us read the Quran in Farsi.

After the reading, we would remain in our original lines and were required to participate in physical exercise intended to wake us up before class. We resembled soldiers in an army training camp. Teachers, who looked more like army sergeants, would monitor us while we executed the drills, to ensure that all the students followed the instructions correctly. The exercises proved to be very difficult in certain weather conditions—at times the temperature would drop to 0 degrees Celsius (32 degrees Fahrenheit) in January. And if struggling to do jumping jacks with mounds of loose fabric around your legs wasn't hard enough, try adding a headscarf that would keep dropping down over your eyes. One of my hands was always shifting my scarf, so I wouldn't bump into the girl next to me. The jump squats were the most difficult though—a recipe for an inevitable wedgie.

Following our daily workout routine, we would walk into the school building, one by one, as the faculty checked our nails to make sure they were not polished or long, our eyebrows to make sure they were not shaped, our hair to make sure it wasn't colored, and our shoes, backpacks, and accessories to make sure they weren't "too stylish." The older we got, the more we found the routine intrusive. As a teenager I wanted to shape my appearance: color my hair, wear fashionable clothing, and manicure my nails. I didn't think it was anyone's business to control my physical appearance, especially since there was nothing offensive about it. And I certainly didn't believe that I was a bad Muslim for wanting to do so.

I couldn't bring myself to conform. I always left my house in uniform, but I would change in the school bathroom. First, I was suspended for wearing Dr. Martens and Converse All Star shoes when the dress code required generic black shoes. How dare they take away my right to wear All Stars?

The principal then unjustly accused me of shaping my eyebrows when I hadn't. Most Iranian girls are fortunate enough to have beautiful thick hair and eyebrows. When you start to develop your individuality, and you also want to look pretty for boys, shaping thick, bushy eyebrows is bound to become a focus. When I was in high school, pencil thin eyebrows were in style. Thank God that trend is out. It made everyone look angry all the time. My eyebrows were naturally thin, so I didn't need to shape them. It came as a bombshell to my parents when I got the boot—expulsion.

Obviously, my parents were livid and embarrassed in front of their family and friends that I kept getting suspended and expelled. I still believe that my expulsions weren't fair or justified. But it was shameful for my parents to have a child who couldn't finish a year in school without getting into trouble. It was hard to make a case for myself. Being a good student didn't matter at that point, because my rebellion overshadowed everything else.

Getting kicked out of school, fighting with my parents, and being scared by government officials didn't stop me from doing what I really wanted to do. No matter how many times I collided with the principles of others, it still didn't scare me off the path toward the woman I wanted to become. It actually made me more resourceful in finding ways to stand up for what I truly believed in. I fought my war of independence with lipstick, shoes, braided friendship bracelets, and clothing. My weapon was fashion, and it was just the beginning.

CHAPTER 8

TEHRAN HIGH

Everyone says the third time is a charm, but my third high school wasn't very charming. It was a brand-new school near my house with a very pricey tuition and only about fifty students. My parents believed it was worth the price because the school had very strict expectations. It didn't turn out to be worth the investment. What my parents didn't know was that, contrary to popular belief, private school doesn't necessarily equal better-behaved girls. In fact, it was quite the opposite.

This small school had much wilder students than the larger public schools I attended. And unlike my last schools, I didn't fit in as easily with their rebellion. My definition of fun and crazy was very different from theirs. I thought that cutting class, smoking cigarettes, and breaking the dress code pushed the limits, but my classmates here were doing much worse. The student body was made up of very troubled rich kids, many of whom had also been expelled from other schools and at fourteen and fifteen years old were already reveling in hard drugs, sex, rowdy parties, and weekend getaways with boys. Some of the girls even smoked hashish and drank alcohol in the bathroom stalls during class breaks. I felt very out of place. To make matters worse, unlike the other two schools I attended, I didn't have any friends I could rely on. I had to enter this new high school jungle solo, and I was worried.

Every high school has one girl that everyone wants to be— Mitra was that girl. One thing I was sure of was that if she had lived outside Iran, a modeling agency would've discovered her. Whenever she entered a room, she looked like she was starring in a Pantene Pro-V hair commercial. Her long, wavy light brown hair blew back and bounced as she walked. Her piercing, bright green eyes trapped people. Her eyelashes were so long that they could've slapped you in the face with a wink. I knew Mitra from before, but not very well. We went to the same parties and coffee shops around town, but we weren't friends. I don't think she thought I was cool enough to be her wingwoman, which intimidated me even more.

I will never forget when I spotted her on my first day of school (it wasn't that hard—she was the tallest girl there). I made eye contact and smiled while a classmate read a *surah* from the Holy Quran in the background. She didn't smile back, so I quickly looked toward the ground. I couldn't wait for the last bell of the day to ring, so I could report to my friends that Mitra and I were classmates. They didn't have to know that she had blatantly ignored me.

The second week of school, she sat next to me in class and acknowledged my presence with a hello. Voilà! That was the deep and meaningful beginning of our newfound "friendship." I felt as though my crown had finally been restored.

Mitra hung out with another attractive girl, Raha, who also didn't interact much. I assumed she didn't like me either. They weren't pleasant girls to be around, but I still wanted to be in their clique. I was worried that they were going to tell the boys in our circle that I was a loser for not having any friends at school. There was no way my parents would accept transferring me to yet another school, so there was no escape. Even under the veil, high school girls can be just as cruel in Iran as they can be in other parts of the world.

One day during break, Mitra and Raha asked me to join them in the bathroom stall in the back of the school. They said that they wanted to share a secret with me. I thought maybe they'd come to their senses, and we could be *the* dynamic trio. We could barely fit in the tiny squatted stall, but we all squeezed in. Mitra pulled out what I thought was a cigarette and asked, "Do you want to smoke?"

Even though I knew we weren't allowed, this was my chance to get them to like me. I paused for a second to think about how I should respond.

She rolled her eyes and said, "Don't tell me you've never smoked hashish before." Then she handed me the tiny black joint.

I should've walked out. Instead, I was too worried about how they would perceive me. I wish someone had told me that being cool isn't about blindly following someone else's lead; it's about being yourself, even if that means you're different from everyone else. Nothing is sexier than being strong and intelligent while embracing your own individuality.

After I finally took a hit, I coughed uncontrollably, and my throat lit on fire. As the smoke hit my lungs and traveled into my blood and brain, I felt like I had gone airborne into another universe and found myself in a wonderland. Then my entire body went numb.

They tried to keep me quiet, whispering, "*Shhhhhhh!*" But the coughs kept forcing themselves from my throat.

I started to become light-headed, to the point that my eyelashes and eyebrows felt heavy. I wanted to doze off. How was I going to go back to class? Anxiety took over. All I could think about was how disappointed my parents would be. Actually, "disappointed" was an understatement. I tried very hard to hide that I was preparing myself for takeoff. I didn't want the girls to think I couldn't *handle it*. They kept smiling at each other and whispering to me, "How do you feel?" "How good is that hashish?"

I was too high to formulate a coherent response.

I felt like someone hit the slow-motion button on my moon-walk back to class. A terrible paranoia crept inside me. You know the feeling when you've done something wrong, and even though no one knows, you feel like everyone is judging you for it? I kept reminding myself not to make eye contact with anyone as I slithered into my seat in history class. I attempted to listen to the teacher talk about some archaic kingdom. This was something that normally interested me, but I was so high that I couldn't get my brain to focus. Out of the corner of my eye, I could see Mitra hitting Raha with her elbow every few minutes. These bitches were making fun of me. I'm pretty sure that's called "bullying."

I felt the cool breeze gusting through the open windows. The sounds of the birds chirping, cars honking, and dogs barking outside were more intense than usual. Did the teacher know what I had done? She kept staring at me suspiciously. I was becoming more paranoid by the minute. I prayed she wouldn't call on me because I wouldn't know the right answer. My mind kept jumping from one thought to the next: *Oh my God! Baba will kill me if he finds out.*

It was obvious now why Mitra and Raha were always so quiet and had puffy eyes—they were high. I didn't tell my friends about what I had done in the bathroom until months later; I thought they would judge me. But Iranian society wasn't so conservative when you dug below the surface. Once I saw my friends starting to smoke at parties, I thought I was safe to let them in on my secret. I slowly realized that almost all my friends smoked.

Mitra stopped coming to class very soon after that. She lived in a mansion next to school, so Raha and I went to check up on her. She opened the door half-naked as clouds of smoke blew past us into the open air. No, her house wasn't on fire. It was from all the joints she had been smoking. A guy in his late twenties was also lying half-naked on the couch in the living room. I had never seen people that high (or naked) before. They could barely open their bloodshot eyes and were drenched in sweat. They had to be doing more than just smoking hashish. The drugs were harder, not something you'd do in the school bathroom stall.

I heard her bedridden father screaming from the second floor, "Mitra, who is at the door?" That was when I realized I didn't want to be Mitra and wouldn't make an effort to interact with her again. We said hello if we ever crossed each others' paths in school, parties, or restaurants, but that was the extent of it. I bowed out gracefully from the crown clique. I would probably be doing crystal meth in some basement in Tehran right about now if I hadn't. A few years later, I found out that Mitra's father had passed away and left her with a huge trust fund. She then married some guy who stole every last penny from her.

The Islamic Republic has an alarming rate of drug addiction, which is shocking given that the government proclaims itself to be a "dry" country in which alcohol and drugs are illegal. According to the United Nations, roughly 2.2 percent of Iranians are hooked on drugs, which is the highest rate in the world. Iran is positioned along the Afghanistan-Europe heroin trafficking route and borders Iraqi Kurdistan, making access to an abundant flow of drugs easier.

The majority of drug addicts live in provinces and regions located along the transit route.

The drugs of choice, for both rich and poor, are crack and meth. Crack is an inexpensive, highly addictive derivative of cocaine and is rampant in the poorer areas of Iran's biggest cities. Crystal meth, which Iranians call *shishe*, is becoming increasingly popular. Both drugs are cheap and easy to produce at home or in an amateur lab. It has become such a problem that young men and women are tested to determine whether they are addicts before marriage. This practice was more common with males, but the number of female addicts is on the rise.

Drug addiction isn't a crime. An Iranian law dictates that any person who abuses drugs without suffering from addiction should be punished. If they abuse drugs like opium or hashish, their sentence can range from twenty to seventy-four lashes and a fine. If they are caught with manufactured drugs like heroin or cocaine, they can be lashed fifty to seventy-four times and also fined. Drug addicts, on the other hand, are seen as ill citizens who need professional treatment.

I can't help but marvel at how many of my friends turned to drugs at such a young age, and I'm not talking about your typical drug experimentation kids do around the world—I am talking about full-blown addiction. Drugs play a major role in the new generation, especially for the young unemployed who are frustrated and have easy access to them. The boom of post-Revolution babies is the most vulnerable, because Iran can't absorb the influx of young, well-educated workers. Those who are stuck in the country because they don't have the means to leave are discouraged and looking for a distraction.

Almost three-fourths of Iran's drug addicts today are between the ages of eighteen and twenty-five. They use drugs at schools, house parties, small gatherings, and even on the streets. Much of it has to do with boredom. After the Islamic regime banned all public entertainment, the youth went in search of other methods of amusement. They can't go to concerts, movies, clubs, or bars. So they run out of things to do in the privacy of their own homes and turn to drugs.

Mitra is a prime example. Behind closed doors, she was part of that tragedy. At first, this beautiful girl had fascinated me. I wanted to be her, until I realized her glossy life wasn't so glossy. People we barely know often fascinate us, but once we learn their reality, we quickly realize they may be the opposite of who we want to become. If you spend too much time wanting to be someone else, then you forget to be yourself.

Drug addiction plagues people of all ages and backgrounds— from the local street vendor to my classmates. Anyone could fall victim. I knew many people who overdosed—from Maman's friend's sixteen-year-old son who overdosed on heroin, to our neighbor's father who had heart failure because he smoked too much opium. Drug usage and addiction was all around me, and it wasn't pretty. People were using drugs for escape, to find temporary freedom— freedom from a land of restrictions to go to some false wonderland, where they could be anything they wanted to be. We are created to be influential and glorious, and I felt nothing but lowliness from the Tehran high.

CHAPTER 9

RESTRICTIONS MADE
ME RESOURCEFUL

The Little Mermaid was my favorite animated movie growing up. I admired the extraordinary mermaid, Ariel. Her character fascinated me. She was beautiful, fearless, and curious, yet extremely naive. She was a dreamer and an explorer, hungry for her freedom. Her father, King Triton, and her fish friends, Flounder and Sebastian, were overly protective because they knew someone out there was evil, deceiving, forceful, unfair, and aggressively trying to trap her. That someone was the cruel Ursula. I compare her journey to that of young Iranian girls. These passionate young women are constantly clashing with both their overprotective families, who are aware of the harsh punishment their children may face for seeking freedom, and the conservative government, whose only objective is to deny them that freedom.

Being young, fearless, and freedom-hungry in Iran is a recipe for disaster. My struggle to fight for my individuality created much tension between me and my parents, schools, and society as a whole. But even growing up as a teenager in Iran, I found ways to beat the system. I still lived a fun and exciting life, and as I sprinted through my teenage years, eyebrows and trends were the least of my parents' worries. My version of being reckless and having fun was to party, meet boys, and dance to Western music.

Like Ariel, I needed to avoid two main groups of people if I wanted to continue with my spontaneous lifestyle. The first was the overprotective King Triton—my loving parents who wanted my brother and me to experience life, but were very frightened about our clashing with government officials; and the second was the villain Ursula—the government that refused to tolerate the youthful experimentation that is typical of teenage behavior. A constant battle raged among these three key players, and our cultures collided in the Tehran bubble. We were continuously clashing with one another's values and beliefs, which resulted in chaos and challenge.

Iran has state-controlled television, and the Ministry of Culture and Islamic Guidance is responsible for censoring the media. Censorship is largely seen as a means to maintain stability in the country. Officials censor the foreign films and documentaries shown on TV and in theaters to make them "appropriate" and "Islamic." Sexual proposals are exchanged for marriage proposals, beer becomes lemonade, conversations about politics are altered, and women's necklines are often covered or completely removed. However, one of the most common ways for the Iranian population to be exposed to Western culture is through satellite TV and uncensored foreign movies. Despite the government's ban on satellite television, because it couldn't censor its content, many homes still had illegal dishes.

Additionally, anyone could gain access to the newest film releases. I began by using Reza, my friend's middle-aged "movie dealer," who delivered movies to her house every week. He could've passed as a businessman commuting to Wall Street, except that he was missing a tie (yet another government restriction on dress). He always carried two briefcases filled with hundreds of movies—from documentaries and cartoons to racier movies like *Striptease* with Demi Moore. My parents tried to confiscate and hide the risqué ones, but I always got my hands on them. In the end, it didn't matter. Watching movies became much easier with satellite television, so I no longer needed Mr. Wall Street! Watching the Western screen would inspire some of my actions and a lot of my outfit choices. My parents and the officials couldn't restrict my freedom once I was exposed to TV shows like *Beverly Hills, 90210* and *Baywatch*. I wanted to jump in with the trends those kids were following.

My friends and family always joked that Baba's eyes bled whenever he saw me wearing lipstick or an outfit he didn't approve of. His eyes turned crimson red out of anger. I wasn't fazed. I wanted to be free to express myself as I pleased. If Brenda Walsh wore something on *90210*, I wanted to wear the same thing on the streets of Tehran. They couldn't tell me not to wear my stylish clothes when the Quran doesn't mention anything about going to hell for being fashionable.

I would hide my risky outfits under my *manteau* and put on lipstick when I went out, then remove it before I came home. One time, Baba found a tissue paper I had used to wipe my lipstick in front of our house. He furiously showed it to Maman and told her I needed to be reprimanded. He would beat his chest like a furious father, but I know that deep down he was just worried I would get in trouble with the government.

A few months before we got arrested, Neda and I attended a house party just blocks away from my house, accompanied by my rebel accomplice Liana. It wasn't unusual for teenagers to have alcohol at parties, but I never had the urge to try it before this night. I debated about waiting to drink, but ultimately decided to forego such restraint. Everyone was doing it! Including my biggest crush,

Omid, who poured my first drink. I blame it on the gaze of his big brown eyes and his long eyelashes!

I tried *aragh sagi*, which literally means "dog alcohol." It is a cheap, heady moonshine made from raisins and was outlawed after the Revolution, becoming a black-market beverage. It is clear and strong, and it usually contains at least 65 percent pure ethanol. I felt woozy after my first sip. With each taste, I tried not to gag. Omid poured some soda into my glass to dilute the alcohol and handed it back to me with a devilish smile on his face. I hoped that would work. I didn't want to puke in front of Mr. Right.

Omid and I sat close together on a velour couch in the living room. He was very funny, handsome, and always impeccably dressed. As Ace of Base's song "All That She Wants" played in the background, I kept thinking, *you are all that I want…* With every gentle stroke through my hair, I became weak in the knees. This was the closest to heaven I had ever felt. He kept telling me how beautiful I was. (Just so you know, when a guy tells you how beautiful you are right before you're about to make out, it's most likely his penis speaking. And I am talking to *you*, all you swooning teenage girls out there!)

He grabbed my hand and took me to the kitchen, where we had a bit more privacy. I was so anxious; the butterflies in my stomach were having a circus. Then he lifted me onto the kitchen counter and opened my legs a bit so he could stand between them. His fingers moved gently up and down my face, which brought goose bumps all over my skin. I could no longer hide my nervousness as all the hair on my body gravitated toward cloud nine.

His head bent closer and closer to mine. I could feel his warm breath on my neck, which sent chills down my spine. Our cheeks brushed against each other's. My heartbeat accelerated. We hadn't even kissed yet. Then he tipped my chin up and slowly rubbed my bottom lip with his thumb. He closed his eyes, and as I did the same I felt his warm, wet lips delicately touch mine. I think I fell in love in that one kiss. He pulled me even closer to his body with a tinge more aggression, and then a really awkward attempt at French kissing followed. I had no idea what I was doing, but the moment was mine. As our lips locked, I envisioned our future together—grand wedding, children, the whole nine yards.

I was abruptly catapulted back to reality when I heard Neda shout that Maman had arrived an hour early to pick me up. *Are you kidding me?*

I was feeling an intense spinning sensation from the moonshine, and Omid was begging me to stay, but I knew I couldn't. Maman would never allow it. I struggled to put on my headscarf and *manteau*, because my balance was off. I got into the car praying that my mother wouldn't smell the alcohol on my breath. It felt much longer than a two-minute car ride around the neighborhood. All the streetlights were blurry, colorful streaks. I couldn't believe I had finished an entire glass of that poison. I was slowly suffocating, hoping she wouldn't find out what I had done as I held my breath.

When I got home I quickly ran to my room and shut the door. I felt a tornado of moonshine wrap terrifyingly around me as my body lurched. A few minutes later, Maman showed up.

"What are you doing?" she asked suspiciously.

"Just changing and getting ready for bed," I replied, the face of innocence. She walked toward my closet, where I tried to hide and desperately fight the awful feeling of vertigo.

While I was pretending to look for clothes, Maman ordered

me to let her smell my breath. I thought to myself: *OK, do you work for the Basij now? Are you serious?* "Why do you want to smell—"

Before I could finish my sentence, she slapped me right across my face. "Were you drinking?"

"No, of course not!" It seemed like every time I tried something new, I was greeted with a well-deserved slap in the face from one of my parents.

Luckily, Baba wasn't home that night. Only God knows what my punishment would've been if he had known I was drinking. Maman firmly told me never to lie to her again, and that I didn't need to get ready for school the following day. She didn't want me to be around my accomplices. I was so scared that I didn't even ask why or try to leave the room. I overheard Maman and Aria talking about the party in the other room. It was just my luck that the host turned out to be one of my brother's friends, and he told her what had most likely happened at the party. Omid. The kitchen. That kiss. I knew I was never going to hear the end of it, and I was livid with my brother for selling me out. Whatever happened to the "bro code?"

The following morning, my mother went to the next extreme to ax my connection with Liana. She went straight to Liana's parents, who agreed that we shouldn't be friends. Maman reasoned that because Liana's mother was a Christian, she was more liberal—she allowed her daughter to drink at dinner and her curfew was much later. My parents grounded me for one month. The only time I was allowed to leave the house was to attend school—the same place where I got educated on how to be wild and reckless.

As unfair as Maman's handling of the situation was, at least my parents weren't the government officials. Possession of alcohol carries a heavier legal penalty than some hard drugs. I could have received eighty lashes for getting caught with alcohol. If Muslims are caught repeatedly, they may even face the death penalty. It seems like a steep price to pay, but that didn't stop my friends and I from breaking the law and finding ways to live like the characters we saw on forbidden TV shows and movies. And we weren't the exceptions; it is estimated that more than one million Iranians are drinkers.

The Islamic Republic's ban on alcohol is just another front in the Iranian "culture war" against Western influence. If a Muslim ever wants to buy alcohol, it's easily obtainable. In fact, alcohol is so widespread that Iranians are the third highest consumers of alcohol among all Muslim-majority Middle Eastern countries. Lebanon and Turkey take the prize for first and second, but it's legal to consume alcohol in both of those countries. Do Iranians drink more heavily because alcohol is prohibited? In a country where drinking is illegal and taboo, it doesn't make much difference whether you have one drink or five, at midnight or at noon, after work or during work.

As with any addiction, the first step to solving a problem is acknowledging that there is one. Recently, the government called its first-ever conference on alcohol abuse in Iran's history, quietly opened its first rehabilitation center, and admitted that there are at least two hundred thousand alcoholics in the region. Even though the figure is said to be much higher, these are baby steps in the right direction. Cheers to illegal alcohol!

Around the time Maman grounded me, I decided that Omid would be my future husband. He was the leader of his group of friends and a notorious party boy. Basically, he was everything parents wouldn't want their young teenage girl to date, especially in such a restricted and conservative society. But, inevitably, we dated. Because hey, girls just want to have fun!

I felt compelled to tell Aria and Maman about our relationship; someone would've probably "outed" us anyway. Iranians sure do love to gossip. Plus, I thought they would respect our relationship more if we were honest. Maman knew that I would most likely find a way to date him regardless of whether she approved, and she preferred to stay in the loop. Omid came from a good family, which made her feel more at ease. But I didn't tell Baba; he would never have accepted my having a boyfriend at fifteen years old, no matter what stock he came from.

Omid was controlling. Iranians call men like him *gheyrati*. They are overprotective and only want you for themselves. He didn't allow me to attend parties or drive around Jordan Street without him, which made Maman grow to like him. She thought he was keeping me safe. But she didn't know that I was accompanying him to all sorts of inappropriate and foolish house parties.

His mother was a well-known fashion designer in Iran who designed custom-made clothing in their beautiful home in the mountains. We spent a lot of time in their basement with friends, playing spin the bottle and cards. I was so charmed by Omid and all the new reckless activities he was introducing me to that his mother's materials and designs didn't even reach my consciousness. Fashion was something I had always been so fascinated with, and now I was surrounded by it, but with one look from this boy's eyes, I was swept away and forgot all about fashion. Damn hormones!

Dating behind the veil in Iran can be complicated. You can go to the movies, restaurants, or public places with the opposite sex, but you could also be stopped and possibly even arrested at any point. If we wanted to venture out and do something different we would go out in public, but only with a larger group of friends. You don't want to draw attention.

One day, I told my parents I was going to my friend Golnar's house for lunch, and she told her parents she was going to mine. We lived next to each other and pulled off this sting quite frequently. We would meet at the bookstore on our street and wait for Omid to pull up with his car so that we could quickly jump in and dodge any passersby. That day he picked us up to go to Alborz, a fancy, overpriced kebab house that was the most popular restaurant in Tehran at the time. On any given Friday afternoon, people would drive up to the restaurant like they were pulling up to a club in Monte Carlo—who knew that overly expensive kebabs could bring in such a high-end crowd?

It was always very nerve-racking to be in a car with members of the opposite sex. We had to look around at all times to make sure we weren't being seen or followed. I was also very worried that someone would see me and tell my parents. It was a constant rush of paranoia. Omid always drove very irresponsibly and blasted music, drawing even more attention to us.

On our way to the restaurant, I suddenly heard tires screeching and heavy honking. I felt my neck snap, and my head hit the car's dashboard. My head felt foggy, and it took me a few seconds to get my bearings.

"That son of a bitch ran a red light!" Omid shouted.

He got out of the car aggressively and started arguing with the other driver. Golnar and I sank into our seats, trying to disappear. Omid was becoming the center of the whole intersection's attention, and we couldn't afford to be seen in that mess.

None of us were severely injured, but when Omid called his parents, they notified mine. Maman arrived at the scene a complete wreck. I think she panicked even more at the sight of all the traffic police, but her worry quickly turned into fury. She didn't want us to be the talk of the town.

The accident was the last straw. I'd had all the school troubles, the alcohol, and now I'd been in a car accident with a boy. After that, I lost Maman's trust. She became even stricter and no longer allowed Omid and me to see each other, which created tension in our relationship. By law, you can't be seen in public with someone of the opposite sex unless he is your father, brother, or cousin. If you are caught, you could be jailed or lashed, and the government could even force you to marry your companion. Our parents had to be strict with us because they were scared we would make the wrong decisions. The only alternative was for me to use my expertly resourceful tricks—lie to my parents and become a master at hiding Omid.

The night that we were arrested, I had pleaded with my parents to allow me to attend that party. I was still grounded and wasn't allowed to go anywhere without my brother. So I made all sorts of deals with Aria to help me get out of the house. I was finally able to convince everyone. But I wish I had stayed grounded and never gone to that gathering. My persistence changed my life forever.

Aria, Neda, her boyfriend, and I took a taxi to the party. When we arrived, Neda and I immediately went to Maryam's room to take off our *hijabs* and fix our hair and makeup. Music was playing, snacks were all over the tables, lights were dimmed, the boys were playing cards, and the girls were dancing to music. There were no drugs or alcohol, just a bunch of teenagers doing innocent teenage stuff.

But there was a small detail that we didn't know at the time. Maryam, who was hosting the gathering at her house, hadn't invited her on-again-off-again boyfriend. They had gotten into another fight a few days before and, seeking revenge, he called in the party to government officials, thinking they would peacefully shut it down.

It wasn't long before the Basijis stormed into the house, looking anything but peaceful. They entered the building following a guest who had just walked in. Everything happened so fast. Everyone was screaming and scrambling around. I didn't know where my brother was, but I just started running, with all that I had, after Neda and Maryam, out the back door into the night...

CHAPTER 10

BEHIND BARS

Vozara Prison was one of the most notorious prisons in Tehran. It was full of criminals, drug dealers, rapists, and thieves. But it was also full of women and men who had done nothing more than play some music or hold hands with their loved one in public. I had heard so many harrowing stories about this prison, and I was about to finally see it for myself. It hadn't hit me yet that this was the beginning of my own story.

I had done nothing wrong. I was scared, sober, and dressed in a skirt that would have been considered an acceptable length in most Western social circles. I had broken lots of rules as a teenager, bent laws, and pushed back. But ultimately, I was just a child, used to the sun and the protection of my loving family and my magical Iran. Now, I was being walked into a cold prison, past the stares of hard-faced officials and violent criminals, like a witch on her way to the gallows.

Inside the jail, the walls and floors were made of concrete. Nearly one hundred women from all different backgrounds and age groups congregated within those walls. They were dressed in dark-colored clothing, headscarves, and *manteaus*. Some wore *chadors*, while others were dressed less conservatively—like my friends and me.

I noticed a very young girl who could not have been more than ten years old. She wore what appeared to be a navy school uniform. When she looked up, I was blown away by the fear and anger flashing through her eyes. I couldn't tell if her expression was from pain, disgust, or a toxic mixture of both.

My eyes fell on a woman kneeling in the corner, weeping into a black *chador*. Her face was streaked with black mascara from the tears streaming down her stunning, but distraught, face. As I studied her more closely, I saw white puffy lace peeking out from the bottom of the black fabric. Then it hit me—this was a bride on her wedding day. Her mother and family attempted to comfort her, but her sobs were uncontrollable. This was supposed to be the happiest day of her life. I'm not sure it's even possible to console such a shattered bride.

To my right were jail cells and never-ending hallways connecting to even more jail cells. To my left was a little hallway that led to an area stacked with dirty pads and toilet paper, empty food cans, and other garbage. A strong stench emanated from the communal squat toilets. We were ordered to sit in this hallway and wait. We got situated a few feet away from the bride and her family.

Even then, sitting next to a crying bride, we still had hope that our parents would come to our rescue. We didn't know when our verdict would be delivered or what it would be. The uncertainty made the entire situation even more tense. But there weren't many possible outcomes: we would either be exonerated, forced to pay a bond, tortured, or locked up. I prayed for the first outcome. For the hundredth time that evening, I wished that I hadn't pressured my parents to allow me to attend the party. It was my fault that Aria was in jail.

At first we played word games to kill time. Being among all my friends helped me imagine that we were having our own slumber party. A few hours passed, and there was no sign of anyone coming. Happily, the bride and her family were released shortly after we arrived, having had to pay a large indemnity. She wished us luck and shuffled away, the train of her wedding dress dragging along the filthy floor. I wished I could hold onto the lacy train and whisk myself far away.

Like clockwork, every ten to fifteen minutes someone would trample over us to get to the bathroom, which was located right down the hallway from where we were seated. Five squat toilets were lined up—each one dirtier than the next. Squat toilets were common in Iran, but I had never seen any as filthy as these. It was extremely uncomfortable seeing women use them out in the open. My friends and I were forced to go to the bathroom in pairs, since the handcuffs remained on our wrists. One would squat while the other stood in front; at least we could use each other as a way to cover ourselves for privacy. The combination of odors emanating from the jail was rancid, not to mention the rats, cockroaches, and ants scurrying all around us.

We began talking to two girls sitting close to us, who both had male names, Majid and Behrouz. They gave us insider information about the other prisoners, almost a running commentary on the other inmates and the guards. You would never believe they were girls. They wore sneakers, baggy jeans, and fairly large T-shirts and had male haircuts. I don't know how they entered the facility without their scarves, but they had managed to circumvent the system. In a way, that daring stance captivated me. I was covering myself as much as I could, even though there were no men around anymore.

I noticed the young girl again when she passed us to go to the bathroom. I wanted to talk to her; she was just a child, and I felt the need to protect her. So I asked her in a concerned tone whether she was alone. To my surprise, she snapped that it was not any of my business and snarled some very graphic curse words in Farsi, which I do not dare to repeat. I wondered what kind of upbringing she'd had that made her capable of spewing such vulgarity. Later we found out from Majid and Behrouz that she had run away from her home in Shiraz, a city in central Iran. During her long journey to Tehran, she was raped by a police officer and was now living in jail until someone claimed her. I couldn't wrap my head around the fact that a ten-year-old could run away from home. But worse than that, I couldn't understand what kind of sick person—a police officer, no less—could be capable of raping a ten-year-old.

Majid and Behrouz talked to us all the time. It was like they wanted something from us or they were fascinated by our situation. They would leave our side and then come back and report everything that was happening. I couldn't tell if they were trying to scare us more, or if they were genuinely trying to help us make sense of everything that was going on.

The night was long and noisy from girls crying, praying, and pleading with the prison guards to bring them food, water, or drugs. We didn't have access to water or food, and none was offered. Some women ate tuna fish out of cans and drank water from white plastic cups, but we didn't have any cash to bribe the guards for food. I could tell that some women had been there for a long time from their tiny, emaciated frames.

At all hours, we heard bloodcurdling screams coming from a small window that was sheltered by black metal bars. Some girls in the holding cell told us that behind that little window lay a torture room. I couldn't help but wonder if the screams were from the women that were leaving the jail. Every time a cellmate left the holding area, she never returned.

The most traumatizing noise came from the girls screaming from the cells on the other side of the jail. Majid and Behrouz told us that female guards were raping the girls with glass soda bottles as punishment for bad behavior. What kind of woman could perform such an animalistic act on another woman? Something horrible must have happened to these women in their lifetimes that made them capable of executing something so barbaric. Sitting in a Tehran prison jolted me from my normal, safe way of life. I felt like I had been dropped into some alternate universe. At sixteen years old, I was getting a huge wake-up call.

The hours ticked by, and at some point night gave way to day. A female guard informed us that a few of our mothers had been cleared to visit us in jail, but we only had a few minutes to talk with them. When they came in it was apparent that they had not slept. Their devastated expressions broke my heart. I was the one responsible for what my parents were feeling, for all the things that I had put them through just to live my life the way I wanted. All those fights, all the times they grounded me. They didn't do it to take my freedom away. They did it to protect me from the thick, metal bars that I was now standing behind.

We now had water, snacks, and warm, comfortable clothes. We were famished and dehydrated, but what we really craved was reassuring news. We bombarded them with questions from all directions: "Where are the boys?" "Why is it taking so long to get us out of here?" "When will we see you again?" They promised us that we would be released by no later than the following day. I believed them.

Back at our spot in the hallway, we put on the sweaters and

other clothing that they had brought us, pulling them over what we were already wearing. Being fashionable was the furthest thing from my mind. I needed warmth and comfort. I was relieved that they had also brought us sneakers, so we could finally slip into shoes and shed our painful high heels. I couldn't help but notice that the government officials had forgotten to remove our shoelaces.

Five times a day when the *adhan* called us to prayer, everyone had to stand up. Immediately afterward, the guards would choose some girls and send them into a room to get lashed. I felt my heart race faster and faster with each *adhan*. It became routine—I would stand up and wait my turn, but every time I stood, I was told to wait until the next *adhan*. Instead of feeling the warm grace that comes with the song of prayer, I felt horror and panic. They were forcing faith, religion, and their rules on us. However, my mind and soul was rejecting all of it. To this day, every time I hear the *adhan*, the hair on my body stands on end.

We were not playing games or laughing anymore. The slumber party had ended long ago. We felt dirty, tired, and doubtful. I could not imagine how some of the other women felt, especially the ones who had been there for weeks. We were all weak and getting weaker, and every hour that passed, our spirits diminished. My anxiety and paranoia were affecting every reasonable thought that tried to enter my brain. I couldn't keep it from going to dark places, but I knew I had to stay composed. I didn't want the other prisoners or guards to know how I felt. It took every ounce of strength I had to stand firm, and especially not to cry. In that moment, I needed to survive; I could cry later.

I became extremely sensitive to sounds. I could hear the pitter-patter of rats and cockroaches approaching me. I would shut my eyes, but I was in the state of consciousness between being awake and asleep, which led to hallucinations and horrible nightmares. Even if I did get to sleep, there was always the possibility of getting raped or robbed. My friends and I created a system where we took turns sleeping around the clock. At night we tied our shoelaces together because we were scared the other prisoners would steal our shoes. We always stayed huddled together, and it certainly helped that there were fifteen of us.

We had been in this bleak pit for five long days and nights before we finally found out our fate. By that point, the sensations had run together until we almost didn't notice the staring women, vulgar stories, and screams echoing from the jail cells. Two female officials came to the entrance of the hallway and fixated on us. They summoned us using Maryam's last name and ordered us to stand and follow them. We all looked at each other with the same glimmer of hope. We were all thinking the same thing—*freedom*. Some women cheered and clapped for us as we walked away.

I turned around one last time to look at the hallway where I had sat for what felt like months, but was actually less than a week. How was I just robbed of those days of my life? I felt that during those days, someone hit the pause button and, upon my release, hit play. I promised myself I would never return. I locked eyes with the ten-year-old girl. She just stared back vacantly. There was so much I wanted to say to her, so much I wanted to ask her. I wished I could've taken her with me. I wondered if she felt the same heartbreak I did.

We walked out of the jail area, and the guards locked the door behind us. I could finally breathe again. We walked up the never-ending spiral staircase. This time I wasn't walking down the pit into hell, I was freed from it. There I was, only days after my birthday party, a forever-changed woman. I could finally see the light at the end of the tunnel.

When I stepped outside, the bright sun was blinding. It felt like someone had stabbed a dagger into my eyes, and I couldn't see two steps in front of me. As my friends and I attempted to adjust and get our bearings, the guards ordered us to board the bus. It felt insanely good to finally sit on a padded chair. I watched people in the bustling streets carry on with their daily lives—people chatting and drinking at juice bars, children in their uniforms walking home from school, and professionals leaving work. It was a typical day for most.

The bus finally arrived at a building in the middle of the city surrounded by a hectic atmosphere. The officials told us to wait in the bus until further notice. I placed my hand on Neda's arm and said in a sarcastic tone, "I'm sad that you won't be next to me anymore." We looked at each other and smiled.

When we entered the building, we soon learned we weren't free after all, that we had been brought to the courthouse for sentencing. I was craving courage in the darkness to be able to see the light. This was better than jail, but I was still terrified to face my sentence, whatever it was.

We were immediately escorted to a room with large glass windows and found the boys from the party already inside. I saw Aria and a flash of heat warmed my heart. I was so happy he was okay, and we shared a hopeful smile. My male friends looked exhausted and miserable. It was quite shocking to see that their physical appearances had been altered, obviously against their will. Ramin, who had entered the jail with long hair down to his neck, was now bald. The religious police claimed that a ponytail was illegal in Iran, so they shaved his head. Shahab no longer had his long, trendy beard. I later found out that a government official had torn it off with a key, saying that it misrepresented a man of Islam.

In the bland white room that was devoid of decorations on the walls, I noticed a middle-aged man with a turban sitting at an old gray metal desk. Behind him were shelves filled with foreign VHS tapes, music cassette tapes, bottles of alcohol, a guitar, some makeup, and other substances banned under the Islamic Republic. Arranged as a wall of shame, these were objects confiscated by the religious police during previous arrests. It displayed items they believed only bad and unfaithful people used—heathens and criminals, like me and my friends.

Through a glass window, I could see our shattered parents entering a special waiting area to learn our fate. They sat mutely as we listened, nervous and empty, to the judge, a cleric who was an expert in Islamic studies, lecture us about our wrongdoings and why we shouldn't act like such reckless teenagers. I thought to myself, *Who in the world are you to tell me how to act? It's none of your business, and more importantly, I didn't do anything wrong.* I knew in my heart that the reason we were being punished conflicted with what I'd grown up trusting and believing in. So I held on to my faith. That is what my parents would have wanted me to do.

The judge went on and on. In my state of anger, I was picturing how I would punish him. I wanted to send him to jail and reprimand him. I wanted to break that guitar on his head. My mind also jumped to my father and the thought of how he would react to this entire situation once we got home. In a way, I wanted to stay locked in jail forever because I didn't want to face him, or my mother for that matter. They were going to be so disappointed and say "I told you so" over and over again. Were our friends in school going to revere us, or were they going to judge us and think we were in the wrong? Would I get expelled—*again*?

Guilt began to take over, but it was crazy for me to all of a sudden feel so guilty for a crime I never committed—or did I? I began to think my friends and family would forever perceive me as a criminal. The awful brand of being jailed could even make it impossible to find love or get married. Thought after thought continued to race through my head, until suddenly I heard, from somewhere beyond my inner consciousness, the dreaded word.

"SHALAGH!"

Lashes.

I felt like I had been punched in the gut. This was a sentence that I never thought would really happen to us.

The boys were sentenced to fifty lashes, and the girls were sentenced to forty lashes. I learned for the first time that there were different types of lashing. The cleric specified that we would keep our clothes on while we were lashed. He said that even though the fabric could get stuck in the wounds, it would be less painful than having our backs bare. Maybe I should have thanked him for his sympathy.

Most of my friends stayed silent as they heard the sentence, but some cried. Others were more audacious, trying to contest their punishments. I looked silently at my father through the soundproof glass window. I could tell he was a nervous wreck as he waited to learn the verdict. It made me sad to see my father break down because of something I had put him through. I showed him the number forty with my free hand. He placed his hands over his face and fell back onto the wooden bench behind him. I exchanged a look with my mother, and in that moment I could see her help-lessness right through her eyes.

All the commotion made me feel light-headed. Our parents tried to tell us through the windows that it was going to be okay, but it was all hitting me like a ton of bricks. Suddenly, the noise of the hectic courthouse fell away from me. I was floating in the air with no gravitational force to tether me to reality; I was discon-nected from my body. I thought about my best friend who had been handcuffed to me for the past five days. She was shaking and crying. How was such a tiny, fragile girl going to make it through this? I thought about the other women in jail and the lonely ten-year-old girl. I wondered what their punishments would be.

I was always one to stand up for my rights and fight for what I believed in, but I didn't react that way this time. I knew no matter what I said, it wouldn't matter. I especially didn't want the judge to harshen our punishment even more. All I wanted was to get it over with—beat me up, and let's all go home.

Inside the bus, some of the girls were in a state of shock, but some of them bawled. We were all petrified. Neda put her head on my shoulder, and I could feel her body shaking next to mine. I placed my head on top of hers and, without making a noise, let tears stream down my face, the first tears since the night of the party. I had held them inside for so long, but I had finally been broken down. I wanted to explode. I don't know how long the bus ride was, but it was way too short. I wanted to stay on the bus for eternity. Couldn't we just drive away? Far, far away…

Hundreds of people stood outside what I called the "punish-ment building," waiting for their loved ones to exit. People cried, argued, and ran around frantically searching for friends and family.

Some of the women waiting outside followed the Islamic dress code by fully covering themselves, while others showed their hair and wore form-fitting clothing. These women were brave to dress as they did right under the government officials' noses. I once considered myself like one of these audacious women, rebelliously wearing what I pleased, but that little freedom-hungry girl inside me had been buried alive.

We entered the dark building and were placed into two separate lines—one for the guys, the other for the girls. There was a large open space with rooms all around and a few wooden benches in the corner. Some of our parents managed to enter the facility and were directed to wait by the benches. But our parents couldn't just sit still. They ran around the building, desperately trying to stop the officials from lashing us. They begged the guards to overturn the verdict and offered money in hopes that they could change their minds. But it was to no avail; as time passed, one after another of my friends entered the punishment room. I could hear them screaming, and some of the girls in line prayed out loud in both Arabic and Farsi. I prayed to myself in Farsi as I watched my friends come back out, one by one, their clothing covered in blood.

I'm not a patient person, and I never have been. I don't do well in situations where I have to wait and languish. I need resolutions, and I need them instantly. And in this situation, I had never been more afraid in my life. I became more and more light-headed at the sight of each girl and boy exiting the room. *If you are going to torture me*, I thought, *don't make me wait for it.*

Finally, it was my turn. Still handcuffed together, Neda and I silently entered a concrete room with two beds on opposite ends. The beds were made out of black metal with flimsy mattresses that were now soiled with fresh and crusted blood. I wasn't expecting to see pristine Ralph Lauren bedding, but it still repulsed me. Two intimidating women covered head to toe in black *chadors* stood by the beds, holding Holy Qurans under their arms and leather straps in their hands. I looked straight into the small hazel eyes of the woman who was about to lash me. Even though I thought she was an awful person, I could see pain and discomfort in her eyes. I wondered if she had a family. I wondered if she had a daughter…

The straps, I remember, consisted of three pieces of leather braided into one large, threatening whip. A round, fairly large bronze-looking bucket of water was perched next to one of the beds. This was used to douse the whip. When they took the handcuffs off, Neda immediately grabbed me and hugged me tightly. This was the first time we had been separated in five days, and it was the worst time to be separated. One of the punishers had to pull us apart because neither of us wanted to let go. We were told to lie facedown on the filthy beds, fully clothed. As we waited for the first lash to slice our skin, Neda screamed and cried out for help. I lay there confused and in a state of shock as I tried to listen to what was happening outside the doors.

I could hear our mothers arguing with the officials, begging them to take it easy on us because we were only kids. A few seconds later, the guard at the door came inside and whispered something to the women. I buried my face into the palms of my hands and ground my teeth so hard it sounded as if they were screaming in my ears. I closed my eyes very tightly and tried as hard as I could to think about good memories. Despite trying to focus so hard on my family and positive thoughts, I started screaming with Neda at the top of my lungs.

Suddenly, I felt the leather whip, drenched in water, lash viciously across my back. The pain was excruciating, and I was so petrified that I lost my voice. I could hear the whip whooshing through the air back and forth, and my back felt like it had just caught on fire. It was burning. I thought I was going to pass out. There were no screams left inside me.

The woman whispered in my ear that she would be gentler, but that I needed to scream to make it believable that she was hurting me just as badly as the first time. I couldn't begin to imagine how painful it must have been for the people who didn't receive the gentler lashing.

And I didn't need to make-believe. It was *torture*. When the whip sliced my skin, I whimpered. I was very light-headed, and all I could feel was an acute burning sensation on my back as the whip penetrated deeper and deeper. Forty lashes later, I lay there helplessly. It was finally over. It was all over. Time had run together like sand. It was over before I could even process what had just happened.

I was terrified when I stumbled out of that room. I was overwhelmed with emotion; I felt disrespected, insulted, humiliated, angry, and relieved all at once. My surroundings seemed to unravel in slow motion around me. As I walked away from the punishment room, feeling as though I had been swept away on dark clouds during a horrible storm, I forgot to even make sure Neda was okay. I could see all the familiar faces of our families waiting outside, looking absolutely devastated. I started bawling as soon as I saw my parents and apologized for what I thought I had done to them. I just wanted to be home. I needed to get out of there. I didn't want to talk to anyone, especially about how I was feeling.

The car ride back to the house was extremely excruciating.

I quickly realized how badly I was hurt when I couldn't sit down properly in my seat. I had to lean forward and prop my body up with my elbow on the door handle. My parents said nothing as we pulled away. They were both concerned and miserable, anxious and angry. I could see it in quick, sudden flashes in the car mirrors. Maman kept looking into my eyes from the front seat, searching for answers. I think she didn't even know how to ask if I was okay, because she knew that I wasn't okay. They had done their best to raise Aria and me in a safe and healthy environment, but we had been punished right in front of their eyes, and they'd had no control over what happened to us. They had been powerless to do anything about it. I could hear my father's voice in my head:

How many times did I tell you not to wear those short skirts?

How many times do I need to tell you that I don't want you wearing makeup and attending these parties?

That was exactly what I didn't want to hear from my parents, but I knew it would happen.

Did I get punished for hanging out with my friends? For wearing a miniskirt? Wearing makeup? Running away? Partying? All of it combined? All I knew for sure is that the punishment didn't fit the so-called crime. As I gazed out of the car window at the fully covered women we passed along the way, I asked myself whether these women believed what happened to me was okay. Could a woman who was covered from head to toe accept someone like me—a woman who chose to express her individuality by not covering?

When I got home, I took a deep breath and looked at my back in the bathroom mirror. The wounds were still fresh. The lash marks were red swollen stripes across my skin, and as time passed they turned yellow, then blue. I stepped into the shower to wash off the blood and dirt from my ravaged body and clean myself. I sat in the bathtub with very little water and soaked my thoughts away. My mind drifted onto a journey of its own making, in and out of consciousness.

What does Islam *really* require, and how did religion come to play such a large role in the Iranian society? I realized that I wanted to explore my Iranian culture and the Muslim religion and find out what it was all about. I wanted to change my now distorted view of those who believed in all this, who believed that my torture was somehow okay and justified. They couldn't all be bad people. And at the same time, I needed to know that I could once again wear a miniskirt without being lashed forty times.

In the days following the punishment, I had to learn how to cope: cope with the principal of my school, who suspended me; cope with my furious and devastated parents, who required more emotional support than I did; cope with the pain and fear associated with the lashes and the five days spent in jail. And I had to wrestle against getting lost in my thoughts about all those poor young girls who weren't as fortunate as we were in our sentencing. I couldn't stop thinking about the bride in her wedding dress, the cursing ten-year-old runaway, and the screams echoing from the other cells. Although I was finally out of prison, the prison wasn't yet out of me.

DON'T GET HOPELESS, GET EMPOWERED

CHAPTER 11

NO CHANGE, NO BUTTERFLIES

Iran is a risky place to be different. People are often victimized for their beliefs. As I learned the hard way from the end of a whip, the attitude toward freedom of expression is very ruthless. It's nearly impossible to feel free, and that is a suffocating sensation. The limitations can be found in almost every aspect of daily life, and they are the main reason people flee the country. It's sad and quite a tragedy to know that people don't want to leave their home but are compelled to because they feel powerless from the restrictions and are in need of the economic, academic, professional, and personal security that other countries can provide. The thing is that everywhere Iranians go, they seem to succeed. They are capable of succeeding because they are given opportunities that they don't have in their own motherland.

Iran has the world's highest rate of "brain drain"—meaning that highly educated people frequently leave Iran to pursue other educational and professional opportunities. Iran is losing its academic elite, which is costing its economy billions of dollars.

Just like many other Iranians who leave the country for better opportunities, my parents believed that Aria and I needed to forge a new beginning, and they hoped for a change of lifestyle for us. They could sense that I was craving more and more freedom every day. But more importantly, they wanted me to have a brighter future. They wanted me to pursue a law degree, get married, and have children— you know, every Iranian parent's dream. But it surely wasn't mine. I didn't want a fresh start, even after facing extreme brutality firsthand. I loved my life in Tehran, and my experience with the government didn't change my views of the picturesque country, its extraordinary people, and its cultural treasures. I didn't want to abandon my magical Iran, and I had no idea if I was ever going to return. But my parents had already made up their minds.

After months of arguing and ignoring my family members for their acts of "human cruelty," I had no choice but to take the tickets my parents had bought for Maman and me to embark on a journey, via Dubai, to the United States and into the unknown. Baba would stay in Tehran. He had too much pride to move, and his status in the Iranian milieu was way too important to him. Even if there wasn't much of a status left.

Before I left Tehran, Omid and I broke up, which made me despise my parents even more. I was convinced that they were the reason I couldn't marry my soul mate and live happily ever after in Iran. Just so you know, now I thank Maman every single day for making that decision for me. I can't imagine what my life would be like today if I had stayed and married Omid.

I had just graduated high school and was off to Dubai to start my new, wonderful, glamorous life (or so my parents wanted me to believe). That's why people move to Dubai anyway, right? Going there would be an opportunity they felt compelled for me to explore. My extended family had business there, and Aria had just moved there for school and work.

The city of Dubai sprang up from a desert in a mere twenty years. Today it's a sparkly new city that was built to have the best of everything—the tallest buildings, the most lavish hotels, the most modern technology, the most glamorous fashion—the list is endless. The sun is even hotter there. The largest indoor ski resort in the world lies smack in the middle of the Mall of the Emirates. The city's affluence is confirmed by its fleet of police cars—which includes a Ferrari, a Lamborghini, and a $2.5 million Bugatti Veyron. If that doesn't scream luxury, I don't know what does. Everywhere you look, there are more wonders to be discovered in this ultramodern, cosmopolitan city. It's become a symbol of prosperity that you either love or hate (or love to hate). Regardless of your opinion, it's undeniably impressive. It feels like living in a futuristic era.

Fashion means business in Dubai. The city has become so involved in the international fashion circuit that it created Dubai Fashion Week in record speed, and it's sneaking up behind Paris, New York, and Milan. Dubai sought a slice of the multibillion-dollar industry. It's the city that wants it all, and it gets what it wants.

Every year, millions of people visit Dubai's enormous malls, designers, and local boutiques to shop. Fashion is much more daring in Dubai, and that's part of the city's culture. The boldness makes sense, given that it's a melting pot of countless cultures. Unlike Iran and some other Muslim countries, there are no extreme restrictions on women's clothing in the United Arab Emirates. Finally, I got to see for myself what it was like to be among women who had choices. It was liberating for me.

When I woke up in the morning and considered what I wanted to wear, I realized that I didn't have to think about rules, restrictions, judgments, or punishments. I wasn't forced into pretending to be more religious than I really was, and I could finally use my clothes to create an identity for myself the way I wanted to. As I stared at my clothes, I saw a future in which I would be judged less for my appearance and valued more for who I was as a person, regardless of whether I chose to cover myself or wear a miniskirt. Freedom is not about the amount of clothing you put on or take off, but about having the choice to do so.

As I explored this new city, I saw women who wore *hijabs*, covered from head to toe, walking on the same beaches as women who frolicked around in their European-cut bikinis. Their freedom of expression empowered me. I found a new respect for women who covered by choice for religious reasons they strongly believed in. They didn't have to fear government punishment for not wearing the veil. I also respected those who wore bikinis in a conservative country. There is something very powerful about standing up for your beliefs, even if you're in the minority. I knew I needed to find a way to celebrate that peaceful coexistence. It all suddenly clicked for me: fashion was a form of freedom.

But I didn't have a chance to fully discover what I was looking for in this city of grandiose buildings and man-made islands, because Dubai was only a layover for me on my way to America. Maman wanted me to move to Washington, DC, so that I could enroll in college. Once again I was on a plane, this time to "the capital of the free world." Leaving for someplace new that second time was even harder than the first transition had been. Dubai was temporary; America was for keeps. Even worse, Aria was staying in Dubai, and I was flying farther away from home and the Middle East, which made my outlook gloomier. I was sick of having no choice in my own future.

Though Maman was only an arm's length away, I ignored her the entire flight. I was devastated and didn't try to hide it. I bawled as if I were traveling into the bowels of hell. I cried more on that plane ride than I did leaving prison. In my mind, I was being hauled away in handcuffs to Guantanamo. It was ungrateful and selfish of me to only think about my future when the woman sitting next to me had sacrificed hers to provide me with better opportunities. She had left her husband and son behind, a beautiful house, friends, family—everything she treasured—for me. I didn't recognize her sacrifice then, but I sure as hell do now.

People around the globe go to great lengths to gain access to the United States of America—the land of opportunity. Your entire life can change if you get your hands on that golden ticket—the green card. You are free to become whoever you want. This is the country that made Kim Kardashian more famous than most world leaders, the country that allows you to purchase a gun and say things like, "Fuck you, president." If you are smart and motivated enough, this country gives you the opportunity to be on the cover of *Forbes* magazine. And last but not least, this country allows you to wear a miniskirt in public without any fear of punishment. It may not sound like much, but it was—and still is—vital to me.

July 5, 2000: Arriving in the terminal at Dulles International Airport in Virginia, my first thought was: *fashion disaster.* Everywhere I looked I saw dirty tennis shoes, very short shorts, way too many flip-flops on non-manicured toes, and eighties haircuts with neon scrunchies. I compared everything I saw in America to Iran, trying to justify in my head why things were so much better back home. Not because they actually were better back home, but simply because I was red with anger from missing my life there so much. Stepping onto American soil made it all real. I put my guard up as soon as I got off the plane, and I didn't want to see positives in anything. Admitting that there was a place better than home would have made me feel remorseful; I thought I'd be letting down everyone I left behind by finding something greater.

I spent the next few weeks at my aunt's house barricaded inside "my" bedroom and crying. I didn't feel like speaking to or seeing anyone other than my friends in Tehran, whom I spoke with every day. (Thank you, AOL Instant Messenger.) At least they could provide me with some sort of comic relief. I don't know if it made things better or worse hearing them share all the fun times I was missing out on. I wanted to go back to the life I knew.

A part of me was so fascinated to be here, but at the same time I was overwhelmed by all the freedom and opportunities I now had. Another part of me felt guilty, as if I were cheating on Iran by enjoying America. Was I giving up my memories of the Rose Garden, Aria, and the wonderful friends and family I left behind? I was in a love-hate relationship with my new home. I felt inadequate, so I ostracized myself until I was ready to confront my fears. And my limited English vocabulary surely wasn't helping me adjust to the United States.

Starting ESL (English as a second language) courses was the first step in acclimating myself to this dream country. I had studied English in high school in Tehran and taken private English classes with Aria and Payam, at my parents' request, but they didn't actually help me learn English. My tutor in Tehran was a crazy British lady named Miss Megly. Her husband worked at the British embassy, which is what brought her to Iran. Our teacher-student relationship was a bumpy one. It was hard to view her as an authority figure when she always had bed hair and a toothbrush in hand. Conveniently, I was stricken with "food poisoning" every other class.

I was basically learning English against my will and resisted it with all my might. Maman wanted me to be culturally well rounded, so she enrolled me in every activity possible—from tennis lessons to cooking classes. Because of my reluctance to learn, I sadly didn't benefit from most of these experiences. Aside from the intensity of learning a new language, the ESL courses were socially difficult for me too. Back in Tehran, I was the leader of my clique and one of the cool girls. Here, I sat like an invisible lump among foreigners of all ages and backgrounds who never gave a single glance in my direction. Going to class was like being in a United Colors of Benetton ad campaign, there were so many different cultures and backgrounds. My teacher was Chinese, the old guy to my right was Indian, and the girl next to me was from Bolivia. The campus itself was massive, and no one cared about my existence. Despite being surrounded by so many interesting people, being in an environment that was so different from what I was used to gave me a sharp shiver of fear every day.

In so little time my life had turned upside down. Each morning, I struggled to wake up, knowing that those dreaded courses awaited me. My mood was tense, and it only grew worse by the day. I was the Debbie Downer in the back of the classroom who didn't utter a word to anyone. The only thing on my mind was what my friends were doing and which lucky girl would date Omid next. As it happened, he dated one of my best friends a mere three months after I moved. I guess my future ex-husband had moved on faster than I had.

I think my parents realized that their dream of me becoming a lawyer was pretty much dead by the time I stepped on U.S. soil. I had already planted the seed in their heads that law school wasn't for me. My future profession was still a huge question mark. All I knew was that I wanted to empower women to celebrate their beauty, but I hadn't figured out how I would do that just yet.

In the meantime, I needed a temporary job. I wanted to distance myself from my family, surround myself with people other than the "enemies" who had brought me to America. It would also help me learn English much faster. ESL class wasn't working as quickly as I had hoped, and I was especially traumatized after a very good-looking guy made fun of my English at a party. It made me inch even closer to total exile. That's when I decided that changes needed to be made. No guy would ever make fun of the way I spoke again. It's ironic that now people think my accent is sexy. Who would've thought that I could ever embrace it?

Fariba, an Iranian boutique owner in Virginia, was the lucky target of my job search. I stumbled upon her boutique one day while I was shopping. She sold dreadful wedding dresses and evening gowns, and she was the physical embodiment of "going overboard." Fariba looked a bit like Michael Jackson. She had more plastic surgery than the entire Beverly Hills community combined. Her face was perfectly pulled back, but her neck was ridden with wrinkles. On top of her overdone face, she caked on makeup an inch thick that was four shades lighter than her actual skin color. I wondered how long it took her to get ready every morning. She was tall, very skinny, and had fried blond hair doused with way too much hairspray.

But thank goodness I found a fellow Iranian! I don't think I would've gotten the job otherwise, given my professional credentials (which were zero) and my extremely limited English vocabulary. I think she mostly felt sorry for me, but in a way she also felt close to me instantly, since we were both Iranian. Fariba hired me on the spot. We find comfort among those who understand us, and having a boss that spoke Farsi was, understandably, comforting.

The store was located in McLean, Virginia, a wealthy suburb of Washington, DC, and it was the perfect place for my new favorite pastime: people-watching. I stared out the front window for hours on end observing what the Virginia fashion scene had to offer. I wanted to change every single outfit. It especially bothered me that these women used their freedom of dress to wear flip-flops and gym sneakers. I missed Iranian underground fashion terribly. My people-watching days were short-lived, as I got bored of being the fashion police. I could only do so many imaginary makeovers.

The store's clients were mainly bridal parties, but the ones who fascinated me the most were the girls shopping for their flashy prom dresses with their fathers' credit cards. While these girls celebrated the beginning of their dating lives, Iranian girls were being punished for merely appearing in public with the opposite sex. Baba would've never paid for a dress meant to be worn on a night where many girls are known to lose their virginity, unless it was my wedding night. I didn't care to go to prom, but I craved that type of freedom for my fellow Iranians.

From a young age, I knew that working for someone else wasn't something I wanted to do, and being bossed around by Fariba for months on end reinforced that. But sometimes Fariba would leave me in the store alone for hours upon hours. It was daunting at times, because I mainly had to use sign language to talk to customers, since my English was still poor. But it also gave me a sense of authority. I was the boss, and that was an exceptional source of contentment for me. During my free time at the register, I would sketch the gowns that hung in the store and then tweak them into better versions. I sketched so much that I actually got good at it. I tried on every single dress at least twenty times to get the functionality in my sketches just right. In those quiet moments of creation, the idea of owning my own clothing line consumed my thoughts.

Before I knew what was happening, an American dream was forming in my head and with it, an acceptance of my new home and community. I started to really cherish my life here. I was slowly making friends and experimenting with different activities. I had gotten a driver's license so I could go anywhere I wanted, and unlike when we were in Iran, Maman would get so excited whenever I went out and did things. She wouldn't even ask me where I was going or when I was coming back.

"Wear some lipstick, for God's sake!" she would say.

Navigating this dramatically different world instilled in me the desire to create more opportunities for myself. What was at first a hopeless place for me had become one filled with countless possibilities. I wished for the same freedom and opportunities for my friends and many others in Iran, who were just as capable, if not more so, than I was. The only difference between them and me was that I held a U.S. passport.

Accepting change is no easy feat—whether it's jumping from one relationship to another, one profession to another, or one country to another. I feared change when I moved to the United States, but I learned to embrace it over time. Fear eventually morphed into nervous excitement. I am where I am today because I grew and learned every time something changed, I discovered fresh insights about every aspect of my being, and I transformed myself. Not all changes will lead you to fairy tales and glory, but overcoming the wickedest, most difficult changes in your life will direct you to what you truly desire. It's about closing one chapter and opening another one. I closed the chapter of living in constant fear and took the pen in my hands to write my own fearless fairy tale. If caterpillars didn't change, there would be no butterflies!

CHAPTER 12

FIRST FASHION STRIDE

I've always lived by the motto, "What doesn't kill you makes you stranger." Yes, you read that right. I said "stranger." It's okay to be strange in a world that is trying to make everyone perfect. The more experiences you have, both good and bad, the better you'll understand what makes you triumphantly stand out. Those who stand out from the masses are the ones who succeed.

The only way to master something quickly and move on to the next challenge is to learn how to be adaptable and wear many different hats. And I had worn so many hats! Before I reached my twenties, I had already witnessed a war, watched my family fall apart, spent time in jail, lived both under a strict regime and in a land of intimidating freedom, and just about everything in between. I knew I hadn't really seen it all, but it sure as hell felt like I had.

I learned how to navigate my way through challenging situations, deal with people, control my emotions, and act rationally. I understood that nothing comes easily and success doesn't come without a fight. Nobody grows through a life of rainbows and unicorns. You only grow when you're faced with tremendously difficult circumstances, and they will prepare you to be greater than you already are. I believed that I had what it took to be a strong woman and comprehended how to "figure it out." I was ready to enter the next phase of my life.

I was no longer looking to be "cool." I wanted to become influential. After becoming fluent in English, I once again became a social butterfly, so it wasn't hard to find a great group of friends. I managed to snag a spot in one of the best social circles in DC by associating myself with people who were motivated and driven, which ultimately put me on the road that I'm on today. My newfound friendships weren't built on the foundation of being reckless anymore. They were energized by encouraging magnificence in each other, and by wanting more and doing more. The people you associate yourself with throughout your life have an enormous impact on the person you become.

One person in my social circle who particularly impacted me was Mark, the son of an Iraqi immigrant. I admired him as a businessman because he was 100 percent self-made. At a very young age, he valeted cars in Virginia and eventually ended up purchasing the valet company and moving to DC. From there he started a money management business and managed the assets of some of the wealthiest businessmen and women in DC. He was driven, always in pursuit of the next big business deal, and simply a genuine person. Mark's entrepreneurial spirit and positivity toward life was striking, and as a mentor he was someone I could look up to. He was an immigrant like myself, which made me believe that the American Dream was real.

When I turned twenty-one, I began playing with the idea of having my own fashion line. I thought about it every day, but thinking about it was the only thing that I was doing. One spring day in 2003, I briefly told Mark about my dream and how I didn't know where to start.

"What are you waiting for?" Mark asked. Don't you just love when people ask you that? He told me that if I kept making excuses, I would never accomplish anything.

He was right. I always made excuses—"I need capital" or "It's so competitive." Instead of spending so much time coming up with reasons why it wouldn't work, I should've spent that time coming up with a million reasons why it *would* work. As fate would have it, I was given the push I needed just a few months later when I attended the Formula One Canadian Grand Prix in Montreal.

Canada's most "European" city comes alive during the races. Hundreds of thousands of people from around the world flood in to be a part of the experience. The weekend offered a party-crowd experience of immense proportions. Every hotel, restaurant, and bar was filled with riled-up fans, and it didn't take long for me to fall in love with the boutiques and the unique street style in the city—from bohemian babes to rock 'n' roll chic. The race-team-inspired outfits were my favorite, though. I loved all the sexy tailored cuts and silhouettes mixed with stand-out, funky trims and logos. The style of a tomboy coupled with the ability to look nonchalantly sexy was a trend that I recognized as ultracool, ultrapowerful, and ultrasexy!

In honor of the impressive race cars, I bought a fitted red Ferrari polo. Mark's preppy, cocky friend Sam, who drove his father's black Lamborghini, made fun of my shirt in front of everyone.

"Where is *your* Ferrari, sweetie?" What an *asshole*! Just because I didn't own a sports car didn't mean I couldn't rock the racer outfit. I needed to plot my revenge, so that evening I went to a small arts-and-crafts store and bought black iron-on letters. I ironed them onto my Ferrari polo to spell out: "Daddy's Car."

The next morning, I met our group in the hotel lobby wearing my newly transformed top. I walked straight up to Sam and said coyly, "Did you say something about my Ferrari?" Everyone laughed hysterically, except Sam, who was embarrassed. I guess you could say that the shirt was a hit, and all my friends wanted one.

Mark saw what I had created and enthusiastically said, "See, it's not that hard! This is a great start."

And he was right. However small, it was a defining moment. People of all ages approached me during the race to ask where they could snag one. I could either kick the idea to the curb and possibly regret it or take a chance on myself.

The second I got back to DC, I got to work. I wanted to test run the "Daddy's Car" model. I bought a dozen short-sleeved T-shirts in a variety of colors. Then I sewed and ironed on the letters. It wasn't exactly high-end, but it worked. Within a matter of days, I had already sold the twenty shirts I had made.

I didn't want to stop at "Daddy's Car" T-shirts. I spent the next few weeks conjuring up idea after idea. In the end, I crafted ten one-of-a-kind designs adorned with chains, fabric swatches, and paint. I thought the forty-dollar price point (and twenty-dollar profit) was reasonable. With every sale, I grew more confident in my products.

Then my masterpiece (and bestseller) came to me: "Forty Lashes."

From the front, it looked like any plain white T-shirt with a circular neckline, but it was much more than that. The back was cut through, representing the forty lashes I had received in Iran. I used a cutter like the one I used to cut my father's leather chair to slash the back of the shirt. My parents would be so proud to know that cutting the leather chair in Tehran would help set me on the path to my new business. It's almost worth the ruined chair, right Baba?

Trials and tribulations happen in your life so that you can rise to the occasion and seize your own power. I now had the luxury of experiencing freedom, and I also had options. I wouldn't allow myself to be a victim any longer. It felt so good to wear something on my body that had blossomed from one of my darkest points and that was now giving me strength. I wore it proudly and told everyone the story behind it. Some were fascinated by it, some couldn't comprehend it.

Although I knew I could take my creations to a wider market, I didn't feel ready, but I don't think anyone truly does. I reminded myself that every big thing starts small. Richard Branson started his brand with a youth-culture magazine called *Student*, which evolved into a multibillion-dollar business. He dropped everything else and just went for it, and that is exactly what I was prepared to do. I was ready to find my greater self—and look good doing it!

CHAPTER 13

DIAMOND IN THE ROUGH

One summer night in 2003, I hit DC's (not-so-big) nightlife scene with some friends. I threw on ripped jeans, heels, and my "forty lashes" T-shirt. An older, mature gentleman in his midforties named Eric was among my group of friends, and his calm composure in the sea of wild college kids dancing and pounding drinks caught my attention. Little did I know, he was an industrial guru turned entrepreneur with a passion for investing in young start-ups. He complimented my shirt.

"Thank you," I replied, flattered. "I made it myself."

"Are you a designer?" Eric asked.

"I'm trying to become one."

He looked at me, puzzled, and asked, "Why are you merely *trying*?"

"It's a very expensive industry," I heard myself answer smoothly. "I need capital in order to take my company to production and market it."

We chatted for about ten minutes, and Eric seemed captivated. A bit of advice: the universe doesn't play favorites, but when I spoke about my dream, my powerful passion came through, and he could feel all my energy simply by listening to me. Opportunities in life come from putting light, energy, and emotion into a specific action or reaction, and that creates possibilities.

"Do you have a business plan?"

I replied confidently, "Yes."

I did not hesitate. I saw a chance, and I jumped (even though said business plan was completely nonexistent). I had created a shining possibility out of a rough situation, but now I needed to follow through on it. It was no longer about faking it, it was about making it. My next hurdle was to learn how to create a business plan—and fast. I didn't want Eric to lose interest in my business. This was my chance to snatch an opportunity, and I had to take it seriously.

A part of me believed that I was being stupid. I thought, *This is never going to happen!* I was afraid I would embarrass myself by even trying. The other part of me urged myself not to listen to the mind chatter of self-doubt and forced myself to take a chance and thrive. *The worst that can happen*, I told myself, *is that you will learn something from it.* As Richard Branson so eloquently put it, "If someone offers you an amazing opportunity and you're not sure you can do it, say yes—then learn how to do it later."

Over the next few weeks, I spent every day at Barnes & Noble. I read all the how-to books on starting a business and writing a professional business plan. I became an expert camper in the business section of the bookstore. All that was missing was my tent.

Three weeks and twenty-six pages later, I was ready to present my amateur business plan. I emailed it to Eric and asked whether we could set up a meeting to go through it. Even if he threw it in the trash, at least I had learned how to write the worst business plan of all time. I have so much respect for those who do this for a living. I would much rather hike Mount Everest in heels.

Weeks passed without a response, and eventually I accepted my fate. Then, finally, an email notification popped up on my phone. It was from Eric. The word *ecstatic* couldn't even begin to describe how I felt. He wrote: "Tala, I will be in DC this week for some business meetings, and I would love to hear about your business plan."

I invited him to Paolo's, a charming Italian restaurant in Georgetown, for dinner. I paired my sharpest black skirt suit with a white ruffled shirt underneath and black pumps. I overaccessorized my ensemble to offset the business look and pumped up my hair to complete my fierce look. To say I was overcompensating for my nervousness would be an understatement.

I packed samples of my T-shirts in a large shopping bag and printed two copies of my not-so-sophisticated business plan. I had memorized my pitch to perfection. How would Baba act in this situation? Serious and confident. Even when he answered questions on a topic he knew nothing about, he made you believe it was his specialty. That was exactly what I sought to emulate.

I saw Eric before he saw me. He was always well-dressed—neat and refined in a charcoal suit with a much lighter-colored casual shirt underneath and leather loafers. He held a briefcase in one hand and greeted me with a firm handshake. When we were seated at the table, he cut straight to the chase.

"Let's get started. Tell me why you brought me here today."

Okay, he wasn't interested in small talk.

I looked at this meeting as a sales meeting. I needed to sell my business, and because my business was just an illusion at the time, I had to sell myself. When you're a start-up, people need to like you to like your vision. Building relationships will always be a key part of building your success. So when Eric brushed away the small talk I got very apprehensive, and my confidence wavered.

I anxiously handed him a copy of the business plan, and we

started to go through it page by page. I sounded awful. I heard myself talking faster, breathing faster, and muttering "um" every other sentence. Maybe I had practiced too much. Would I have been better off winging it? After the fourth page, he held up his hand and firmly said, "Stop."

My heart was beating like a drum. *Shit. Eric hates it*, I thought. Then he said, "Tala, you clearly can't write a business plan. No offense, but this is dreadful. I tried reading it last night and didn't make it past the second page." Well, thanks for the blunt letdown! I had only spent hundreds of hours and three weeks camping out at Barnes & Noble creating it, and it still sucked!

After a long silence, he finally said, "Forget about the logistics. Why don't you tell me about your plan—your *personal* plan? What do you envision for your company?"

Forget about the logistics? That was all that I had researched. My entire business plan consisted of market research, fashion history, and all that factual yet one-dimensional stuff you can find in books and articles. I guess learning about the history of polka dots wasn't going to help me in this situation. I needed to bring out my street smarts. I was on a scorching hot seat, and I had no choice but to deliver the pitch of a lifetime.

I took a sip of my drink to buy myself a few seconds. I knew exactly what I wanted, but were my dreams too big? He was a person who could either make or break my dream. My legs shook, and my palms started to sweat. I put my hands on my legs firmly in an effort to get them to stop shaking. The convulsions were something I had never experienced before. *Stop. Stop. Stop.*

I finally said, "Well… I'm going to tell you what I feel in my heart. Don't judge me. I may sound crazy." I pulled out the T-shirts and showed him what I had created in my bedroom. I told him about my friends and I being arrested. I explained how that event inspired me to start a fashion business to empower women to follow their dreams and celebrate freedom. He stared at me through his thick glasses with his arms crossed. At some points he nodded his head, indicating that he understood what I meant—or perhaps it was a "fuck-my-life" headshake from how bored he was. But it didn't matter. Voicing how passionate I was about my mission, and how deeply it came from within my soul, felt incredible. All of a sudden the shaking ceased, and I felt a kind of relief blossom from within myself.

Then he abruptly said, "Okay, that's enough." My heart plummeted to the bottom of my gut. Did I lose him again? *God, I suck at this.*

Eric grabbed his whiskey glass from the bottom and swirled the ice in it. Then he said, "Here's the thing. I don't know much about the fashion industry, but there is something about your passion that I can't overlook. I see the fire inside you. I can feel it pouring out of your skin."

I thought it was a polite way of rejecting my business plan. I was trying really hard to keep a confident face and not cry from embarrassment. He calmly looked down at his cell while I was shaking, once again, in my pumps. I seriously considered grabbing his phone and throwing it out the window.

After about a minute, he said confidently, "Let's do it." All the air left my lungs in one giant gasp. I could feel my face shaking from my effort not to scream in excitement. Before he could even finish his sentence, I was already picnicking on cloud nine, envisioning my future, surrounded by my T-shirts, a brand-new design studio, staff, fashions shows... Then Eric interrupted that vision by asking, "How much do you need to start this business?"

Well, that's a thought. I had no idea. Numbers kept flashing in my head, but I didn't know which one to choose. I didn't want to say a number that was too high because I was afraid he would walk away.

Eric insisted, "Come on. Give me a number."

I said, "Twenty thousand."

He asked, "How much equity will you give up for that number?"

I said the first number that popped into my head, without calculating any business terms. "Three percent."

Eric started laughing hysterically. *Shit*, I thought. *That was too low.* He was laughing so much that he had tears in his eyes, and I had to fight away my humiliation. Then he took out a pen from his jacket pocket and grabbed the dampened napkin that was underneath his whiskey glass. He wrote: "I, Eric R. XXX, will invest $20,000 in Tala Raassi's T-shirt line for 3 percent of the company." Then he signed the bottom of the napkin and handed it to me. I couldn't peel my eyes away from the soggy white napkin. Was this the start of my glamorous destiny?

"Is that it?" I asked.

"I will have someone from my staff draft a legit contract tomorrow and send it to you. My signature on the napkin shows you my commitment to this. Now it's up to you to figure out how to make this successful. You have a lot of work ahead of you." Then he stood up, shook my hand, and said, "Thank you for dinner. I have an early meeting tomorrow." He walked out of the restaurant leaving me alone with my thoughts. I had just survived an earthquake of emotions.

I stared out the window at people walking through the

bustling streets of Georgetown and attempted to process what had just happened. Getting a successful businessman to invest in my business at twenty-one years old had appeared impossible. But I had conquered my fear and managed to secure a freedom that I never thought I would be able to get. This was the kind of support that I needed to move forward in my hopes of inspiring young women through fashion.

It is very rare (but, fortunately, becoming less so) that a young person has the self-esteem to maneuver through life as an adult businessperson. But if you're open to the unexpected, life will always shed light on an area of opportunity. You have to identify that opportunity when it comes and realize why it's there to serve you. Once you identify your open door, you must plan a course of action toward that light to manifest the destiny that you crave. Eric was a guy I met in a nightclub, but he ended up becoming my investor with a contract written on a soggy napkin.

CHAPTER 14

THE WORLD'S LONGEST RUNWAY

Welcome to a new chapter in my life: Tala Raassi, *CEO*.

Wow, a business owner. I felt like I was following in the footsteps of my father and rebuilding my family's entrepreneurial legacy. The role of CEO brought me countless sentiments and responsibilities. On top of that Eric was counting on me to make his investment worthwhile. I was experiencing a high like I never had before, but at the same time I was scared. There was no going back now!

The first step was to register my company. I researched how to legally set up a company online and then registered my new T-shirt line as Tala Raassi, LLC (limited liability company). That was the easiest step. The next part involved using some of the investment to purchase material and start creating T-shirts. Spending money was always easy for me, but this time I was really terrified. The future of my newborn business was based on this investment.

I wanted to be as resourceful as possible, so I turned my bedroom into my workshop and "hired" Maman to help. It took me several weeks to produce fifteen styles, and Maman was instrumental in helping me create them. She was much better at sewing than I was and obviously there was no charge for her labor. My poor mother has helped me with so much throughout my life and has never asked for anything in return. She is and always has been full of strength. I think she wanted me to follow my dream so badly because she never really got to follow hers. She saw bits and pieces of herself in me.

Each T-shirt sold for around fifty dollars, and I made a twenty- to thirty-dollar profit. Despite that, my expenses were adding up so quickly that in a few short weeks, I had already spent more than $5,000 in material and equipment.

I needed to get some exposure before I ran out of money. All my friends and family had already bought my T-shirts, and it was essential to find more customers to generate a better cash flow. I decided to advertise the birth of my brand by hosting a fabulous fashion show in DC. At this point in my life, I thought you were only a real fashion designer when you had real runway shows, models, celebrities, and all the other glamorous things that outsiders associate with the industry.

I had never hosted a fashion show before and still had a lot to learn. I watched a myriad of them on television and the Internet, but hosting your own is quite different, especially if you're preparing for it solo. I knew influential people in the nightlife business. (Let's give a round of applause to my years of partying.) I got in touch with a friend who promoted the hottest DC clubs, and he loved the idea. Who wouldn't want a bunch of hot women strutting down a runway at their club? We settled on Pearl nightclub, one of the most popular venues at the time. My target market would be there—young, good-looking, international college students who could afford a fifty-dollar T-shirt.

The crowd was perfect, but the logistics on-site couldn't have been more imperfect. The venue was *enormous*. The only way for all the guests to see the models was to create an L-shaped runway that started from the bathrooms, passed by the bar, went around the table service area and ended at the entrance. Welcome to the world's longest runway. I convinced the club manager to purchase a red carpet and ropes to glam it up. Despite what seemed like miles and miles that the models would have to traverse in high heels, my vision was beginning to take shape.

Hosting trunk shows to sell jewelry in Tehran had taught me about the effects of "word-of-mouth marketing." So I personally called, messaged, or emailed every single person I knew and made sure they were aware that if they weren't in attendance on the night of my fashion show, I would never talk to them again. This is how I created my guest list—by force! Then I used social media as my second tool for publicity and marketing and began arranging the details for the show.

My budget was a massive: zero dollars. I wanted brand exposure without spending a dime. This was going to be my inauguration as a professional at making people do things for me for free. I realized that I had what club promoters hunted for on a nightly basis—stunning women and a large crowd, which is ultimately why they covered all the costs for the event. I approached college students from George Washington University, American University, and Georgetown University and eventually found ten fit, good-looking girls who were willing to model in the show for nothing. So far, so free!

I made all the bartenders, cocktail waitresses, promoters, and managers wear "I am with Tala Raassi" black-and-white T-shirts as a marketing tool to promote the line. They all agreed to wear the T-shirts, but I'm pretty sure they weren't thrilled about having my name plastered across their chests. I mean, who the hell was Tala Raassi to them anyway?

On the night of the fashion show, I arrived on-site early. Although I have never been married before, it felt like it was the night of my wedding. I was so anxious. I sat in my car outside the building until one of the managers came to open the door. The lights were off as I dragged my skidding suitcase across the quiet, bare venue to the back room. The place was so empty that I could hear my voice echo when I chatted with the staff. After helping place all the ropes and the red carpet to create the extended runway, I went to the storage room and started setting up for the action.

That night my problems seemed endless. An assistant like Andy Sachs from *The Devil Wears Prada* would've really come in handy right about then. Three models backed out at the last minute, but I remained calm (even though I was having mini panic attacks on the inside). My two best friends and Samira, my cousin, filled in.

Samira is a gorgeous, tall, thin brunette, and at first she was reluctant to walk the show because of her father. She didn't think he would be pleased with her walking around a club half-naked. And she was right: if my uncle ever found out that she wore booty shorts in a nightclub with her butt cheeks hanging out, he would've killed us both! But I knew once she got out on the runway she would work it. Leave it to me to corrupt all the Raassis, one kid at a time. After I assured her that her father would never find out, she agreed to do it.

Working with what you have takes resourcefulness and a dash of imagination. The girls showed up at 8:00 p.m. to get ready in Pearl's glamorous storage room—complete with trash bags, boxes, ropes, and unused club inventory. I used the boxes as chairs and the ropes as clothing racks. I hung my designs up with their "name tags" (pieces of paper with the models' names written on them in permanent marker). I did the girls' makeup and told them to blow out their hair with big, loose "Victoria's Secret" curls. I saved money, but prepping ten girls was a challenge, even for me. Despite the somewhat grungy aspect of the venue, I felt that this was the beginning of something awesome.

A sea of enthusiastic guests had packed the club by 11:00 p.m., and the show was scheduled to begin at 11:30. The front row was filled with club promoters, horny college boys, and a bunch of other sloppy drunks. I assumed all the guests had showed up for my big debut, not just to see hot girls and drink until they couldn't see straight. Where were the fashion editors, buyers, "it" girls, and fashionistas? I'm sure Ms. Wintour was devastated that she didn't get an invite to such a lavish affair.

The promoters had the genius idea of giving the models a bottle of Grey Goose as they got ready. By the time the show started, there wasn't a drop left in the bottle. Their blood-alcohol level didn't bode well, especially given their strappy sky-high heels. I was afraid they were going to trip and fall or throw up on the never-ending runway. All I could do at that point was wish for the best.

When it was finally showtime, I peeked my head out from the storage room to get a glimpse of what I had worked so hard on. It felt great watching the girls wear my designs on a runway for the first time. My creations had come to life under the club lights. A sense of pride overtook me, and I desperately wished that my family was there to see my first runway show. I wanted to make them proud.

After the last model strutted the runway, the DJ announced my name and welcomed me for the last walk. I held on to Samira's hand tightly and walked out, with the rest of the models clapping behind me. An electrifying power rose up through my body with each step down the runway.

I waved to my friends and the rest of the crowd. It was beyond amazing to hear everyone cheering and shouting my name. The crowd merged together into a sea of faces, and for a moment they could have been anyone. I could have been anywhere. I had goose bumps all over my body as I envisioned myself walking the runway during New York Fashion Week, surrounded by an audience of celebrities and fashion icons. That day couldn't come soon enough.

Given my budgetary limitations, all the models looked incredible. The venue was packed, and I had very positive feedback. Unfortunately, the show didn't generate much money or press for my line. But on the upside, the show ended up being pretty popular with the guys around town. Many of them got in touch with me asking for the models' contact information. Perhaps if a career in fashion didn't work out, I could become a madam or start a dating business.

It became very clear to me that it wasn't about getting an investor or hosting a fashion show anymore. Runways and word-of-mouth advertising just weren't going to cut it. I needed to figure out a way to sell my products to people outside my social circle and a real strategy for the bread and butter of my business. It would have to begin with a better production process—one that would be more cost effective, have a faster turnover time, and still produce high-quality products. I couldn't make everything myself or with the help of Maman anymore.

To jump-start this new plan, I put all my energy into finding the right facility for making high-end T-shirts. I contacted everyone I knew (social media to the rescue!) and quickly realized that most of the factories that I needed to work with were either in Los Angeles or overseas. I had always wanted a jet-setting life, but this was different. I didn't have a lot of money left, and it surely wouldn't cover the cost of traveling. I needed a way to get to these places without drying out my bank account. I had no choice but to get creative.

Imagine that you have to cross a body of water and in front of you are stepping-stones. Some of the stones are close together, which makes it effortless. But then you look down and notice that the next stepping-stone is farther away, and there is no going back. Your options are to stand still, paralyzed with fear forever, or to challenge your inherent capabilities and remember that fear only has power over you when you doubt yourself.

I thought about a friend of mine who worked for an airline company at Dulles International Airport. She was always traveling around the world on discounted buddy passes. But buddy passes were only available for airline employees and their families. I figured I could either pay full price to visit these factories and run out of money for production, or apply for a job with the airline so that I could go for free.

I didn't know anything about the airline industry, but that didn't matter. I would just have to jump to the next stepping-stone and figure it out! I got a job at the airport and was given an airline uniform with a hat. I put that hat on knowing that in life you have to wear many different hats. And even though this navy cap with a silver metal airplane glued in the center wasn't the kind I wanted to wear, it was the one that would get me closer to my goals.

I created the freedom I needed to explore my options further. You just have to do what you have to do, even when it's scary!

CHAPTER 15

COLLECTING PASSPORT STAMPS

After doing a great deal of research, I decided to visit two factories with my new buddy passes—one that produced fabrics and one that created T-shirts.

I arrived in sunny Los Angeles and began my descent into the vibrant Fashion District, where any shopping addict can buy directly from wholesale vendors and manufacturers. Pop hits blasted through storefront stereos to get shoppers' blood pumping, which created an electrifying energy among the busy buyers. Store owners stood outside their shops trying to snatch the attention of tourists or any potential customer who happened to be passing by. They sold everything from racks of hats, sunglasses, and shoes to colorful wigs and fake eyelashes. The crowded streets were packed with people carrying black plastic bags so full they were ready to burst.

As I stood in the middle of the glorious, colorful mess, the size and scale of the place felt overwhelming, especially when I had no clue where to go. I got lost in the rainbow of fabrics for hours. LA's Fashion District is home to the largest selection of textiles in the country—from exotic silks to novelty fabrics, sold on long cardboard rolls or just in piles on the floor. It's a place where negotiating is not only acceptable, but welcomed. I was in a magical forest of fabrics.

I made my way to the factory. *Boom! Boom! Boom!* The sounds of the factory machines seemed to pierce my eardrums. Yards upon yards of colorful thread appeared on cardboard combs. The machines looked like submarines, twisting, turning, and blowing on the materials. The thread they use is so fine that it's impossible to work with by hand, so workers use compressed air guns to meticulously fire it directly into the knitting machines. Large crates filled to the brim with thread were maneuvered around the space, waiting to be thrown into the next machine.

The factory produced immense amounts of fabric each year. I could hardly imagine all the fantastic T-shirts that I could make. I was blown away as I walked past the factory employees in their surgical masks and the various large machines performing each step of the fabric production process, their clunks vibrating through the floors. It reminded me of Baba's leather factory, except that he wasn't there to kick me out. Workers operated at lightning speed. They looked like Olympic champions, and each worker had clearly mastered his or her craft.

I shook hands with a factory sales representative, who gave me a thorough tour and showed me the cutting, pattern, printing, packaging, and shipping rooms. This was my chance to witness firsthand how the process worked, step-by-step. I was deep in the trenches of the manufacturing business, and it was like going from black-and-white to Technicolor. I was mesmerized. I was also in the big leagues now, which meant I needed to brace myself for a large quote.

All I needed to do was email the design of the T-shirt in a PDF version with the graphics and specifications, and *voilà*! That sounded easy enough! But the financial reality of this business slapped me in the face. After discussing the factory's pricing and minimum orders—at least one thousand per every size and style—I had to conclude that it wouldn't make financial sense to move forward. I guess I wasn't quite ready after all. It was hard to fight back my disappointment. How could I sell one thousand T-shirts?

On the plane ride back to DC, I wondered how other independent designers dealt with production. I needed to look into different manufacturing options, but the only alternative that would offer better deals was to work with factories abroad. I had my work cut out for me to research that, but God never gives you something you can't handle.

Eric put me in touch with Dana, a factory production manager who worked in Lima, Peru, which is a known destination for manufacturing. I didn't gather much information before I received my buddy passes. All I needed to know was that the factories she worked with were known for producing high-quality T-shirts and executing beautiful print work.

Maman didn't take the news of my trip lightly. She was convinced I was going to get kidnapped and never return. Truth be told, I was a bit nervous to travel there alone too. I had heard stories about kidnappings and robberies, which didn't help, especially since I was planning on spending my time in industrial locations. As a twenty-one-year-old Iranian girl who didn't speak a lick of Spanish, I was definitely embracing the concept of "fearless."

Bienvenida al Peru! When my plane landed, Dana was waiting to greet me at the airport. She was a short, chubby woman, with a black pixie cut, who loved to talk. Dana didn't speak English very well, which worried me, but it was comforting to have someone waiting for me at the arrival gate. I got into her old burgundy pickup truck and watched the sun set beneath the horizon as we made our way to the hotel. The run-down, hectic city flashed past the car windows, dotted with numerous casinos. I was there for a different kind of gamble though. Hopefully my luck would change, and I would leave Peru a winner. Beyond the grit and grime of the urban center, the backdrop of the mountains and water was absolutely breathtaking.

The following morning, I got a much better impression of life around Lima. The people walking around the bustling streets of the city, which is nearing nine million in population, were from a blend of backgrounds—Spanish, Italian, German, and neighboring South American countries—that had inhabited the land for centuries. Modern skyscrapers mingled with colonial residences and mud houses. The style of architecture depended on which neighborhood we were in. The districts, as Peruvians called them, were separated by a clear class divide. The wealthier districts were situated on the coastline, whereas the poorer ones were farther toward the mountains.

Dana took me to different factories to give me a well-rounded idea of how they operated. Once again, I was reminded of the factories Baba owned in Iran. Their workers were just as friendly and hospitable. Upon entering, they greeted me with hot tea and other Peruvian beverages. Men smoked cigarettes while they worked, just like Baba and his friends. The rigid rules of corporate America clearly didn't exist there. Although I was far away, I felt very close to home, which I took as a good sign about my prospects.

We visited three factories. The first two required that I order very large quantities. It was LA all over again. Dana had originally promised that these factories offered low-quantity production, but to her that meant orders of two or three hundred, not twenty or thirty.

The last manufacturer we visited was the smallest of the three, measuring the same size as a typical suburban two-bedroom home.

I wasn't impressed with the facility, but I was hoping they could craft what I needed. The owner was much more flexible with his minimum order requirements and willing to create my patterns and samples for a good deal. I could still make a small profit after manufacturing, shipping, and customs costs. Any seasoned businessperson wouldn't have accepted such a small margin of profit, but in my mind—a small profit was still a profit.

My prayers had finally been answered. I not only felt like I had grasped the manufacturing process, but I found a way to produce my line quickly and efficiently while offering great quality. I had to travel to South America to find it, but I loved the small factory and the warm family who worked in it. I couldn't wait to see my final products and develop our ongoing business relationship.

A few weeks after my trip to Peru, disaster stuck. The factory owner passed away, and his family was taking time off to grieve. They couldn't start working on my line for another few months, at the very least. They were already behind on orders from many other brands. I was very saddened for the lovely family who had been unbelievably hospitable and accommodating to me.

But still, this setback landed me back at square one. I continued to research factories and wasn't able to find a facility that could help me get started. I didn't know what else to do.

My friend Faisal suggested that I travel with him to Amman, Jordan, to visit factories there. I had met Faisal through mutual friends and, conveniently, he had solid connections with many Jordanian factories. His mother owned a very popular boutique in Amman. It was an in worth exploring. It didn't matter that it was so soon after my Peruvian setback. I was ready to travel to the moon and back to find a manufacturer.

Faisal and his mother put me in touch with Raj, a production manager. I sent Raj a few of my designs and within a few days, I received the green light. Once again, I was on a long plane ride into the unknown. As they say, the world is a book and those who don't travel only read one page.

Amman was a beautiful city made up of cream-colored buildings and desert sand. All the buildings seemed to be the same short height, and the city felt like a land that time forgot. If I wore a red shirt, I would look like the target in a bullfight. Among the ancient monochromatic buildings were more modern buildings, but according to municipal law, all buildings must be faced with local stones. This rule created a rather odd uniformity, yet a comforting continuity in the city.

The call to prayer, which echoed from the mosques' minarets, still gave me chills. It was a strange mix of emotions. It reminded me of waiting in line to be lashed in prison, but it also brought back memories of my childhood and walking home from school in my uniform in Tehran. God, I had missed the Middle East.

While Amman is quite liberal compared to some of its neighboring countries, I still needed to be cautious in my outfit choices. Most people who roamed the streets were conservative. Of course, Western women are held to a different, more tolerant standard, but the more liberal locals only appeared at chic restaurants, clubs, and house parties. It had been such a long time since I'd had to worry about my appearance being offensive or disrespectful. I had gotten so used to wearing what I wanted all the time. Having to think about that again reminded me of how much freedom I now had. It was that simple joy that I needed to remember not to take for granted.

Every day, we drove an hour outside Amman on extensive,

dusty highways to visit factories. Sidewalks and curbs didn't exist. By the end of the trip, we had visited half a dozen factories. None of them honored the initial quotes they had given me or anything else we had agreed upon in our preliminary conversations, before I'd flown halfway around the world. Talk about a curveball.

Omar, Faisal's father, accompanied us to the factory meetings. He was an older, witty man with a calm spirit. He warned me that I wouldn't be taken seriously because I was a very young girl and said that his presence would get us better deals. He was right! I was a woman in a man's world. If you thought the glass ceiling in the United States was bad, it's like societal discrimination against women was on steroids in Jordan. We aren't just talking about men thinking little of my company's finances or my business abilities— they completely disregarded my presence in the meetings. They only addressed Omar (unless they wanted to ask me my age). I was treated like an incompetent child. How could I expect to foster a business relationship if these manufacturers couldn't look past my age and gender? Omar reassured me that I shouldn't take it personally because culturally, they were used to dealing with men. Theirs was exactly the stereotype I was hoping to break.

With that, I left yet another country feeling completely helpless. There wasn't a next step. I had used up all the money, and my T-shirt line was halted. And that is how you lose $20,000 in 120 days! Did I learn a lot? Yes. Did I figure out who I couldn't work with? Yes. Did I make many connections? Yes. Did I find a facility to produce my line? Yes. Eventually. But I wish someone had given me a step-by-step guide on the process of manufacturing for an independent designer.

I'd had absolutely no experience and no guidance on how to

start a clothing line. I did it all backward. I think Eric wanted me to learn as I went along, and then learn from my mistakes. I told him exactly what happened, all the bumps and bruises, and his only response was, "What's your next move?"

I felt like I had failed Eric and myself, but my passion for fashion didn't die. I was given the opportunity to witness the inner workings of the fashion industry. Being behind-the-scenes of the most glamorous industry in the world couldn't have been more unglamorous, but that didn't stop me. Traveling to those factories made me recognize that the people who made my clothing were an essential part of my business, almost as much as I was. It wasn't about getting the most for the cheapest price but about finding someone who excelled at the craft and could create exceptional pieces. Learning about the process of making clothing excited me. I remained fascinated and craved more knowledge with each passing day.

Fashion isn't just about the perfect photo on the cover of *Vogue*, the awe-inspiring fashion shows during fashion week, or the breathlessly sleek people in head-to-toe designer clothing. Fashion is also about the brilliance behind creation and craftsmanship. The designers who got famous on a reality show or by having famous billionaire parents didn't interest me. I wanted to know more about those who started their brands from scratch and were now leaders in this multibillion-dollar industry. Because if they could do it, then so could I. It became my mission to figure out how they became successful and how I would too.

CHAPTER 16

THE BARE BONES OF THE CRAFT

L adies and gentleman, flight 629 is now ready for departure. Please proceed to gate B23…"

What the fuck am I doing here?

After traveling all around the world in pursuit of a manufacturer and working my ass off to the best of my ability, I *still* failed. No T-shirt line, no money, and I was back where I started. Well actually, I was at a gate in Dulles Airport, wearing an airline uniform, sketching T-shirts.

I was disappointed in myself and embarrassed of my failed business and defeat, but being an ordinary employee at another company wasn't feeding my creative soul. I was curious and wanted to pursue other opportunities. I was always speculating, "What if this" or "What if that."

My failure provided me with enough valuable information to know what I needed to avoid. I knew that I wasn't a quitter when I realized that I feared quitting more than I feared failing again. I hadn't selflessly put all my energy into my dream just to walk away and work at another job. As excruciating and regretful as that first failure was, I wanted to try again. Because I had survived, and that was all that mattered.

I had to come at my problem from a different angle. No more factories, no more patternmakers, no more looking for someone else to do something that I could do myself. And no more sitting at the airport and wondering. The manufacturers weren't the problem, I was the problem, and I needed to fix that. I needed to become familiar with the foundation of the industry that I was trying to take over.

At the advice of a friend, I found a small facility in Florence that offered a three-week program in high-end production. I was excited to learn more about the industry from people who knew it best. Let's be real; I don't think anyone can beat Italian design quality. It was time for me to learn how to perfect *patternmaking*.

One buddy pass and passport stamp later, I was sitting on the steps of the famously breathtaking Basilica di Santa Maria del Fiore, admiring the city's unique style: gorgeous men whizzing by on their mopeds, their hair fluttering in the wind; lively conversations; and tourists capturing every picture-worthy moment with their cameras in one hand while juggling a delicious chocolate gelato in the other. *Ciao Florence!*

Florence is small relative to its many marvels. The buildings and monuments tell stories of art and war. I felt honored to roam the same streets that Leonardo da Vinci, Michelangelo, and many other distinguished artists had done before me. Street artists painted pictures on the sidewalk, and handcrafted goods lined the pathways. The piazzas were overrun with tourists and students on school trips, not to mention the hoards of pigeons constantly landing and taking flight again as children scrambled to disperse them. Every day I spent in Italy, I felt inspired, much more inspired than I did sitting at gate B23. It was impossible not to envision my future in fashion as I took long walks through the cobblestoned streets and piazzas.

Italian fashion is undoubtedly the envy of the menswear community, with its fine leather goods, unique tailored cuts, shoes, accessories and all other types of goodies. I also must point out that Italian men are extremely sexy. There is something about their thick, dark hair and olive-toned skin combined with their outrageously stylish fashion sense. Of course, there are also Italian men with potbellies and anger-management issues who couldn't dress to save their lives, but let's just stay focused on the could-be movie stars who embellished every other street corner.

Having dark hair, eyes, and skin, I could pass as an Italian; nonetheless, it was extremely difficult to communicate while I was staying there. Locals spoke little to no English. All the menus and street signs were strictly in Italian. But even when we couldn't communicate verbally, the locals spoke the universal language of love, meaning they always made an effort to help me without any hesitation.

I felt like ever since I had moved to the United States, I had been on a nonstop mission to succeed, and I didn't make enough time for myself. Learning how to relax was probably one of the biggest takeaways from my trip to Italy. Other countries need to take a page out of their book. After a while, I actually felt European. It was easy for me to adapt to their way of life.

My course at the very small patternmaking school only had fifteen students. Most of them were European and Middle Eastern fashion students who were also looking to learn about patternmaking on a more professional scale. It was refreshing to surround myself with artsy and free-spirited people from different backgrounds who shared the same passion.

The small building was only one level, but it never felt crammed because of the large, bright windows that circled around. I walked in and chose the desk by the window, which had a beautiful view of an old Florentine street. Each student had his or her own workspace. My table was already filled with equipment, including a roll of pattern paper, scissors, pins, pens, a sewing machine, and everything else you could imagine we'd need. I was so excited about the course that I had bought all the materials beforehand and packed them neatly into a separate suitcase, like a kindergartner on her first day of school.

Everyone said hello, and some even came up and introduced themselves with a handshake. They were all so enthusiastic and reminded me of myself. It was a universal eagerness, and it felt great to finally be among other motivated designers. Even better, as I worked with them more and more, I found myself feeling honored every day to be in the presence of such talented people. They knew their craft, and they knew it well. The teachers taught us the tricks of the trade (thankfully, in English), and I made many horrible garments in the process. But I also learned so much about clothing, proper fit, fabrics, and construction techniques. It was addictive, and the more I learned, the more fascinated I became. This was my first step toward expanding my knowledge of the creation of patterns, texture of fabrics, cuts, fits, and styles. I wanted to live and breathe in all of it.

I was in a new world, and things moved quickly as I tried to adjust and digest all the new information I was learning! This class made me discover who I really was as a designer, what I wished to create, and how I would want my designs executed. It gracefully brought light to my vision. I was aiming for perfection and realizing that I wanted to construct things that were different, that would appear sexy, sophisticated, and elegant while also being effortless to wear.

I couldn't have made it through this incredible experience without my tall, gorgeous, gay right-hand man, Lorenzo. The first time I met him, he was so obnoxiously brassy, animated, and outrageous. At first I thought he was judging everything I did, but I soon grasped how detail-oriented he was. One of the first days in class I was struggling to sew together an awful skirt. I could see him sitting on his chair, just staring at me. He had finished his project in no time, and I felt like he was just sitting back to critique me. I wanted to throw my scissors in his face and say, *We get it, asshole, you are good at what you do.* He wanted everything to be flawless, even if they were pieces he didn't make himself.

It wasn't long before Lorenzo came up to me, literally pulled the skirt out of my hands, and started going on and on about what it was that I was doing wrong. At first the critique hurt, because he was stepping on my pride, but when I realized how legitimate his analysis was, I took a breath and watched him show me how it was done. In his expert fingers, it took only minutes.

And just like that I started to admire Lorenzo's talent, and I picked his brain for the rest of the course. He helped me with assignments, and I learned a great deal from him—inside and outside the course. His talent was remarkable, and he was by far the best in the program with a wicked sense of style—and humor.

Lorenzo always gave me unsolicited fashion advice. He would say things like, "The more holes in your jeans, the more expensive they are" and, "The higher the heels, the more important your social position." It was as if he thought he understood fashion better than me because he lived in the center of the European fashion scene and I lived in the United States. Okay, maybe he had a point.

One blissful afternoon, while roaming the streets, he made

me take off my pristinely white Converse. "Look at you," he said, motioning crazily with his hands. "You look like a nerd in your brand-new Converse!" I threw him an annoyed look, but I removed the offending shoes and stood barefoot on the crowded sidewalk. People passing by were turning their heads and staring at us. He took both shoes, threw them on the dirty ground, and stomped on them until the dust and grime of the street—and hundreds of Florentine feet—smeared and streaked across the bright white fabric.

"Hey, I just bought those!" I stood there in complete disbelief.

"They look too new," he replied. "Don't you see?" But I couldn't help notice that Lorenzo didn't have a single crease in his perfect white button-down. I grudgingly took my shoes back. My new, dirty shoes made it seem like I cared less about my outfit than I actually did. Although I took Lorenzo's craftsmanship very seriously, I still didn't think style was about following what others believe in. I recognized that style is about wearing something you love with pride and confidence. It's about staying true to your vision and to yourself, even if there are people who are not going to like it.

On the weekends, I split my time between Milan and Rome, visiting some of the most well-known fashion showrooms in the world—a perk of the program. We are talking the best of the best: Valentino, Gucci, Versace, Armani, Prada, Dolce & Gabbana. You name it, I visited it. These designers had twenty to forty years of experience under their belts, and their racks of clothing priced up to ten thousand euros a gown could still make a girl drool. Visiting the showrooms was a reality check though. I had a long way to go in my scuffed-up Converse before I could achieve my goals.

When my Italian adventure finally came to an end, and I waved good-bye to Lorenzo and his European expertise, I felt more confident and secure in myself than I ever did traveling to LA, Peru, and Jordan. I no longer needed to find a factory to make my patterns. If I could ever be granted a professional do-over, I would've taken the Italian patternmaking course before going crazy with airline buddy passes.

Your priorities as an independent designer shouldn't only be securing an investor, finding the best-quality production, or trying to compete with the most successful brands in the pages of every magazine. It's first and foremost about learning *who you are* as a designer, the craft behind the product, and the pins and needles that go into everything you're creating. You can always be a better version of yourself, but there isn't always a shortcut to get there. The more you practice, the more you learn; the more you learn, the better you become; and the better you become, the more likely you will be to succeed. I came to this conclusion a bit later than I would've liked, but better late than never.

CHAPTER 17

NEVER TRUST CAPRI PANTS

sn't life all about figuring "it" out? It's a never-ending quest to make our existence meaningful, from the moment we are born until we die. We take our first step, get through school, navigate relationships—the list is infinitely long. So what's the difference between figuring out how to live and making your dream a reality? There isn't one. Your passion is your life, and to live your desired life, you have to take the journey. You must make your passion a part of your daily routine, so it becomes less of a task and more of an innate habit. Just know that you don't always have to figure everything out in order to move forward, because once you're on the right track, it will take you where you need to go.

Over the next few years, I dabbled in nearly every profession imaginable to further my knowledge and ability in the fashion industry. I was a makeup artist at a cosmetic company, a sales representative at an apparel company, a regional manager for a retail chain, an assistant at a law firm, an office manager at a doctor's office—I did it all. I conquered everything from cleaning the store and buying merchandise to marketing products and training hundreds of people on the art of selling.

These jobs were mainly in fashion and beauty, which is a fancy way of saying that I worked retail, which is another fancy way of saying that I got screwed. You can work 24–7, 365 days a year, and no one will feel sorry for you. Not to mention that you don't make much money. In some cases I was taking jobs just to get by while pursuing my dream, and although I moved up in my positions pretty fast, there was always something missing…

Have you ever wanted to pursue something so badly that it hurt your soul? I have. I wanted to be around patterns, fabrics, clothing, fashion weeks, models, photographers, and makeup—the whole nine yards. You're probably thinking, *Who doesn't?* But for me, it was much more than just the glamour of it. I was captivated by creating and the journey of constructing a business.

If you go to work every day and count the hours until you can leave, you are not being your best self. We only get one chance in this life, and for me, whenever I was on someone else's clock, I made it a point to learn something new that would better my future. I had realized what I wanted in life, and if a job I was in wasn't going to challenge me or help me achieve my goals, I needed to search for something else that would. Don't waste time at an unchallenging job. Figure out what will challenge you, move on, and find something else.

To get your foot in the door of the fashion world, you would typically start out by interning for a successful fashion house. But I had taken an unconventional approach by starting my clothing line first. I confronted challenges as they came my way, and when it didn't work out, I learned a great deal from my mistakes. My mistakes were my best life coaches.

Despite that, I didn't want to allow my past mistakes to define my career. I knew what I wanted, and I wasn't ready to accept anything less than that, or to admire anyone else's success from a distance. I knew that if I remained persistent, one day I would achieve my dream.

With that desire nearly carving out my heart, I wanted to bid regular employment adieu and became an entrepreneur again. I sought to open a boutique specializing in high-end apparel, which would give me an opportunity to sell my own designs next to well-respected brands. With the knowledge I had acquired over the years, I was convinced that this step fit my long-term vision. It would provide me with the opportunity to learn the inner workings of the fashion industry, and it would get me closer to my target market, buyers, and the most popular showrooms around the world. Most importantly, it would be taking a step out of corporate America.

In the spring of 2007, I decided that I was going to take a leap of faith. Being the dreamer I was, my boutique was already open and ready for business (in my head)! Faisal, the Jordanian who helped me find factories in Amman, had become a very close friend of mine. He was in finance, so I asked him to help me execute my financial plan for the boutique. At the beginning stages of drafting the plan, Faisal decided he also wanted in on it!

While I wished I could be the sole boutique owner, I knew that his expertise could be a huge bonus. He also wanted to bring a third partner into the deal, Moe, an Iranian businessman who I had never met before. I didn't know much about this mystery man, but Faisal vouching for him sufficed. I thought the fact that they were in the same social and professional networks was at least enough to warrant an interview with him. Plus, the added twist of three partners made the situation undeniably more interesting. I could see the headline: *Three Middle Eastern musketeers take over the fashion scene by storm in the land of opportunity.* Okay, maybe it sounded more like an act in some sort of "axis of evil" stand-up comedy tour.

I arrived to the meeting like a proper boutique owner would—decked out! But my eyes almost popped out of my head when I saw Moe for the first time. I'm pretty sure I looked like Jim Carrey in *The Mask.* I had hoped to meet a fashionable man in skinny jeans and a blazer with a pocket square—the type of guy who is so fabulously dressed that you're convinced he's gay. Instead, I saw an orange bodybuilder wearing a formfitting, very deep V-neck T-shirt (perhaps a U-neck) that exposed his curly chest hair, backless sandals, and *capri pants.*

Oh my God! Please let this be the wrong guy.

Thankfully Faisal was dressed decently, like a typical finance guy, which barely balanced out Moe's fashion gaffe. The first impression you make in the fashion industry is based on how you dress. I assumed Moe didn't get the memo that morning about impressions.

When Faisal introduced "Capri Pants" to me, we exchanged an awkward handshake. Moe was very proper and polite, while at the same time managing to be obnoxiously cocky. "Nice to meet you," he said in a very deep Iranian accent with a faint touch of British.

After getting to know each other informally, we delved into our professional backgrounds. Despite my first impression of Moe, I tried very hard not to judge the book by its cover. I settled in and focused on what he had accomplished in his past fashion expedition. I kept telling myself that many designers and other people who work in the fashion industry dress eccentrically and are often unique. Above all, I knew that, ultimately, I needed his capital contribution. I had to look past the capri pants! But could I?

Throughout the meeting we discussed our hopes, dreams, and

plans for the store, and I took many mental notes. We brainstormed for hours about everything from where the store would be located to who our target market would be. We wanted the store to be trendy and high-end, concentrating on a mixture of haute couture and edgy independent designers. High-priced items with extraordinary quality. The store would offer personal shopping, and the decor would be modern, chic, and sophisticated. I was already in love.

Our initial investment would be split in thirds, making us equal partners. Faisal worked at a major finance company, but he was prepared to resign to take on this opportunity. He was familiar with the fashion world since his mother owned one of the most popular high-end boutiques in Jordan. Coupling his fashion and business backgrounds, we agreed that he would handle the financial and business aspects of the boutique.

Based on Moe's experiences, we agreed that he would run the operational side of the business. He had recently moved to the United States for family reasons, but he expressed that his passion still lay in the fashion industry. We agreed that he would be the general manager and run the company's day-to-day operations.

I had access to Brazilian and European showrooms through my previous occupations, as well as vast experience doing fashion shows and marketing around DC. Additionally, by that point, I had gained years of experience working in retail management, merchandising, and customer service for many well-known brands. I would handle the marketing and buying, as well as being the face of the company. My soul was so happy, because finances and administrative work and I just don't get along.

The meeting helped me realize that we all needed each other. On the road to success you should always focus on doing what you are really good at. With start-up businesses, entrepreneurs are often stuck doing things that they hate or can't do very well. Having more than one cook won't always spoil the broth, and can allow the soup to become richer, more complex, and balanced! Having three partners who could each focus on their own area of expertise was ultimately going to be the reason for our triumph.

I believed that our respective experiences would make for a great partnership, and it was especially helpful that the investment would be split among us. When we shook hands I felt like I was once again on the right track toward my dream. I had found a new purpose and was ready to give it my all. This was the meaningful challenge that I had been missing in my life, and it was going to set the wheels of my passion in motion. I closed my eyes and hopped on the carnival ride, praying that Moe's outfit choice wasn't an indicator of how the boutique would end up.

CHAPTER 18

FASHION IN THE HAUNTED TOWN HOUSE

The energy between us—the three musketeers—was high. We were on a mission and shared the same passion, which created a highly motivating situation to feed off of. As the days went by, we continued brainstorming and worked tirelessly to solidify a business plan (which is, as you know, my absolute favorite thing to do in the world!).

Our plan was to put enough money in the company's bank account so that the business could operate for two years without making a profit. We needed to cover rent, utilities, inventory, and staff, along with costs associated with building a corporate identity. An exact figure for the budget was difficult to determine until we knew how much we needed to allocate for rent.

It doesn't take a rocket scientist to figure out that when it comes to a boutique retail business, it's all about the location. This principle was crucial for us to follow, and my new partners felt the same way. We found a real estate agent to scout a location for us in Georgetown, a neighborhood in DC that's popular for its high-end shopping, dining, hotels, and invite-only lounges. It's a quaint area filled with Victorian-style row houses and cobblestoned roads lined with lush trees, which adds to the picturesque neighborhood. The most stylish people in DC walk along these streets, so it would bring the right clientele, and being one of the nicest areas of the city, it also attracted loads of tourists. There wasn't a better location to fit our vision for the boutique.

Real estate in such a prime location doesn't stay on the market for long, so when we heard a space was opening up we had to act quickly. As soon as I walked through the front door, I immediately fell in love with the vintage feel of the three-story brick-walled building. The stock room in the basement was spacious, and there was even an office on the top floor. Pinch me, please!

But before we could sign the lease, Faisal broke disappointing news. He had been offered a fantastic job opportunity in Dubai that was too good to pass up. *Are you fucking kidding me?* I was devastated. We were on the verge of signing the lease, and I had already told everyone I was opening a boutique in Georgetown.

Moe and I discussed the possibility of moving forward with the store without a third partner. Even with Eric, who was still my business mentor investing in my share, there was no way we could afford to pay the operational expenses for that location in Georgetown. Was I really left with Capri Pants?

A few days later, Moe called me with a "brilliant idea" and wanted to know whether I was interested in hearing him out. I thought long and hard about the different possibilities he could propose, and what I was and was not prepared to accept. I was skeptical about his potential in the fashion business, but I was also beginning to feel for the first time that my dreams had an expiration date on them. I agreed to meet with him. His proposition turned out to be one that I hadn't considered.

He told me his family had a town house in an up-and-coming

area called U Street. *Dum dum DUMMMM!* All I heard was U Street. The words "town house" and "up-and-coming" were lost under the lightning flashes and thunder echoing in my ears.

To give you a better idea of what this area is like, there is now a Hipster Express bus that runs from U Street, Washington, DC, to Brooklyn, New York. Its passengers are people with messenger bags, nonprescription vintage glasses, lots of facial hair, and iPhones loaded with brand-new bands that no one has heard of. But that being said, U Street is also ranked one of the greatest places in America by the American Planning Association because the neighborhood turned around after facing several decades of economic difficulties. It's largely Victorian, having been developed in the late eighteen hundreds, and the majority of it has been designated a historic district.

Moc proposed that we renovate the town house into a trendy boutique. We would make money in that location for a year, and then move the store to Georgetown. I looked at his loose belt buckle, dreadful leather jacket, and bell-bottomed pants and said, "Let's check this place out." The rent was one-tenth that of the Georgetown location, so I owed it to myself to at least look at the property.

We met at what I call the "Haunted Town House on U Street."

I parked my car and stared up at the graffiti—I mean *street art*—outside. The town house was connected to a fairly large parking lot with broken fences on one side and a dusty bar on the other. Residential apartments mixed with a few old restaurants, and low-end stores lined the block, selling anything from sparkly stripper shoes and sex toys to skateboards and skater T-shirts.

I looked up at the dodgy three-level town house and thought, *It's going to take a great deal of magic to turn this place around.*

The little gate in front opened into a tiny yard filled with cigarette butts, a brown patch of grass, and lots and lots of garbage. As Moe struggled to open the door's century-old lock, he explained that no one had lived there for about eight years.

A few homeless men stared curiously at us from across the street. I wondered if they were laughing at the sight of us. My very high heels and dress didn't help the ridiculous scene. I definitely didn't belong there in that outfit. On second thought, they probably thought I was a stripper who bought my shoes next door and fit in just fine.

Moe finally managed to open the door. I took my first optimistic step up the stairs, praying in my heart that this was going to be a temporary new home for my second baby. By the second stair I was already trying to fight off rapid disappointment, and when I finally walked up the third stair, I scoffed loudly, "What the fuck is this place?"

"I never said this place was nice," he replied defensively.

The brick walls inside were cracked with chipped white paint. A hallway led to a broken staircase that resembled the stairs from *The Exorcist*. I couldn't see what lay beyond it because it was too dark, but I prayed that the creepy Regan MacNeil from the movie wouldn't suddenly appear and crawl backward toward me.

To my right was a battered glass-paneled door. Some pieces were broken and scattered all over the crooked gray-stoned floors, while others were covered with blue duct tape. Through the glass door was a midsized room that overlooked the yard. I guessed that this was where we could display the merchandise. Wait—was I actually starting to envision a boutique here?

There was a very antique-looking fireplace and a small room that we could potentially use as a fitting room (and where a few ghosts could watch over us). Dammit, I was doing it again!

With each step up the spooky stairs, loud screeching ricocheted off the walls. After a few more steps, we entered a spacious room with sky-high ceilings and an outdated kitchen. The short wooden staircase in the back led to a small bricked loft that had a bathroom inside. I observed my surroundings in silence. My mind bounced from thought to thought. I was making decorative plans for every wall and room. I was forcing it to work in my head because I wanted the boutique to work so badly. I looked at Moe and said, "We should have a bar in the store."

"What?"

"Listen," I continued, biting off the skepticism in his voice, "obviously this place looks like hell and there is no way that we can get rid of this kitchen in the middle of the room given our budget. We have to make it part of the decor. So we can set up a bar and offer cocktails and personal shopping. The first floor will be for men's apparel, the second floor for women's apparel, and the third floor will be the office. We'll put the register across from the bar, and the kitchen pantry will be the ladies' fitting room. What do you think?"

He shrugged, unconvinced. "If you think that would work."

"We need to use all the vintage furniture already in the town house to make it cozy and antique looking," I continued enthusiastically. "We could use vinyl records and newspaper as wallpaper, and then put antique masks and other props on top of that backdrop." I was becoming inspired as my mind opened up more and more to the space.

It's important to be flexible in business, but you should never deviate from your original plan to a point where you're settling. Perhaps I got too excited, too soon. I thought it was necessary to reevaluate our plan and shift our vision if we wanted to make that location work. I wish someone had slapped me across the face and told me to wake up. But isn't hindsight always twenty-twenty?

After I gave myself a little golf clap, I called Fadi, a dear friend who owned a very successful construction company, for a renovation estimate. I knew I could count on him for the best possible deal. The tricky part was that we were only going to be in that location for a year, and neither Eric nor I wanted to spend an enormous amount of our capital on construction costs.

Fadi met us the following day at the town house. He is a short, bald Egyptian with a straight-shooter approach, which I appreciated. And whether I liked to hear his honesty or not, I needed to know what he thought about my new business venture. After walking around and analyzing everything for about an hour, he disbelievingly turned to me and asked, "Do you really want to go through with this?"

I could tell he really didn't believe this was a good idea. I answered that I was 100 percent sure (even though I was lying to him and to myself) and explained that this was a temporary solution for our bigger plan. Even though I had learned from my father's past mistakes that you shouldn't make temporary plans for your long-term goals, I was still hoping the risk would pay off.

When Fadi estimated the construction work at $50,000, I swear I could hear my heart begin to ugly cry. Moe and I could never afford that. After Fadi left, Capri Pants and I stood in the middle of the empty space on the second floor and just stared at each other in silence.

Suddenly, my mouth drew up into a smirk as I leaned over the kitchen counter and asked, "Have you ever done any construction work?"

"Only minor stuff here and there with my properties," he

replied. I assured him that I was a skilled construction worker, given my long list of high school punishments, like painting school walls in Tehran. Once again, my parents would be so proud!

Then I continued, "Why don't we do this ourselves? I have friends who can help out, we can borrow tools from Fadi's company, and there is a Home Depot a few blocks away."

He chuckled. "Faisal told me you are ambitious, but that's just crazy."

But it didn't take much persuading for him to agree to my proposition, and the next day, we met to plan the town house renovation. We needed a clean slate, so the first phase was to empty out the space completely. I walked up and down the creaky wooden staircase, with Regan MacNeil by my side, dragging out bags and bags of garbage. During my garbage commute, I spotted Edward, the older homeless man who always sat across the street. He kept quiet, but I could see a look of curiosity on his face. He probably hadn't seen any activity around that place for years. He was perched on the curb next to the parking lot, and when he saw me, he politely said, "Hi, Miss."

I wanted to hug him. He seemed like a good man, and he must have had friends and family at some point in his life to make it into his sixties. Moe and I discussed the possibility of hiring Edward to help us with the store, in exchange for money and food.

So the following morning, we approached Edward and proposed our job offer. His entire demeanor suddenly changed. A glimmer of hope shined in his eyes. He expressed his gratitude, stuttering with excitement, and said he was ready to get started. His first duty was to clean the little yard in front of the store, then fix up the dead grass and broken fences. Freshly motivated, Edward didn't waste any time and got to work instantly. There is nothing better than helping someone who has little hope. Even though I had never been homeless and couldn't know what Edward was feeling, in a way I felt like we were both finding a new sense of purpose, and helping each other fulfill it felt very sweet.

That day I took a little trip to Home Depot to teach myself about construction. I thought to myself, *This is no fashion glamour.* There was an excruciatingly long list of tools and equipment that I needed to acquaint myself with that I had never even heard of before: speed and framing squares, carpentry crayons, framing and finish hammers, core drill, hammer drill, and the list goes on. What the hell were all of these things used for? My simple vision of grabbing some wood, nails, a hammer, and paint was painfully unrealistic.

While walking through the aisles of a home-improvement store for the first time in my life, I realized that I needed to love every second of this process if I was going to love my boutique. With that in mind, I suddenly transformed into a giddy schoolgirl at the sight of the paint mixer. Mixing colors together to create the perfect shade for the boutique's walls? Sign me up! Where was my hard hat? Let's get this YMCA party started! As many wise people have said, it's not always about the destination; the journey itself is the brilliant challenge that makes it all worthwhile.

When I got back to the town house to talk to Moe about my new discoveries, he immediately wiped the big smile off my face. He had learned that we needed about ten different permits before we could even start construction. We could potentially run into major delays because of the time frame it would take to get the permits and the poor condition of the building. *That's it*, I thought, *who cursed me?*

Moe and I didn't waste any time. We went straight to the District of Columbia government center to inquire about the permits. The morose expressions on everyone's faces waiting in the long line didn't bode well for what this experience might be like. We waited in line for hours, which meant more time for Capri Pants and me to bond. Unfortunately, the more time I spent with him, the more I couldn't stand to be around him. He always thought he knew everything, but when it came down to it he couldn't act on anything. He would make insulting jokes, and as time passed that polite and proper guy I had met began to disappear.

When it was finally our turn, I filled out mounds and piles of paperwork while Moe just watched. I was convinced he couldn't read or write. We were told that the entire process could take a few months, we needed to schedule an inspection, and blah, blah... Wait! A few months? We did *not* have that kind of time.

I spent the next few weeks, five days a week, at that government center. The first couple of times Moe accompanied me, but then he had the bright idea that I should go alone, because I was an attractive woman and the men seemed to be friendlier with me than him. But, in reality, it didn't matter. I was much better and faster at getting things done on my own anyway.

The last missing piece to the puzzle was to have the space inspected post-construction, and we couldn't do that until we had a solid, standing, beautiful building to show. Luckily, I got every permit we needed within a record breaking *five weeks*. I would walk into the facility every day as though everyone there was my buddy. I greeted each person with a smile and asked how they and their families were doing. I tried to be as pleasant as possible, which was hard at times given that I spent some sleepless nights at the town house. As much as I hated the lengthy ordeal, I learned so much about the business and administrative sides of construction.

When I finally had all the permits in hand, I was ecstatic to share my big accomplishment with Moe and Edward. I rushed into the town house bursting with excitement and shouted, "Look what I have, boys," while waving all the permits in the air. If you put your heart, mind, and soul into something, the impossible will never seem out of your reach.

We spent the next six months working on the renovations. Yes, it took more than six months—we did everything from breaking down walls to sanding the hardwood floors. On the flip side, we saved a tremendous amount of money. During that time, you could either find me at Home Depot or the boutique. I even knew most of the Home Depot employees by name. I lived and breathed that boutique, which meant I barely had time to do anything else. Occasionally, my friends would stop by to visit. They always seemed surprised that I had traded in my stylish outfits for leggings and basic Tees. I was permanently covered from head to toe in paint or dust, with no makeup, my hair pulled back in a bun, and a hammer or paintbrush in hand. Sometimes they helped me paint, but I needed them more for companionship. I was getting really lonely.

There are many challenges to being an entrepreneur. You're essentially working for yourself, which means that you'll also be working a lot *by* yourself. You have to put in long hours; you are creating something from nothing, and that requires your full attention. Your business is your new best friend, it's your family, it's your baby, and it's your everything. It's not that you are always feeling lonely because you want a companion, friends to party with, or people to go on vacations with. It's a kind of loneliness that comes from thinking, "I am absolutely insane to think that what I am doing is going to work." And you have no one to tell you otherwise.

Entrepreneurs are also built differently from other people. We think differently, we act differently, and we want different things. Often people around you don't understand what you're going through, and when you're so focused on bringing your idea to life, it's easy to start distancing yourself from others. This is the worst thing you can do. Yes, you'll get exhausted, and you may not want to talk to others about it because "they won't get it anyway." But it's very important to keep your family and friends close so that you have a shoulder to cry on, even if you don't want to explain why you are crying. And of course, it's an amazing feeling to have people in your life who you can share all the high moments with as well.

Many times I wanted to have a nervous breakdown or run away and never come back. Having friends and family around made me realize that I am not alone in this world, as much as it sometimes felt like I was. People need people, and remarkable concepts can come from the most unexpected places. The people you surround yourself with could inspire those concepts. You have to open yourself to the world around you and allow people in.

CHAPTER 19

NAUGHTY SÃO PAULO

The famous Brazilian novelist Paulo Coelho wrote: "You have to take risks. We will only understand the miracle of life fully when we allow the unexpected to happen." Coelho had a point. We certainly took a big risk opening the boutique. How much I had learned about the miracle of life remained to be seen.

Halfway through construction, it was time to shop designers' spring collections for the boutique's grand opening. Moe and I planned a five-day trip to São Paulo, Brazil—the fashion capital of Latin America. People in the industry predict that Brazil's fashion week will shift into the top five over the next decade, which is no surprise. Brazilian fashion is out of this world. Because of its major influence on international fashion trends, I wanted to incorporate its flavor into our boutique.

I had already been to Brazil numerous times and fallen in love with the beautiful people, delicious food, and over-the-top fashion. In the winter of 2006, I went to São Paulo for Fashion Week, and one of the exhibitions that blew my mind the most was a swimwear runway show. I watched the perfectly toned, tanned, and spectacular Brazilian models strut down a miraculously elegant runway. It was absolutely inspiring and dreamy. The magnificent fabrics, vibrant colors, unique styles and cuts, and the confidence of the women showcasing them were dazzling to me. That experience encouraged and influenced me, and it definitely inspired my creative juices.

My friend Renata, who worked at a renowned, high-end Brazilian showroom, had provided me with the Fashion Week passes for that trip, so I got in touch with her again in hopes that she would whip out her Rolodex and put Moe and me in touch with her long list of contacts.

On the plane ride, I couldn't stop thinking about all the high-end, perfectly executed merchandise that we could find at these showrooms. I created a merchandising strategy that would help shape our brand. I even color-coordinated everything. I wanted the boutique to be flawless and to make it a one-stop shop for all the trendy, fashion-forward people in DC. I knew our clientele would love it and that it would mesh well with the exclusive, charming boutique that we had been building.

When we arrived in São Paulo, it soon became apparent that there had been a huge miscommunication between Renata and me. She had thought that we wanted her to be our tour guide, not our fashion liaison. She hadn't made any appointments, so I took the lead and started contacting showrooms immediately. I knew that getting angry or disappointed wouldn't get me anywhere, so I put my energy into finding a solution.

My first experience with Moe buying as partners was a disaster. I was worried about how the designers would react to his fashion sense, and I thought he wasn't the least bit familiar with how showrooms worked. I found myself teaching him Fashion 101 the entire time. Most concerning was that we couldn't see eye to eye on our store's merchandise.

As it turned out, our opposing tastes weren't going to matter anyway, because no one was going to want to work with us. He constantly raised his voice at me in front of designers and their teams for trivial reasons. Building business relationships with these contacts should've been our top priority. We weren't on the set of some tacky reality show! What kind of impression was he creating, not only of himself, but of *me*?

Things went from bad to worse. Our second day in São Paulo, we went to a grungy showroom that was recommended to us for having cheaper clothes. From the minute we walked in, it was obvious that the styles wouldn't gel with our original vision; Moe, however, still wanted to consider the merchandise. Of course, I understand that some designers produce inexpensive, low-quality clothing that can be profitable, just like a restaurant can choose to serve either warm lobster bisque or a hot dog to make their bottom line.

I calmly went up to Moe and whispered, "What are you doing?"

"I know this isn't something you would want to sell," he replied, "but my friends will love these T-shirts, and we are going to carry them."

When I explained that we were trying to create a lifestyle brand, his brows started to furrow. I could tell he was getting angry again. His voice rose as he said, "People in U Street want cheap T-shirts, not your fancy Brazilian dresses. I am just trying to make money and all you care about is being chic." I reminded him that we were going to move the store to Georgetown a year later, and for that reason we had to stay consistent for our clientele. I became uneasy at the sight of his lips pursing tightly, his nostrils flaring, and his heavy breathing.

"I will buy these whether you like it or not!" he shouted. And at that, I walked out with Renata in tow.

She sat quietly next to me on the stairs, rubbing my back. I was boiling inside like a teakettle. I didn't like Moe's personal style, business acumen, or personality, but it was too late. I was already in too deep. I wanted the store so badly, and I had just spent months working my ass off on this project. There were so many times I wanted to succumb to the temptation of quitting, but it was as if I were in a broken relationship or marriage; I rationalized that the bumps were just part of the ride. I knew somewhere deep down that there was no way this could end well. But instead of acting on that instinct, I convinced myself that it was all just part of the business.

That evening, Renata said she was going to cheer me up and give me a taste of São Paulo's nightlife. My mind still wasn't clear or calm after Moe's blowup earlier, so going out seemed like the perfect way to release all the tension. I wanted to listen to music, people-watch, and get lost in my own thoughts with a drink in my hand. Renata and I dashed into the evening, away from our troubles and into a trendy Brazilian dinner spot, and sipped delicious, Moe-free cocktails.

We were clearly in a major fashion capital, because the bars and clubs were filled with leggy models who could've easily graced the cover of *Vogue*. As we approached the club, a security guard patted me down from head to toe, then confiscated my camera and phone. Was I entering Al Capone's nightclub? A blond, fake-breasted cocktail waitress wearing nothing but a thong and chunky jewelry escorted us to our table. I could barely see two steps in front of me as we walked through the dark, smoky club. I took a seat on the purple velvet couch lined with tacky, furry pillows and tried to get my bearings.

I quickly realized that many of the women weren't just half-naked, but completely naked—Brazilian and French waxes, bushes, and every other type of shape imaginable obstructed my view of anything else. They were dancing on top of tables and along the massive bar. No one was fazed by the nudity.

I looked at my friend and asked, "Am I losing my mind or are we at a strip club?" Renata shot me a funny look and grabbed my hand. I followed her around the circular venue lined with floor-to-ceiling glass windows.

Behind the glass were about two dozen people having sex. I froze in disbelief. It wasn't just sex, but a full-blown orgy. My first reaction was: there are some flexible people in the world! Have you ever seen a woman upside down on a pole while a man is thrusting inside her from the back? I hadn't either. Even more surprising was that the people who partook were your typical Joe Schmoes, John Does, and Jane Smiths. And every few minutes, new people would open the glass doors and join in.

I tried to hide the shock that must have been written all over my face. I didn't want to offend Renata. She was unduly amused and shouted over the loud music, "Isn't this crazy?"

"Are those screens showing porn or is this actually happening live?" I shouted back, unable to take my eyes off these people. There was a part of me that wanted to get the hell out of there, but there was another part that was slightly intrigued by how they were celebrating their sexuality.

Then Renata pointed to private wooden rooms in the back of the club. Only one person could fit in the small, claustrophobic space at a time. They looked like the dirty portable potties any sane person would refuse to use at grungy outdoor concerts. But when I got a little closer, I realized that all the wooden boxes had holes where you could stick your hands, feet, mouth, or whatever else you could fit through.

I didn't want to touch anything. I was afraid that I was going to catch a disease! Was this place even sanitized? Tears welled up in my eyes. The combination of jet lag, the argument with Moe, stress, and shock overwhelmed me, and I ran out of the club.

Renata came after me. I was hyperventilating and could barely get a word out, but I said, "Why the fuck did you bring me here? I don't want any part of this."

"I thought that this was something you should see at least once in your life," she replied defensively. "Everyone I bring here is fascinated by the entire experience."

I guess live porn wasn't my thing.

In Iran women are both encouraged and forced to protect their beauty and only share it with people they know very well. I grew up in a part of the world where premarital sex was illegal. It wasn't even acceptable for me to speak about sex publicly, or in front of my family—I still feel uncomfortable watching a movie with Maman if there is a sex scene—and here I was in Brazil, experiencing this expression of freedom on an extreme level. It was a culture shock for me.

I think it's healthy for people to be open about sex. Quite frankly, I think sex is beautiful when it's shared between two people who are extremely attracted to each other physically and emotionally. But there is nothing romantic about a public orgy.

The rest of the trip was very busy and hectic, but we managed to get merchandise from some of the best Brazilian brands. We ordered unique low-cut jeans, very high-end cocktail dresses, chic T-shirts, shoes, jewelry, and—my personal favorite—the most striking swimsuits I had ever seen.

But socially, our little group was extremely awkward. Not only was I expecting Moe to apologize for being so rude and disrespectful to me (which, of course, he didn't), but I also couldn't look my porn chaperone in the eye.

As a serial entrepreneur, I have launched companies mainly on my own, but I have also realized the importance of finding a partner who can both complement my skills and work toward the same agenda. But communication is something I didn't do much of growing up. Ever since I was a little girl, I had learned to put my problems aside, ignore them, or simply find a way to get through them on my own. People, including business allies, can't read your mind. The adage that two brains are better than one was one of the reasons that I went into a partnership with Moe. But our personalities didn't work well together, and this experience was another example of how our very minimal communication ended up hurting our relationship and the business itself.

Like any relationship, a business partnership may hold a great deal of potential, but it can only survive if all parties involved can work together and openly discuss issues. Moe and I didn't have an ongoing dialogue. It got to a point that we just didn't talk to each other anymore. That caused us to make assumptions and think the worst of each other, and it prevented us from staying focused on our shared vision. Instead, we became increasingly divided.

CHAPTER 20

GOD DOESN'T HAVE PARTNERS

O nce I returned to DC, after sanitizing my body and clearing out the hard-core sex images that had been burned into my brain, I continued the construction on U Street in full force. I made picture frames, racks, shelves, and other decorations from scratch. I found random pieces of material on the street and built "art pieces" out of them. Maman had taught me much more than I realized.

In the midst of all the preparations, it occurred to me that I was nearly a solo act. In the time it took Moe to make the shelves in the men's area, I built the fitting rooms, set up the bar and the office, painted the walls, obtained all the necessary permits, decorated the entire store, took care of all the orders, and recruited my friends to help out. I even constructed an entire wall in the women's fitting room with cutout photos from newspapers and fashion magazines. It took me four days just to cut out all the articles and modish images I wanted to use. I felt like the work wasn't being distributed evenly, but our line of communication had been completely disconnected by this point. I was afraid to say anything that might make the situation even more awkward.

Almost a year after I first stepped foot into the Haunted Town House on U Street, we were finally ready for our grand opening. Moe, of course, didn't think a grand event was necessary, especially after he heard what I had in mind. I wanted the opening to be so big and lavish that the entire city would hear about it. We weren't going to have much foot traffic because of the location, and it was my mission to make our name known.

My friends Mark and Antony had created the High Rollers Club, an exclusive luxury sports car club that brought liveliness and lavishness to hot events around DC. I saw their concept in action at a Gucci store, and my eyes lit up like fireworks. They had been on my radar ever since. The High Rollers Club was just what we needed to take the event to the next level. An appearance from them would link our brand with a high-end lifestyle and generate more buzz at our opening.

Once they were on board, it was much easier landing an alcohol sponsor, given the stampede of models and sports cars that would be at our boutique. Our guest list was comprised of five hundred movers and shakers who I had personally invited by phone, text, and email. I also asked some of my club promoter friends to help me blast the event. After racking up an A-list crowd and an alcohol sponsor, I snagged *Washington Life* magazine's attention, and an editor agreed to cover the grand opening.

Happily, pounds had shed off my body like wool from a sheep thanks to my recent construction-worker gig, which meant that I could fit into my fabulous, couture dress. Ten of my girlfriends slipped into glossy black dresses and worked in the boutique that day. I also asked some of my friends to model our merchandise and walk around the event as succulent eye candy. Maman catered the party. Of course, she made the most delicious, visually appealing food. She hadn't lost her touch from her party days in Tehran. She even spelled out the name of the boutique in her *salad olivieh*.

The sports cars arrived one by one. Around fifty antique and brand-spanking-new Ferraris and Lamborghinis filled the parking lot adjacent to the boutique. The street art and the broken fences didn't even look so bad anymore—they blended in as part of the decor. The beautiful models strutted up and down the boutique to music spun by two popular DJs. The store was out of control. Moe sat in the men's section and chatted with his girlfriend throughout the entire event. When I asked him to mingle and network with the crowd, he laughed at me and said, "These are all your friends. I don't know anyone."

Up until the very last second before the grand opening, I had been busy doing paint touch-ups, hanging and tagging clothing, and perfecting every tiny detail. But now, I finally stood in a corner with a glass of champagne in my hand and took a deep breath. Looking around, I wanted to cheers myself for how exquisitely the boutique and the opening had turned out. I could finally take a moment to appreciate the long, eventful journey of creating my second baby. I felt accomplished as friends and family congratulated me on my success. And at least for tonight, I would try to ignore the trouble in my relationship with Moe and the obstacles I would need to overcome to keep the store afloat.

The event was a hit. We sold thousands of dollars of merchandise, met some of the most successful people in town, and were featured in DC's most popular blogs and magazines. I had created an event that *had* to be written about. After living in Iran and having to navigate its strict laws, I knew how to be resourceful. I reached out to my network and made the best out of what I already had at my fingertips for free.

Unfortunately that promising moment was short-lived. The

credit crisis that crashed Wall Street in 2008 changed everything. It was the worst financial disaster since the Great Depression. I was on such a high, just to have it all come crumbling down so rapidly. Our clientele wasn't growing because they didn't have money to spend anymore. The boutique was severely affected, and the future of the store seemed bleaker with each passing day. In addition to that, Moe and I had become like an old married couple that couldn't stop bickering even if we tried. The fights between us seemed endless. Our conversations got shorter and shorter, and we finally reached the point where we communicated solely through emails—even when we were in the same building.

I had to get ready for damage control.

Eric's company was struggling too, and he couldn't fulfill his financial end of the bargain (i.e., half of my share). Moe didn't want to front any more money than I had, so we were strapped for cash. I was put in a pretty tough position and became the intermediary between Eric and Moe. The tension between all three of us was unbearable. Every part of me was beginning to suffer—emotionally, psychologically, financially, and physically. I was a ticking time bomb waiting to explode. I had to either fix the situation or plan my escape.

Finally, I confronted Moe about the grim reality of our store's future. We needed to work as a team more than ever, but the fact that we didn't have a contract made things even more complicated. When Faisal pulled out so long ago, I went full steam ahead with building this company, forgetting the most critical part of the business, which was the contract. Moe and I never signed one! ALWAYS SIGN A CONTRACT!

I knew in my heart that I had fought as hard as I could for six months to keep the store afloat, and there was no fight left inside of me. I couldn't magically make the investment appear out of thin air. There was nothing more I could do to create a successful future for our business without money coming in. As Donald Trump once said, "Sometimes your best investments are the ones you don't make." I needed to remove myself from this situation before investing any more time and energy into a dead end. That night, I consulted a lawyer who was also a good friend of mine. He suggested that I offer Moe three options:

1. Hand the company over to me. I would stay at his family's building for another year and pay his investment back with the store's profits. Then I would move the store to another location.
2. Pay me back my investment, withholding the profits from the costs of my construction work, and he could keep the brand.
3. Split the merchandise and furniture fifty-fifty and walk away.

Moe didn't want to buy me out because he had no experience in women's clothing. Instead, he said that I could buy him out, but I would have to move out of the space immediately. You would think he would be more grateful for my months of free labor, and the property's value increasing because of it. And he had no interest in the third option.

My two biggest regrets from this experience were not being a cotenant on the lease and not signing a contract. I got so caught up in the idea of owning the boutique that I failed to cover my ass. Technically, all the merchandise inside the store belonged to me too, but I didn't have the money to battle it out in court. Legally, I wasn't allowed in the building after-hours, and he had changed the locks; besides, seeing him would've triggered a panic attack for sure.

After weeks of arguing, we couldn't come to an agreement. Ultimately, Moe decided to change the company's name and run the business under another entity, with the help of his girlfriend. I don't know what happened to me, but I had lost my will to fight. I wrote it off as a huge loss and just walked away, which was a very hard pill to swallow. Moe and I never spoke to each other again.

It broke me into pieces every day knowing that my company had been snatched away from me so easily. I had no control over what I had worked so hard to build. But on the other hand, I also felt freed from what had become an increasingly difficult situation and a terrible burden. I cried myself to sleep for months. Why was reaching this American Dream so hard? Thousands of dollars and a whole lot of time and energy later, I still didn't get what I believed I deserved. Money wouldn't repair me. I walked away from this chapter of my life realizing, "If partners were good, God would have one." That is what my father said for many years after his business partnership failed. At the time I thought his saying was funny, but it wasn't funny anymore after it happened to me!

CHAPTER 21

STARTING OVER

Devastation…weakness…disappointment…*failure.*

These words were etched in my mind. Even when I tried to sleep, the boutique haunted me in my dreams. Whatever I did, I was reminded of that damn place. A part of me wanted to curl up in a ball and disappear for all eternity, but a larger part of me didn't fear failure anymore, because it had already happened and it was making me stronger each time. Failure is not a bad thing, but only if you learn from it. I put my loss behind me and recognized that every path to success has a trail of failures behind it.

After I left the boutique—and lost my life savings—I could no longer afford my apartment, so I moved in with one of my best friends, Mariana. I hadn't earned a steady income for nearly two years and was left with nothing but debt, attorney fees, and PTFD (Post-Traumatic Fashion Disorder).

I was petrified to discuss yet another business disappointment with my parents. I could already hear their voices saying things about responsibility and law school and "I told you so." I had done absolutely everything in my power to save the boutique from ruin, but they didn't know that. I wondered whether my father would sympathize with what it was like to be involved with the wrong partner.

Dear Mother and Father, I felt like saying. *I get it! Law school would have come in handy!*

"The quicker the better" is my motto when it comes to delivering unfortunate news. I told my parents that the boutique had taken a serious hit because of the economic crisis, and that I wasn't able to keep it afloat despite my best efforts. I said I would push my entrepreneurial spirit aside and focus on a career with a steady income, to ensure a "safer" future (as many people viewed it). My parents suggested that, in the interim, I should start studying for my LSATs to get into law school, advice that I respectfully ignored.

At first, I applied for jobs in the beauty, fashion, and marketing industries in Dubai, Los Angeles, and New York. I wanted to move as far away from Washington, DC, as possible. I was very apprehensive about how people would judge me around town after yet another business catastrophe. In my mind, it felt very likely that they would label me a failure forever.

But of course, that was ridiculous. No failure is forever; there are always more and more chances. Things don't go wrong in your life so that you can give up with a broken soul. They go wrong so that you can learn from them and rebuild yourself with even more knowledge and strength to become the person you were intended to be.

Eventually, I came to realize that my ego was actually hurting me more than anything. It wasn't the failed businesses or the million other glitches I had to deal with in my life. Oh trust me, those did hurt, but what made things the most difficult for my heart, soul, and mind after every single one of these situations was my ego. My ego made me feel embarrassed of my failures. It made me hide my feelings from the people who loved me the most because I was scared and convinced that they would judge me. My ego almost made me put my dreams behind me.

Fuck your ego! Because your ego is the only thing standing between you and your dreams, the only thing stopping you from asking the questions that could change your life, the only thing stopping you from starting over again. It stops you from being fearless. I had spent my entire early adult life building my network in DC. It was time to shove aside my pride and get back to work. I didn't want to quit before the race was over.

One morning I jumped out of bed feeling a sudden urge for change. After one long look at myself in the mirror, I headed straight to the hair salon—I needed a fresh, new look to go with my fresh, new attitude. Everyone needs to spruce up their appearance every now and then. After the haircut, I was actually quite pleased with what I saw in the mirror. Even though people say you need to be happy with yourself on the inside before you could be happy with yourself on the outside, sometimes your glammed-up appearance can make you smile from within. But let's not get too deep here.

It was like the universe recognized the change too. I walked out of the hair salon with confidence and noticed a missed call on my cell. I called the number, and the voice of the male who picked up sounded wired, like he had been up for days. He identified himself as David from a company called the Startup and said he was calling about the vice president of marketing position that I had applied for online.

David, who sounded like an overadrenalized entrepreneur, explained that their company's genius purpose was to help others launch their businesses, from concept to market. Their clients ranged from government contractors to busy businessmen and women who didn't have the time or resources to accomplish their visions alone.

Where in the world have you guys been all my life? I thought to myself. It's ironic how much I could have used their services when I first got started.

He spoke very passionately, and, quite frankly, I admired his vision. I never criticize those who dream big. I've always had big dreams, and I would never want someone to judge me for them. Whether their company was ultimately successful or not, I knew he had a drive that I admired and could feed off of daily.

David wanted to interview me for the position, and I needed a steady job to help me get back on my feet before I could tackle another business. So I was more than ready to convince him why he needed me on his team. Just one short month before, I had been the commander of my own little world, and now I was gunning to become a slave in someone else's.

It had been such a long time since I'd been on a job interview that I was a ball of nerves. I arrived at the Startup thirty minutes early. Being the fashionable girl I am, I wore a sexy office dress and very high heels. The dated, bland office building in the suburb of Tysons Corner, Virginia, sent shivers down my spine. Since there was no receptionist in sight, I saw myself through the quiet lobby and took the slow, squealing elevator up to the third floor. The raggedy, dull-colored carpeting and depressing green-colored walls left much to be desired. I took a seat on one of the old "vintage" chairs in a room that felt more like a doctor's office waiting room than the lobby of an exciting new start-up. But then again, no start-up is ever really that fancy.

It felt very strange to sit in someone else's office when just a few months before I had been a boutique owner traveling the world. I grabbed the latest copy of *DC Modern Luxury* on the table next to me for a distraction. While flipping through the pages, I landed on an article about me and my boutique. So much for distracting myself!

They had interviewed me a few months prior to when this issue ran and included a photograph of me standing proudly in the middle of the store. I couldn't believe I was reading about such a trendy boutique in DC that had once belonged to me. People were going to congratulate me on this, and here I was interviewing for a new job. It's incredible how your life can do a complete 180 in a matter of weeks, or even in some cases a split second.

In my peripheral vision, I saw a couple of men chatting and approaching me. As his colleague departed, I boldly stood up to give my potential new boss a firm handshake. David was a tall, good-looking man in his early thirties (about a decade younger than what I had imagined). His wrinkly, colorful button-down shirt was tucked into his worn jeans, which he paired with beaten-up loafers. He said animatedly, "I'm sorry I'm wearing jeans, but it's casual Friday at the office." It looked like I was back in corporate-freaking-America after all. Bruce, his partner, was already waiting for us in a conference room.

David and Bruce explained that the Startup would deal with the administrative side of clients' businesses, register their companies, develop their corporate identities, and in some cases even handle things like manufacturing and marketing. By this point in my life, I was an expert in start-ups, especially what you *shouldn't do* when starting one. My credentials fit the position perfectly. I killed it at the interview, and they offered me the job on the spot.

When you work for a start-up, you must be prepared to get involved in all aspects of the business—from marketing, sponsorships, events, and finances to administrative tasks, making coffee, and cleaning the office. In that spirit, I soon realized that my duties at the

Startup would extend way beyond my position description. But that never fazed me; I knew there was always something I could learn.

Working at the Startup had its pros and cons. It felt amazing to advise others on their business ventures and use all of my past mistakes as a learning tool to help them succeed. I also felt undoubtedly safe and comfortable knowing that I had a nine-to-five job with a solid paycheck every two weeks. My evenings and weekends were free to do whatever I pleased, as long as I performed well at work. But I wasn't wired for a nine-to-five life. I needed more out of my career.

As they say, if you don't work hard enough to achieve your own dreams, someone else will hire you to make theirs come true. Despite my previous failures in starting a T-shirt line and opening a boutique, I wasn't ready to become a nine-to-five person forever. I didn't have the capital to start another business yet, but I knew if I wanted something badly enough then I would figure out a way to make it happen.

One day as I sat at my desk feeling inspired, I grabbed a pen and a piece of paper and wrote down the headings of a new skeletal business plan. The essentials of my fashion business consisted of a name, a website, deciding which articles of clothing I wanted to produce, and my marketing strategy. Clearly, I had climbed a monumental step in creating my five-sentence business plan.

We are surrounded by opportunities, and if we don't take them we will never create for ourselves the freedom to do what we truly desire. I wanted the freedom to follow my dreams, and unlike in Iran, there were endless possibilities here in America. I couldn't allow myself to get comfortable at the Startup and forget about all those possibilities. Knowing that made me want to take another risk, and even though the risk of starting a fashion line was much greater and scarier than the boutique had been, I knew I was ready to take it on.

So there I was, sitting in my office behind my dark wooden desk at the Startup, gazing out the window through the dusty blinds at my breathtaking view of a parking garage and dumpsters, when it clicked. I grabbed a pink highlighter and highlighted the word *swimwear*. It all made perfect sense. I always knew I wanted to have my own line, and the swimwear fashion show that I experienced in Brazil had obviously left a lasting impression on me.

I thought back to life in Iran, where female individuality is stifled. My clothing line would empower women to wear whatever they desired without being judged and punished like my fellow Iranian women were. Despite the Islamic regime's dress code, we found a way to be stylish and feel beautiful. It was our way of empowering ourselves, and here I was, once again, fighting—albeit in a different way—to help women be stylish and feel beautiful. My line would represent much more than fashion. I wanted to broadcast a broader message—that "Fashion is Freedom."

CHAPTER 22

BORN TO DESIGN

Dar be dar in Farsi slang means "lost and all over the place"—that surely sounded like me. I didn't have any direction and navigated through the rough terrain alone. I had embarked on a country-to-country journey to find an investor, partners, sponsors, and ultimately to figure out how to succeed in the fashion industry. I had knocked on any door that I could for answers, to get where I wanted to be. So I decided on the spot, still sitting at my desk at the Startup, to call my new baby Dar Be Dar, which also means "door-to-door." How fitting! And just like that—the Dar Be Dar swimwear line was born!

I immediately went online and registered Dar Be Dar as an LLC. In a record thirty-minutes' time, I had a name, a registered company, and the type of product I would produce. Now all I needed was money, a website, designs, and actual products. Sounds easy enough, right? I was fired up.

Martin Luther King Jr. said, "You don't have to see the whole staircase, just take the first step." You will never be able to know how stable that first step is, but you have to have faith. Even though there is a chance you may fall off that step, there is also a chance that you could sprint up the entire staircase. So you just have to get out there and step up onto that one daunting stair!

The Startup was beginning to work to my benefit. My colleagues and I spent the majority of our time creating corporate identities for our clients' companies, so I learned from all the business models we worked on for them. I had easy access to web designers, business plans, marketing strategies, and many other resources. But what I needed most of all was money, and a lot of it.

One Saturday morning, I drove past a man dancing erratically at a popular intersection. His oversized headphones must have been blasting loud, bumping tunes. Give me whatever he was having! His energy level was off the charts. He twirled a large neon-yellow sign that read "We Buy Gold." I had seen him many times before but never thought twice about stopping by the pawnshop—until that day. Desperation is a ridiculously powerful force.

In Iran, gifting gold coins is a well-known tradition. They aren't used as currency, but as an investment. People usually wait until the price of gold skyrockets to trade them in for cash. They come in different sizes and have different values, depending on their weight, style, and age. At every stage of my life, my friends and family had gifted them to me. Some of my one-of-a-kind coins dated back to before the 1979 Revolution.

My gold coins and jewelry were going to jump-start my new empire. I turned my car around toward home and put the pedal to the metal. I sifted through my most expensive Iranian jewelry and gold coins to find the perfect ones to exchange for cash. But I wanted to research and familiarize myself with each step I needed to take, so I checked the value of gold before going in to negotiate my terms. I walked into the store and spotted the scrawny, bald, older man who kept his thick glasses so low on his nose that I worried they were about to fall off. Gold wasn't the only thing the store sold; from jewelry, antiques, and electronics to useless knickknacks, it was packed with goods waiting for jubilant new owners. I walked straight toward the old man's vintage register.

I asked whether they bought gold, and he responded in a very deep Iranian accent, "Vat else vould ve be doing here, my lady?" I took the little bag out of my purse and showed him each item I wished to sell. It didn't take him very long to figure out that I was also Iranian. His eyes sparkled as he curiously asked why I wanted to sell them.

"I need the money for an urgent matter," I responded, like a paranoid felon in an action thriller.

Our negotiations started out congenially, but slowly escalated. We argued, joked, and fought. It didn't help that we were both Iranian—negotiating was in our blood. I knew he felt my urgency, but I wouldn't give in without a fight. We went back and forth in the boxing ring, which prompted spectators to gather around us to watch.

I needed to bring out the big guns—I could feel him slowly starting to budge, especially after I explained how much the items meant to me. Then all of a sudden, he said, "My lady, I can't do this." I took a seat in the chair next to the register, exasperated. After a few moments, he started tapping away on his calculator again. Then he signaled for me to approach the counter and gave me one final price, which I accepted. The price he gave me was relatively close to what I had expected from my research, and secretly I was over the moon. A small victory is still a victory. After the exchange, we shook hands, and he said, "*Khoda negahdar*" ("May God care for you"). My Persian charm had worked.

With my crisp $3,600 in hand, I went straight to the bank to open a new business account with my new tax ID number. I was hopeful that this investment was a step in the right direction, and the corners of my mouth lifted into a smile. I had been waiting to put my creative energy back into motion. All that was left to do was create an entire collection, and I would have my very own swimwear line. Like magic!

Sometimes having something to prove to others (and yourself) can be your biggest motivator. I was going to prove to my parents that I could be successful despite not becoming a lawyer, and show everyone else that I was worth more than two failed businesses. What happened with my boutique wasn't because I lacked the ability to be a successful businesswoman, but because of bad timing and getting involved with the wrong partner. I couldn't allow life's pitfalls to stand in my way.

That evening I eagerly sketched on the carpeted floor of my tiny room while my roommates, Mariana and Lina, got ready for a night on the town.

"Babe, are you not coming out with us?" Mariana asked, walking into the room all dolled up. She looked at my drawings suspiciously. "What are you doing?"

"I'm sketching bikinis for my new swimwear line," I told her, nervously searching her eyes for a reaction.

She gazed back at me with a you've-got-to-be-kidding-me look.

"Did you already forget what you went through just a few months ago with your boutique? Why would you want to start another business?" Mariana had watched me go through the entire process of opening and losing the boutique, and she'd seen me deal with every single emotion possible, from excitement and anger to sadness and devastation. So she was shocked that I was in the emotional, mental, and financial position to even consider another business venture. But that was exactly what I was ready to do.

I spent the entire weekend sketching swimwear and brainstorming styles I wanted in my first collection, and at 6:30 a.m. on
Monday morning, I was standing in line to get on the four-hour bus
ride to New York's Garment District.

My first stop was Mood Designer Fabrics, known by many for
its recurring role on the hit reality show *Project Runway*. This enormously famous fabric store measures forty-thousand square feet and
offers endless amounts of material—from silk to cotton to chiffon—
that is made around the globe. I walked into Mood Designer Fabrics
with Tim Gunn's "make it work" mentality.

In the past, I'd had a habit of getting overly excited and forgetting to focus on the details, like signing a contract before spending
an entire year building a business with someone. True to my character, from the moment I entered Mood, the store spun around me
like a carousel of fancy dresses. *Snap out of it*, I thought, and I forced
myself to hone in on what I'd come to buy, while keeping my eye on
the prize—becoming a well-known and respected fashion designer.
I needed to let the fabric rolls inspire my ideas and build a firm
foundation from the inception of my company, so that my empire
wouldn't crumble in the future.

But as determined as I was, and as hard as I searched, Mood
Designer Fabrics didn't have a suitable selection of materials for
swimwear. I walked away from the colorful fabric bolts discouraged,
wishing that a fashion wizard would whisper in my ear what my next
move should be. I didn't even have a plan B, because I had believed
that Mood Designer Fabrics could change my "mood" and be the
answer to all my supply problems.

While the barred metal doors of the elevator closed, an older male
elevator operator in a costume-like suit asked, "Ma'am, which floor?" I

was so upset that I didn't even realize he was talking to me. He finally got my attention when he raised his voice a few notches, "MA'AM?"

"Lobby please," I replied. "I'm sorry, I didn't hear you the first time."

"You didn't find what you were looking for?" Was it that obvious?

"No. I own a swimwear line, and I'm looking for very specific, high-end swimwear fabrics," I answered dejectedly. "The selection here is not something I can work with." He suggested that I check out Spandex House. *Oh my God*, I thought to myself as I stepped off at the lobby, *there is a* Spandex House?

A block away, on Thirty-Eighth Street, stood the fabled Spandex House. It's the headquarters for all things spandex and Lycra, brimming with designers searching for fabrics for activewear, swimwear, ballet, and dance clothing. When I walked in through the doors, I thought I had finally arrived to the magical, fairyland forest of stretchy fabrics. Inside, I found heaps of colorful materials, but much to my dismay, I wasn't able to find anything that fit my vision. Strike two!

The key to thriving in a dog-eat-dog world is the ability to roll with the punches. This was one of those times! If I wanted to leave New York with anything to show for the trip, I would need to change my original designs, and I would have to choose the fabrics right then and there, since the minimum orders were extremely high, and I didn't have enough money to travel back and forth.

I asked a salesperson for a pen and paper and sketched an entirely new twelve-piece collection using six different fabrics. After purchasing them, I headed to another store on the same street to buy chains, clasps, and other accessories to add to the bikinis.

That evening I finalized my designs on the twenty-dollar bus ride back to DC. I felt like I was going backward, departing the most cosmopolitan place on earth where dreams are made to return to a city where two of my dreams had already bitten the dust. Through the bus windows, I faithfully stared at the sparkly stars winking at me and felt a thrill of anticipation run through me as I sketched my swimwear on the bumpy roads. Great ideas don't just come to you when you're behind a desk during business hours. Sometimes the most vivid concepts appear amidst the most random circumstances.

The next step was to create the prototypes myself. So what if I had never made swimwear before? The program in Florence provided me with a solid enough foundation to create patterns. How hard could it be? I was a disheveled mess from traveling eight hours to and from New York in a twenty-four-hour period, and from lack of sleep from the weekend, but I didn't waste any time when I got home. In my frenzy, not only did I ruin the fabrics, but I also created horribly fitted swimwear that I would never be caught dead in. The fabrics themselves were difficult to work with, and each itty-bitty piece must be perfectly tailored to a woman's body.

There will always be some obstacles where no matter how hard you try to tackle them on your own, you won't be able to. Don't be afraid to ask for help. When a friend of mine put me in touch with a New York-based company called Magic Samples, I immediately got back on the bus to visit the factory. It was known for design development and production. This was the real deal.

The sample house was located in an old building in the Garment District. No one looked up from the organized chaos around them when I walked in. Patterns, fabrics, and samples were scattered around the left side, and a small factorylike space with twelve sewing machines was on the right side. About eight hardworking women worked furiously behind the machines while they chatted away in their native tongue. I immediately spotted Mik, the company head, and his wife. He gave me a little wave, and his wife nodded her head in my direction, then they both carried on with their work. I was praying that this man could be my saving grace.

When he invited me to his office, he got comfortable behind his desk while I tried to find a place to sit. I spotted a chair stacked with fabric swatches and papers. I didn't want to move anything, so I placed myself on the edge—I was scared to sit on something important—but he smiled and said, "Get up!" He cleared the chair so that my entire butt could fit, then he kindly shuffled some papers around to make space on the desk for my things.

Over the next hour, I barely managed to explain my vision, sketches, and quantities I could afford because eager youngsters from massive fashion houses constantly interrupted us. They were frantically looking around for their samples or dropping off sketches for new garments. Mik kept the door open throughout the entire meeting, which was meant as an open-door policy for the interns to get what they needed. I admired his supportive attitude, and the interns' enthusiasm reminded me of myself. I could see just how much effort and care they were putting into their missions, and how much faith they had in Mik.

After my pitch, he looked at me as if my request were outrageous. Thankfully, I was getting used to rejection. He said, not unkindly, that the quantity I wanted to produce wasn't worth his time. I guess my offer amounted to peanuts in his eyes. He was used to producing quantities in hundreds and thousands, and I only wanted to manufacture about a dozen of each style. I begged him to reconsider. I was a dreamer, and if I wasn't going to believe in my own dream, there was no way I could persuade anyone else to. "Believe in yourself," said author and humanitarian Cynthia Kersey, "and there will come a day when others will have no choice but to believe with you."

By the end of our meeting, Mik decided to believe in me, and two weeks later, I went back to New York to pick up my new collection. The crammed bus, frequent bumps and jerks, and the girl vomiting next to me didn't matter. I couldn't wait to finally see my prototypes come to a tangible fruition.

Except that when I arrived, they hadn't yet. The seamstresses were scurrying around like little mice as I sat in the pattern room. I stared at the cutout patterns hung all over the walls, daydreaming about the day I would have my own pattern room. After a few hours, Mik and his wife finally presented me with my 108 bikinis— nine samples of twelve different styles. I wish that I could say I was pleased, but I was far from it. The bikinis were just as bad as the ones I had made myself a few weeks before.

I attempted to explain that they were not up to par with my expectations or industry standards, for that matter. The sizes were off, the strings were either too short or too long, and they didn't sit well on the body because the sewing was poorly executed. But Mik had no interest in hearing my complaints, so I unwillingly took the pieces and returned to DC crushed. What other option did I have? I had depleted my funds, and this is what I would have to sell.

The entire journey back to DC, I worried about how potential clients would perceive my brand. The key ingredient to a successful fashion line is high-quality products. I had to find a way to sell these suits so that I could use the money and create better quality products the next time around. I'd have to swallow my pride and make people feel like they had to own one of these suits. Being resourceful means tactfully doing what you can with what you have.

I searched for a model (and by "model" I mean a good-looking friend who was willing to wear my bathing suits and have her picture posted on my website) and a photographer who would work for free. Then I created a simple marketing plan, which I quickly implemented. I would sell these bikinis no matter what.

That was the beginning of Dar Be Dar. I still had a long journey ahead of me, but I kept my vision like a jewel that would remind me of my final destination. Don't ever forget the reason why you started. Remember, even if the road to that dazzling prize at the finish line is bumpy, it's also full of lessons that only experience can teach you.

All the experiences, challenges, up and downs, and people that you meet along the way will open up many more doors than you could ever imagine. Enjoy the ride and gain as much as you can from it. You will develop an epic set of skills that will set you apart from others. Besides, if someone were to hand you your true desire without your having to work or fight for it, it would never mean as much to you as it does when you hustle for it.

CHAPTER 23

THINK BIG

E ventually, the Tala curse lifted. A few weeks after the disaster with my first swimsuit collection, a friend of mine named Josh, who owned a men's T-shirt company based in DC, approached me about the possibility of collaborating with the Washington Wizards NBA dance team. Sign me up immediately! I played basketball in high school, and Aria was really into it and watched every single game. I couldn't wait to tell him that I was going to design swimwear for an NBA team. This is a great example of the unexpected opportunities that the entrepreneurial journey can bring.

I was overjoyed about the sponsorship. This type of offering from heaven doesn't present itself every day, especially when you're a brand-new swimwear designer. I gifted the dancers Dar Be Dar bikinis for their yearly calendar and hosted a fashion show to promote it. In exchange for Josh's introduction, I imprinted his company logo on one of the photographed bikinis. This was not only the perfect marketing opportunity for my line, but also, to top it all off, the proceeds went to charity.

The calendar shoot was scheduled to take place a few weeks later on the gorgeous beaches of the Virgin Islands. I found myself, eager and overwhelmed, in the Verizon Center's changing room for my first Dar Be Dar fitting with the Wizard Girls. My roommate Mariana helped with the fitting process because of her love for NBA players. (Hey, I'll take all the help I can get.) My staff has always consisted of my friends and family, thanks to their incredible support for me and my cause. I'm sure some of them would argue that I conned them into helping me, but whatever the reason, thanks a bunch guys!

The sample-size bikinis from Mik didn't fit the dancers' athletic body frames, but we made them work by mixing and matching tops and bottoms, cutting the sides of some, and adding fabric to others. I had to roll with the punches again and recreate my designs under pressure. The women were extremely nice and supportive, which is always refreshing in an industry where people can often be intimidating. The photos in the calendar turned out decently, but my overly critical self knew that I could've done better. Regardless, I was still proud of what I had accomplished. I was just two months into creating my line, and I had already sponsored the Wizards dance team.

Now that I had the Wizards sponsorship under my belt and Magic Samples as a supplier, I felt like I was ready to attack something bigger. I was clearly overambitious, or shall I say, delusional. Whatever it was, I felt confident enough to call Eric for another investment. After contemplating over the next few weeks, he got back to me saying, "Just the fact that you never give up gives me a reason to invest in you." I treasured his belief in me. His investment, albeit small, was enough to produce more samples and get me to Mercedes-Benz Fashion Week Swim in Miami.

Every July, thousands of hopeful swimwear and beachwear brands crowd into Miami for the biggest swim fashion week and trade show showcasing fashions from around the world. Only select, well-known designers can participate in the runway shows. These designers are usually familiar names whose lines are displayed on supermodels strutting down the catwalk. But hundreds of other designers, like me, who can't participate, can show their seasonal designs to international media, buyers, and swimwear *fashionistas* at the Miami Beach Convention Center, which has hosted the trade show for the past nine years.

The designers here set the beach and poolside trends for the following season. They plan for months, and most of their energy is spent creating their newest collections and picture-perfect booths to showcase them in. The trade shows and runway shows are compiled into a five-day fashion week event, with satellite events in ritzy hotels and restaurants around town. More than 2,500 lines have been exhibited at the trade show, which has attracted thousands of buyers from more than sixty countries. This was such a big undertaking that, as an amateur, I probably should've thought twice before signing myself up. But hey, at that point I was thinking either go big or go home!

However, when I got in touch with the swim show's VP, she informed me that registration had already closed months ago. I asked her to reconsider and immediately emailed her images of the Wizards dance team photo shoot along with pictures of my stunning friend modeling the bikinis. I even mailed her physical samples. Something must have caught her eye, because she gave me the green light. Win! Who cares that the small booth she gave me would end up being a very costly investment. I could simply kiss eating for the next month good-bye. Hello, ramen noodles! *Hola, Miami!*

All my time leading up to the show was devoted to preparing for this giant opportunity for my line. In addition to my signature styles, I designed eight new ones. My original twelve-piece collection wasn't enough. I made and printed lookbooks (crafty catalogs) and flyers to present to the thousands of buyers who would visit my booth. Wowing them was obviously my goal. I went shopping for over-the-top accessories to decorate the booth. I purchased some fancy round metal hangers for all the swimwear to hang on, as well as an elegant vase to put flowers in.

I arrived at Miami International Airport and headed straight to the convention center. My friend Lauren and I, dressed to the nines, dragged my two large suitcases across the hallways of the convention center, in heels no less. Unfortunately, we stuck out like virgins at a porn-star convention. Our dressy outfits on setup day, friendly attitudes, and naive optimism were all dead giveaways.

A few years ago I worked as an event coordinator for an IT company and was sent to a few trade shows to support the sales team. Exhibitors at those shows would high-five each other, closing millions of dollars' worth of deals, but that is not the vibe at a fashion trade show. People barely wanted to talk to us. No one thought we were cool, and the energy was very hot-and-cold.

All I could think about as we navigated through the massive building was how insignificant I felt next to all the well-established brands. Some designers set up runways and hung chandeliers, while others set up bars, fake pools, and beaches. These weren't booths—they looked more like high-end boutiques! How could I compete? Even the simplest booths were more extravagant than mine. They were overstuffed with more products than I had created in my entire career. I was barely a minnow in an extremely large pond.

My tiny booth was all the way in the back and almost didn't measure more than the length of my body lying flat on the floor. It consisted of three flimsy cardboard walls with my logo imprinted in the center. A few rails for the hangers, two plastic chairs, a table, and a trash can awaited my arrival. Let's not forget to mention the plastic bag that was already in the trash can—thumbs up to that.

I looked at Lauren and said, "We are fucked."

"No, babe, your designs are beautiful, and we're going to rock this," she reassured me.

I replied with another, "Trust me, we're fucked."

I knew that my booth wasn't going to be impressive enough to catch any of the buyers' attention. I didn't have any press, my swimsuits were never featured in any upscale magazines, and no celebrities had ever worn them. Sponsoring the Wizards dance team meant nothing here. My twenty tiny, colorful bikinis hanging from the round metal hangers I'd once believed were dazzling quickly became nothing more than ordinary.

It took me a record-shattering thirty minutes to set up the booth. Learning that other designers had spent days on theirs with the help of a full staff didn't help my faltering composure. Although I loved my designs, I could instantly tell that the quality of my suits was very poor next to my competition. I was embarrassed. I wanted to hide under the table when others informed me of how many years they had been doing this trade show, and how many appointments they already had.

At the time, I thought the swim show was a complete failure for Dar Be Dar. A total of five buyers stepped foot in my booth, and two orders were placed—for a whopping twenty-four bikinis, one from a store in Miami and the other in Hawaii. At least two stores believed in me, but overall it wasn't reassuring. I could feel this once-in-a-lifetime opportunity slowly slipping through my fingers.

I needed to formulate a plan to make this trade show worthwhile. I was around the best of the best in my industry. What better way to learn than from the people who do it best? I decided to leave my corner to walk around and network while Lauren manned our station. Many people didn't want to talk to me, which was very humiliating and intimidating. But you will always come across people who, no matter how badass they are, stay humble. And luckily for me, I found the people I needed to set me in the right direction.

Upon my return to DC, I emailed everyone I had met—half of whom didn't reply, which I expected. Several seasoned swimwear designers finally answered my questions about fabric distributors, manufacturers, and suppliers. The trade show wasn't a total loss after all. I acquired the most useful knowledge I could have in this business—how to achieve high-quality production—from a place I had originally gone to in search of sales and buyers. Sometimes the real gems are the opportunities that are the most unexpected—the diamonds in the rough.

CHAPTER 24

MY MISSION PUBLISHED

After the swim week experience, I visited Magic Samples in New York one last time. I still had to fulfill the orders from the stores in Miami and Hawaii. On the same trip, I met up with my cousin Samira—the cousin who modeled in my very first runway show in DC—at her cute little SoHo apartment. I hadn't seen her since I left the boutique, and we had much to catch up on.

She sat on the windowsill of her apartment with her feet dangling over the ledge while I sat on the stairs of her fire escape. It felt good to be with family, especially someone with such an uplifting spirit. The tone of our conversation turned deep after a few glasses of cheap red wine. Samira seemed very concerned about me. I knew she had heard about the boutique from her father, and I got choked up when she brought it up. She listened to me talk for hours about growing up in Iran, my failed business ventures, and why I was so determined to follow this dream of mine. Despite her being born in the Middle East, she had moved to California as a baby, so we didn't share the same experiences growing up.

It was easy for me to open up to her because we shared the same blood and last name. I told her why I wanted to broadcast my "Fashion is Freedom" message, and how it all started by growing up in a country where freedom of choice was limited. She couldn't know firsthand how it felt to rebel against limitations to express her personality and individuality through the way she dressed. I constantly clashed with my parents, school officials, and the government about the dress code. I wanted to stand out from the masses, I told her, but was judged for wanting to be fashionable, stopped on the street by the religious police for wearing lipstick or colorful scarves with a smidgen of hair peeking out. My "Fashion is Freedom" message was born when I moved out of Iran and was exposed to women wearing whatever they wanted without being judged, scrutinized, or punished.

My cousin was fascinated to hear about the restrictions imposed in our home country. In my mind, a woman dressing how she wants is a form of freedom, and the women in Iran are denied this every day. Despite that, they remain some of the most stylish and beautiful women I've ever seen. Women in Iran are mastering high-end style while loosely abiding Iran's continuing restraints—no bright colors, minimal skin exposure, and the mandatory *hijab*. They strut down the streets of Tehran as though it's their own personal catwalk, giving Paris, Milan, and New York's street styles a run for their money. Even since I left, it's evident that Iran's fashion has evolved. Women are making bolder decisions as they become stronger and more progressive, and I look up to them for this.

And, as for occupations, running a fashion business in Iran is like being a drug dealer. You have to hide all your products and activities. Marketing is only done by word of mouth. Modeling is not a career option, and fashion shows don't exist. Most women use their friends as models and host women-only fashion shows in the privacy of their homes. But even with all those limitations, these girls are making it happen, and in the process they're inspiring some really amazing creations. Some are even making an outrageous amount of money from it. Compared to them, I had so many more options and opportunities. So if they could manage to be successful with all the restrictions they faced, then I could do it too.

My journey captivated Samira. She lived a comfortable and safe life here in America. Cigarette and glass of wine in hand, she looked at me curiously and asked whether I had ever tried publishing an article about my experiences. She believed it could inspire and teach others, like herself, and she offered to share the story of my mission with Michele Shapiro, a freelance writer, whom Samira had interned for. It felt wonderful to see her be encouraged by my journey and message.

Back in DC, I continued to hold trunk shows and fashion shows, but I needed more exposure. I soon realized that the Startup wasn't bringing anything valuable to my life or business anymore. I was waking up every day feeling anxious and stressed, knowing that my time and attention was going toward anything other than my dream. Feeling like I was traveling on a dead-end road, I decided to get off at the next exit and quit. It was time to say good-bye to yesterday's doubts and worries. I couldn't remain where I felt caged.

My voracious hunger to learn and move up in my career as a designer propelled me to seek jobs in beauty and fashion. My options proved to be very limited because Washington, DC, isn't necessarily a booming hub of fashion design. Anna Wintour doesn't come and sit front row at DC Fashion Week, and there's a reason for that. Despite this obstacle, I was persistent in applying for every position I believed would advance my career in these fields. I figured that if Laura Bush needed a makeup artist or a fashion stylist, I had to find a way to be the one she called.

A cosmetics company hired me to serve as a regional retail director. Working full time at the cosmetics company while also running Dar Be Dar was challenging, but I had no other choice. I needed the money, and in order to accomplish my long-term vision, I had to do both.

Months later, as I walked to work one fall morning, I slipped into a daydream. As usual, I envisioned walking into my very own office as the CEO of a Fortune 500 company. I was snapped back to reality by a *ding!* from my BlackBerry. I glanced down absentmindedly and saw a new email with the subject line: "Marie Claire Magazine Inquiry." I spilled the hot green tea I was carrying all over my new suede Prada shoes (which I could barely afford).

Dear Tala,

I used to work with Samira Raassi, who told me about the story of how you created your clothing line. I freelance for Marie Claire *magazine, and I would like to talk about profiling you for the magazine. I think your story is inspirational and your clothing line is wonderful. It would make a fantastic story. Let me know if you have a moment to talk. You can reach me at 917-XXX-XXX or let me know a good time and number to call you at. I look forward to speaking with you soon.*

Best,
Michele

I walked into my small, windowless office, grinning from ear to ear. I was euphoric. After briefly pondering the multitude of possibilities that this email could single-handedly create, I wrote her right back.

Wow, I thought. I couldn't even dream of being published in such a renowned magazine. I reminisced about my childhood in Tehran when I would flip through the pages of my mother's illegal *Marie Claire* magazines. Would it really be possible for me to be in those pages that I had fantasized about so much growing up?

A few weeks later, I headed to New York by train to meet Michele and tell her about my mission and clothing line. I couldn't wait to inspire young women to pursue their dreams. She hadn't told me whether I would be featured on *Marie Claire*'s website or magazine, but I would've been humbled by either. I just assumed it would be on the website.

I was scheduled to meet Michele in Manhattan's Lower East Side at the Bowery Hotel, a boutique hotel with the feel of an English manor. I walked in wearing black jeans, a tank top, and a blazer. You can never go wrong with wearing all black. I borrowed a Louis Vuitton purse from my mother to complement the look.

The hotel was piercingly silent, but the dim lighting gave it a warm and inviting feel. The front desk directed me toward the lounge area, where I sat on a large red velvet sofa. It resembled a cozy home in Britain, so it was only fitting that I ordered a steaming cup of Earl Grey while I waited.

I thought about the kinds of questions Michele would ask and how I would answer them. Samira spoke very highly of Michele and always told me how she'd enjoyed working with her. She seemed very pleasant over email and phone conversations, but I was still a bit nervous. Michele's accomplishments were impressive; she was a very successful writer for the nation's top magazines, including *Forbes*, *Glamour*, and *Marie Claire*, but her greatest passion was race-car driving. She had competed in and won major rallies around the world. It takes purpose, discipline, and ambition to achieve all that, and she had all those characteristics. I felt very excited and honored to meet with her.

A few minutes later, a lean, petite woman walked into the hotel. Her long, jet-black hair touched her lower back, and she wore a simple outfit. She was very different from how I had envisioned her. I'd pictured her in head-to-toe designer clothing, with a fancy updo and a bitchy personality. Instead, she was a very straightforward, calm, and polite woman. As we exchanged small talk, she removed a tape recorder from her oversized purse and asked if I minded her recording my answers. She had a pen and paper in hand and began firing questions.

I prefaced the interview by saying that it was extremely important that the article wouldn't focus on religion or politics, but that it would be centered on the message I had drawn from my friends and my experiences in both the Iranian prison and America. To be honest, I had never acquired any in-depth knowledge on religion or politics, and I didn't want to discuss controversial topics on which I wasn't well versed. I didn't want the article to sound biased in any way in regards to Islam and the regime in Iran.

Instead, I wanted the article to focus on women around the world who suffer from cruel and inhumane acts. My goal was to inspire women to cherish their lives and follow their dreams, because those unlucky girls in the Iranian jail and many other women around the world will never have the opportunities that we do. We have to do it for them.

The meeting was pleasant, and I felt as though my story was

in good hands. She asked me many detailed questions, especially about how I'd felt during my time in jail. It was more difficult than I thought it would be to dig deep within myself and bring to the surface old feelings that I never wished to experience again.

After the interview was over, we shook hands. Michele assured me that she would keep me posted about the progress of the story, and I believed that she would honor my only request to not make this about politics or religion. This was one of those moments where I didn't want to hope for the best. After experiencing many failures throughout my life, I had finally learned to keep my expectations low so I wouldn't get disappointed.

Shortly after the interview, a *Marie Claire* employee contacted me about doing a photo shoot for the story. She told me that they were going to send a photographer to my design studio to take pictures of me, and that's when I started to panic. *Oh my God!* I didn't want *Marie Claire* to photograph such an unglamorous setup. How embarrassing!

My design studio was at a friend's warehouse in McLean, Virginia. It was very simple—a large wooden table (once used as someone's dining-room table) where I cut patterns; a sewing machine (taken from my mother); two mannequins (borrowed from a friend's store); and a large Dar Be Dar banner (made at a friend's print shop). There were pieces of fabric, magazines, and useless items scattered throughout the studio. I didn't think anyone would want to see such a modest place in the glossy pages of *Marie Claire*.

Melissa, the photographer, a beautiful redhead with striking blue eyes, arrived for the shoot the day after the North American blizzard of 2009 hit. The snowstorm produced record-breaking December snowfalls in the region, forcing several counties to declare a state of emergency. The district went into panic mode. Schools closed, the government shut down, the whole shebang. In Iran, people still went to work every day during the Iran-Iraq War, despite daily bombings. I have seen the incredible ability people have to adapt to the circumstances that are happening around them, so I have to admit that I was amused by how, in America, it seemed that small disasters and temporary inconveniences could quickly feel like the end of the world.

Melissa explained that the article would be published in April as part of the May issue, so she needed the photo to seem like it had been taken in the spring. There was only one problem—massive amounts of snow still covered the streets from the blizzard. Luckily, the skies were blue and the sun was shining. After she photographed me inside the not-so-fancy studio, we went outside to snap more pictures. We scouted areas where the snow was already cleared, and the parking lot of the Tysons Galleria mall was the winner.

It was *freezing*. I took off my five-inch heels and put on my comfortable boots so I wouldn't slip on the icy parking lot. I stood outside in a black-and-gray short-sleeved dress, my arms wrapped around myself in an attempt to stay warm. I couldn't see much because of how the sun reflected off the icy snow, and my eyes kept involuntarily squinting. I was relieved when she finally took the winning shot and the shoot was over.

While driving to work a few days after the photo shoot, I received a phone call from an unknown number. Abigail Pesta, editor-at-large for *Marie Claire* was on the line. She informed me that my story would be featured in a five-page spread in their May issue. I calmly thanked her, hung up the phone, and continued to drive in silence.

It didn't take long before I pulled over to the side of the road and exited my car. I leaned back on the cold hood and pinched my face. For the first time, I had accomplished something that could inspire other people, something that had more meaning than just a owning a business. I couldn't believe it. I wanted to shout out loud and high-five myself.

I called Maman first to tell her the news. She said, "You talked about Iran?" *Seriously?* All I wanted was to hear my mother say she was proud of me, and instead she was talking about politics. I wanted to share the news with someone who wouldn't worry about the consequences and focus instead on the present. Someone who would understand the sensation I was experiencing. So I called a friend who had been arrested with me in Iran.

"Shut the fuck up!" she screamed through the phone.

That's what I wanted—we shared the same reaction.

One night in April, I woke up in the middle of the night to the sound of my BlackBerry vibrating. I silenced it the first few times it vibrated, but it wouldn't stop. I finally checked it to see what was going on and found that I had hundreds of emails popping up. I turned on the lamp by my bed and opened the most recent email, which was titled, "Fan from Texas."

> *Hello my name is Maha, I am 13 years old and I live in Houston, Texas and I am Muslim and i'm from Jordan and Palestine and I was very much intrigued by your story in* Marie Claire *and your fashion line. I am inspired so much more to fulfill my dream to be an international lawyer and to go to Harvard Law School because of your story. It has made me want to*

leave a mark on the world that much more. I also have a passion for the art of fashion I love to compare looks and mix and match. I just wanted to say thank you so much your story has made me want to succeed that much more!

—

shoot for the moon even if you miss you will land among the stars!!!

I read this email over and over again. I wrote back to Maha to encourage her to follow her dreams—not only for herself, but also for those who never get the chance. I sat in my bedroom, finally having touched someone's soul eleven years after being in prison. In that moment, I thought, *Screw all those people who thought I was a failure, didn't believe I could make a difference, and never supported my dreams.* My story had inspired Maha from Texas, soon-to-be Harvard graduate and international lawyer extraordinaire! Her email triggered in me a new determination to take over the world, one bikini at a time.

I Googled "Marie Claire Tala Raassi," and my photo popped up. *Oh shit.* I thought I looked awful. My eyes were squinting because of the sun, and my body language communicated arrogance.

The next thing that caught my attention was the article title: "How I Survived Forty Lashes." And directly underneath that, a blurb read: "The crime? Wearing a miniskirt—in the privacy of a friend's home—in Iran. As protesters increasingly take to the streets to oppose the oppressive regime, Raassi, now a fashion designer in the U.S., describes the punishment that changed her life."

I was in shock. Could this article be any more political? My family was going to disown me.

I read the endless emails. I couldn't believe how many remarkable people took the time to write to me. It took me hours and hours to read them all. I was blown away by what they had to say. Women wrote to me about their abusive husbands, young girls wrote about how the article had inspired them, fashion students inquired about working for Dar Be Dar. The emails didn't stop. I wanted to write everyone back.

But there were also some upsetting emails—religious people wrote about their disapproval of my designing bikinis, and others questioned my faith in Islam. The more I read the hate emails, the angrier I became. How could these narrow-minded people judge my faith solely by my decision to design bikinis? Faith is an internal journey, and no one can know the depth of anyone else's trust in God based on what they do or do not wear. In my opinion, wearing a bikini doesn't make you less faithful. There was no difference between these people, who were judging me for designing swimwear as a Muslim woman, and the government officials who judged me for carrying a Quran in my purse during my arrest.

Still seething, I suddenly saw an email that made my mouth drop. It was from the legendary swimsuit designer Monica Wise.

Good morning Tala,

I just finished reading the article about your story. Such an inspiring story Tala!

I too am in the swimwear industry. My journey has been much different than yours and after reading

the article I felt compelled to reach out to you and wish
you all the best in your business endeavor. I'd love to
meet you in person if you plan to be in Miami again
this summer.
        Best of luck, Tala!

                                        Best Regards,
                                        Monica Wise
                                        *L*Space*

You win some, you lose some. And then you really and truly *win* some.

The following morning, I attempted to go about my work normally at the cosmetics company. I didn't end up staying at the office very long because my phone wouldn't stop ringing. I attempted a few times to put my phone aside and focus, but I couldn't. Every time it rang, I rushed to check it. The buzz surrounding the article grew rapidly, and more magazines, newspapers, TV stations, and bloggers contacted me for interviews.

My friends and family suggested that I shut my phone off and stop reading the emails, but it became addictive. I felt obligated to reply to those who were seeking help. It was emotionally draining to read the difficult paths that some women had to navigate. Young girls asked me to "please write back." And when they reached out, I felt it was my duty to try to help them. These women were inspired by my journey and shared their life struggles with me as though they had known me their entire lives. What if I could help even one woman with her struggle?

I chose not to reply to those who criticized me for designing swimwear as a Muslim woman or urged me to practice another faith, although it took every ounce of my being not to reply. I refused to stoop down to their level. I had to stay strong. Some people will always find something to disapprove of, regardless of what you do—even if I were covered from head to toe, they would say something. At the end of the day, they were really judging me for being a woman who is taking a stand.

I experienced many different emotions from the media's interest in me and the way in which readers reacted to the article. Even though I was feeling a rush of excitement and inspiration, I didn't really want to talk to anyone else. I wanted to go into hiding—it would be safer there. The media attention scared me. I was worried that the story was becoming too political.

In the end, I was right. My story spiraled out of control. I lost all power over its content. In a matter of weeks, I had more than ten thousand search results on Google from blogs and news hits. The meaning behind the story of what my friends and I had experienced in Iran was lost, and the message that was being communicated was no longer about following one's dreams or about abused and mistreated women around the world. It was no longer about fashion, nor was it about freedom. It became exactly the opposite of what I wanted it to be. It had twisted into a controversy over religion, politics, and diplomatic relations between Iran and the United States. And it didn't help that, at the time, the biggest political uproar since the 1979 Revolution was exploding on the streets of Iran.

CHAPTER 25

THE LIPSTICK REVOLUTION

Journalists rarely travel to Iran to cover positive stories about this remarkable country—the warm, welcoming, and beautiful people; the stylish fashion, delicious food, and rich culture; the kind hearts of the Iranian people and its extraordinary history. That's not sensational. The media chooses to focus on the dark side of Iran—protests, war, nuclear weapons, and the restrictions of the Islamic regime.

In the summer of 2009, protests against the presidential election results broke out in Iran's major cities. President Mahmoud Ahmadinejad had been reelected on a platform of helping the poor, strengthening the economy, and promoting freedom for young people and the media, but most Iranians knew that those were empty promises. The protesters disputed Ahmadinejad's victory and supported reformist politicians Mir-Hossein Mousavi and Mehdi Karroubi. Their movement was called the Green Revolution, named after Mousavi's campaign color.

The protests were relatively peaceful at the beginning; however, the police and the Basijis soon attempted to suppress them with physical force. In Tehran, it became violent. International media outlets described the demonstrations as the largest protests since the

1979 Revolution. Everyone I knew believed that the government was going to collapse and Iran would be free once again. The city's streets became a place where people could finally vocalize their discontent with the government, and hope for change briefly emerged.

My story went viral largely due to the Western media's interest in the Green Revolution and the election. The media wanted to use my journey from Tehran to the United States as an example. They wanted to expose why people in Iran were frustrated with the government and their lack of freedom, and they were looking to tie my personal journey into the protests. But I didn't want my story to be associated with the protests. My single traumatic experience in Iran was nothing compared to the thousands before and after me who were arrested and punished.

Unlike the 1979 Revolution, when the government censored everything that the media released, during the Green Revolution, control of the media fell into the hands of the Iranian protesters themselves. They used social media, especially Twitter, as a means to organize protests, which resulted in unified demonstrations in the streets and squares. Social media allowed Iranian protesters to engineer one of the greatest protest movements in Iran to date. I was proud.

Of course, it didn't take long for the Iranian government to ban all protests and shut down all forms of electronic communication, including the Internet, cell phone, and telephone usage. But Iran's youth always found ways to break the rules—they managed to hack into Iran's digital communication system and leak photos and videos for the whole world to see.

Hundreds of thousands of Iranians and millions more around the globe responded to the censorship by uniting together to defy

the law and challenge the Islamic Republic. Their unity caught the
government and the international community by surprise. The protesters' motto became "Where is my vote?" and they used sayings
like, "Down with the dictator," "Death to the dictator," and "Give us
our votes back."

One of the most critical moments of the protests occurred
when a Basiji shot an innocent woman, Neda Agha-Soltan, in the
chest. Neda was a twenty-six-year-old living in Tehran who had
withdrawn from college because Iranian authorities pressured her
to change her appearance and dress. She and her music teacher
wanted to observe a protest on a street in Tehran. As she peacefully
watched, a Basiji, who later claimed that he didn't mean to kill her,
shot her in the heart. Screams of horror rang out, and people rushed
to her aid as she fell to the ground. Neda lay motionless in a pool of
her own blood. Her face was bloodied and her eyes were wide open
while bystanders attempted to revive her. But it was useless. She was
already gone.

The images and videos of her bloody and heartbreaking death
were uploaded to YouTube for the world to witness. Some news
outlets labeled the footage: "Too disturbing to show in its original
form." My heart broke into pieces every time I watched it.

Often we watch the news and feel sad about what we see. For
a few minutes it can even make us cry, or we may spend the next
few days talking about it. But as our lives go on, we tend to forget.
There are other sad stories the next day, or we are simply so caught
up in our own lives that we quickly move on. For me, this was a
story that *stuck*. Watching Neda die devastated me, not only because
of how brutally she was killed, but also because it really hit home.
She reminded me of myself; she reminded me of my friends. The

streets she was killed on were the same streets where I had left half of my heart. They were the streets I wanted to be on. I so desperately wanted all the protesters to get what they rightfully deserved.

Neda's video spread quickly and gained the attention of international media and viewers. Her death made her an instant symbol of Iran's antigovernment movement. The government released a propaganda statement saying that the protesters had shot Neda and that the videos uploaded on the Internet had been fabricated by Western news agencies. Luckily, these claims were quickly dispelled.

There were reports of thousands of victims being arrested, tortured, raped, and even murdered. Family members of those who were killed were forced to confirm unrelated reasons for their family members' deaths. The Iranian government denied all the allegations and only admitted to thirty-six people's deaths during the protests. I wasn't surprised.

Funerals in Iran have long served as a political rallying point, because it's customary to have a week of mourning and a memorial service forty days after the death. It gives people time to come together. During the 1979 Revolution, funerals were used to initiate protests, which in turn resulted in more deaths. During the Green Revolution, families weren't allowed to host memorial services for their loved ones because the government feared that people would use the funerals as a platform to protest.

In all this disquiet and violence, Iranian women were a driving force behind the Green Revolution. They no longer rebelled by means of subtle civil disobedience—like brighter nail polish or sheerer headscarves—but participated boldly in the fight for their country's future. The images published on the Internet clearly showed women of all ages present in the protests and made evident the bravery of Iranian women risking death and imprisonment. Christiane Amanpour, chief international correspondent for CNN, called the Green Revolution the "Lipstick Revolution" because of the impact Iranian women had on Iran through their protests. More power to them!

For a few weeks, Western news channels' primary focus was the Green Revolution. Iran was finally at the forefront of the media. People were being educated about President Mahmoud Ahmadinejad's shortcomings, as well as Iran's deep-rooted issues. The world was interested to find out whether the government would crumble and faith could be restored in Iran.

My eyes were glued to the TV for hours on end. I monitored the story's progress with Google alerts, tweets, Facebook—anything and everything to keep myself up-to-date. But all I really needed was to follow my friends' postings on social media. They posted updates on the situation before news outlets even got the chance to.

Would Iran be freed? Would the protesters prevail in bringing down the government? Would women be able to wear bikinis by the Caspian Sea and hold hands with the opposite sex in the streets of Tehran once again?

Then Michael Jackson was pronounced dead.

The media's focus suddenly shifted. The attention was no longer on protesters who fought for their freedom and a better future, but on the death of a music legend. His music changed the world—that's true. His dancing inspired people—also true. But the people in Iran who were being tortured and killed fighting for a bigger cause suddenly became old news.

A news correspondent for Fox News in DC contacted me to do a live interview, which I graciously accepted. I was very nervous.

I asked her to send the questions she planned to ask me in advance, so I could prepare my answers. The interviewer said that Fox correspondents didn't usually provide questions before a live interview, but she would make an exception because this would be my first time on the air and I was worried about the political side of the story.

On the day of the interview, I sifted through the questions and realized that I couldn't be a part of this. Her questions centered on my thoughts on the Iranian regime and the current political situation, and I knew it was wrong to go on television and talk about my fashion business and what happened to my friends and me eleven years ago when some of those same friends were fearlessly protesting in the streets of Tehran at that very moment. I didn't dare put the spotlight on myself. In my heart I wanted to be out on those streets with my friends, protesting and tweeting videos to the world, exposing the cruelties being inflicted on the Iranian people.

Soon after I declined to do the Fox interview, I sat on my bed in my room clenching my huge Tweety Bird stuffed animal and reading more emails. Suddenly, I received an email titled: "I read your story on MSN." What story on MSN? Once again, I was inundated with hundreds of new emails. I searched for the article and saw the same picture *Marie Claire* had used of me on the home page of MSN.com. I clicked on it. It was the same story that was featured in *Marie Claire*. I couldn't believe I was on the home page of MSN!

I sifted through thousands of comments. I started with the most recent one and couldn't stop reading them. But the more I read, the harder it was to breathe. The comments seemed endless. They ranged from people wanting me dead to people defending my situation. Tears streamed down my face as I read, "She should be stoned to death in Iran for breaking the rules"; "She will go to hell for putting girls in bikinis"; "The United States is using this story to go to war with Iran"; "This is politics, and this girl works for the Iranian government." I kept wiping away the tears, but they wouldn't stop. I began sobbing.

I threw my computer across the bed and cried until it pained me to take a breath. I design bikinis for a living. I love to dress fashionably and travel. I party with my friends, date, and have grand adventures. I have a massive Tweety Bird on my bed, for goodness' sake! But I was also arrested and punished for attending a party with my friends when I was a teenager. From then on, my sole purpose in life was to inspire people to follow their dreams and bring attention to the atrocities women face every day, because I had witnessed a place where all hope was lost. Violence against women doesn't only happen in Iran but around the world—forced prostitution, rape, abuse, and mutilation—and now people thought I should be killed for designing bikinis as a Muslim woman. How could the world view me as a political figure? As a proponent of or dissenter against my religion?

I called Michele Shapiro and explained the fears I had for the safety of my friends and family. It was a difficult decision, but I felt that the story had to be taken down from MSN. If I could go back in time, I would leave the story up and ignore all the threatening comments, but in the moment, I felt alone and scared. Dealing with the media is a skill that I hadn't mastered yet. Talk about cyberbullying. People don't realize the effect their words can have on others.

As usual, Michele was calm and comforting. She said she would have MSN take it down, but she explained that this type of reaction from readers was normal following the release of any controversial story and that I shouldn't waste my time feeding into the negativity.

People will always have their own opinion, regardless of whether it coincides with your intentions and beliefs. She also warned that because *Marie Claire* had posted an online version of the story, I was sure to see it reposted on other websites.

About two hours later, the story was taken down from MSN and a weight was suddenly lifted off my shoulders. But sure enough, over the next few days, it was posted on many other online outlets. The story's publication was out of my hands and out of control.

I had been completely naive to believe that there wouldn't be any negative backlash from a story that had originated in a country that is riddled with political and religious strife. But if I had kept my story only to myself, my family, and my friends, I would never have had the chance to inspire other people and raise awareness about an injustice that happens daily in my home country. It was worth sharing. I wouldn't be the person I am today without living through that chapter in my life.

Despite the harsh punishment I had suffered from the government, my home and my heart will forever remain in the most beautiful country in the world—Iran.

A few days later, Abigail Pesta phoned me to ask if I was interested in going on the *Rachael Ray Show* for an interview. I felt much more at ease at the thought of appearing on this show; it was mainly viewed by women—more specifically, *modern women*—and it rarely delved into politics and religion. This was a once-in-a-lifetime opportunity that I couldn't forgo.

At the studio in New York City, a producer asked me the same questions for more than an hour, expecting me to have perfected my answers by the twentieth time. Then the editors cut it down to a three-minute segment that would air during my live interview the following day. They combined the footage with flashbacks of photos from my childhood and teenage years in Iran, which the producers had asked me to send in advance. It was difficult to find photos without my family or friends in them. I guess selfies weren't as popular when I was growing up.

I asked Michele Shapiro to accompany me to the live interview, which she graciously agreed to do. As I walked to Rachael Ray's studio that morning, my nerves were twitching. A part of me was proud to be there, and another part of me was questioning whether I should have come at all. After the reaction to my MSN article, I was hesitant to face any consequences that could come from being on television. I was escorted to a room where "Tala Raassi/Rachael Ray" was written on a plaque on the door. I took a picture of it and sent it to my friends. Despite how nervous I was, I still felt like a badass.

As I waited in the room, images flashed before my eyes of me tripping on set or forgetting how to speak English. I even thought about what type of underwear I was wearing in case I fell and it showed. I couldn't sit still. I just walked back and forth in my heels across the small room until Michele arrived. Her presence calmed me.

After about an hour, I was escorted to a small makeup room adorned with bright lights and mirrors. I wondered how many famous people had sat in the very same chair I was sitting in. A hairstylist sprayed and styled my hair, then applied makeup. I felt like a little girl getting to wear makeup for the first time as I got star treatment for my first TV appearance.

Rachael Ray came to speak with me moments before I walked onstage. She was picture-perfect and very calm, and I appreciated how she approached me. She complimented my outfit and reassured me, saying, "I know that you don't want to talk about politics, so just tell me what you want to talk about and we can talk about that." I was overcome with a sense of relief, and my nerves startled to settle. I finally felt like I could pull this off.

I heard her introduce me to the audience while I stood behind the curtain. People were scurrying around the set getting ready for my entrance. Before I walked out, she showed the audience the clip they had made the night before. I thought I looked awful on TV. What was wrong with my hair? There were photos of women covered from head to toe flashing between my face and childhood pictures. I guess they needed to show the dress code in Iran, but it made me feel uneasy.

Then Rachael Ray announced enthusiastically, "Please welcome Tala Raassi!" I shot a quick look at Michele, who smiled encouragingly and said, "You are going to do great." I smiled back and walked onstage—actually, it was more of a sprint. I couldn't get to the couch fast enough. I kept reminding myself not to fall as I sailed past a sea of four hundred women standing and clapping.

I thought I did a decent job with the interview, considering my heart was pounding out of my chest. What if people could hear the thumps through the microphone? *Focus, Tala, focus.* Comfortingly, Rachael let me take control. When she asked me questions, they were quick and to the point. I felt like I was talking to a friend in her kitchen. All that was missing were homemade cupcakes and some hot tea. And it was over in the blink of an eye.

The show aired a few weeks later. I had completely forgotten which day it was supposed to air, but I was reminded by a phone call from Maman, who told me proudly, "I am watching you on the *Rachael Ray Show* as we speak." I am extremely critical of myself, so when I flipped on the TV to watch, it only made me anxious. I didn't like the way I looked or my hand motions, and I couldn't even count on two hands how many times I said "um."

My website crashed once again from the traffic surge, and I got another storm of emails—some positive and others negative. But this time, I was ready. I was used to the criticism by that point, and it was much easier to let the negativity bounce off my back. The words no longer had power over me. Instead, they ignited a fire in me that continues to burn today.

Bring it on.

They say haters are going to hate, but sometimes that can be hard to ignore, especially when you want to do something for a greater good. The key is to know who you are, believe in what you do, and realize that the negative things people project to you is nonsense. No matter how kind and remarkable you are, there will always be someone who is not going to like you. These people are simply resentful and bitter about their own lives, and they often try to find fault in others to make themselves feel better. Don't allow their pessimism to leave a negative mark on you; learn how to be better for yourself. Remember that the judgment of others doesn't define you—it defines them.

WHERE IS *MY CROWN?*

CHAPTER 26

A GOLDEN OPPORTUNITY

In the weeks that followed, I received a great deal of media attention—but I didn't want it. I had already lost control over the message I wanted to convey, and I was also slowly losing control over Dar Be Dar. I appreciated how lucky I was, but I couldn't handle the number of orders that were suddenly coming in. I only had twenty-four bikinis in stock! I was still working full time at the cosmetics company, and I was answering all press inquiries on my own, without a publicist. I felt like I was stuck on a wheel of fortune and I was never coming to a stop anywhere near the right direction; I just kept spinning round and round. The length of my to-do list made me feel nauseous.

Once again, I had to come up with another strategy, and this time it was going to require that I rebrand the company, create a new collection, hire a publicist, and find time for all the press. I was in need of a bigger investment and a legitimate business plan.

Eric and I discussed the necessity for a larger capital contribution to Dar Be Dar. He has always said that an entrepreneur's most important quality is knowing how to rebuild yourself from scratch. I respect him tremendously, and his life lessons have been

instrumental in my success. My favorite words of encouragement
from him were, "Some of the most successful people in the world
fail at first, and some even fail many times."

Consider these famous examples:

BRIAN ACTON

When he applied for jobs at Twitter and
Facebook, they both rejected him. Four years
later, Facebook bought his creation, WhatsApp,
for $19 billion.

VERA WANG

She failed to make the U.S. Olympic figure-
skating team. Then she became an editor at *Vogue*
but was passed over for editor in chief. She began
designing wedding gowns at age forty and is now
the premier designer in the business, with a multi-
million-dollar company.

WALT DISNEY

He was fired by a newspaper editor because he
"lacked imagination and had no good ideas."
Several of his businesses failed before the premiere
of his movie *Snow White*. Today, most childhoods
wouldn't be the same without his vision.

OPRAH WINFREY

She was fired from her television news-reporting
job because the network didn't think she was fit to

be on screen. But she rebounded and became the undisputed queen of television talk shows. She is also a billionaire.

DR. SEUSS

His first book was rejected by twenty-seven different publishers. He is now one of the most popular children's book authors ever.

Devastating failures are just another stop on the road to success. Drive is something that no one can put a price tag on, and that is why Eric continued to invest in me. He knew that my drive would continue to motivate me to move forward.

This time Eric's investment in my company would be different. I had acquired so much more knowledge of the fashion business, I already had sales lined up, and I had access to media. I felt more confident than ever before. Again his investment was relatively small, but it was the first building block in a series of interlocking pieces that would ultimately lead to the creation of my empire. We agreed that I would use the investment to hire a publicist; attend trade shows in New York, Miami, and Vegas; and then create more well-rounded collections, which I could present at these shows.

I instantly started researching renowned PR companies and interviewing publicists who could potentially help me build a brand and handle media. After reading through the contract terms for several companies in both Washington, DC, and New York City, I realized that a substantial PR company wouldn't be a good fit for my needs (and budget). First, some asked for monthly payments as high as $20,000. If I had that kind of money to spare on PR representation, I would use it to hire an actual staff. Second, there was a strong likelihood that I wouldn't receive the amount of attention I needed from them because of how much of their resources are spent on their A-list clientele. I was really searching for someone that wouldn't just be in it for the paycheck, but would understand my vision, be passionate about it, and help me maneuver my way around the fashion industry step by step.

A dear friend of mine, Erika Gutierrez, who is the daughter of the former U.S. secretary of commerce, worked for a PR firm in DC. She confided in me that she was planning to leave the firm soon and was thinking about starting her own PR company.

A few weeks later, Erika and I met at Starbucks for coffee. I always thought she was an outstanding woman. She owned every room she walked into, which I admired, and I knew she had the ability to ace the PR business. I couldn't handle the media alone, and I needed someone who could take the pressure off that aspect of my life so that I could focus on building my brand. Could she be the one for Dar Be Dar?

I explained my vision and what my business plan entailed. She was enthusiastic about my strategy, and I felt she truly believed in my mission. A few days later, we signed a contract! I would be her first and only client for the next six months. It was so energizing to work with someone who embodied such strong and influential characteristics. People either inspire you or drain you, and I wanted to surround myself with people who would inspire me to reach higher. Her enthusiasm was infectious.

Shortly after signing our contract, Erika and I were going over media questions when I received an email titled "Miss Alabama." The email read:

Dear Ms. Raassi:

> *I am the current Miss Alabama, and I am getting ready to compete in the Miss USA Pageant. I came across your story in a magazine and was amazed by your inspiring story. I was wondering if you could help sponsor my swimwear portion. I would love to talk about your story and represent your brand at the Miss USA Pageant.*

I read the email aloud to Erika and said, "How cool would it be if we could actually sponsor the Miss *Universe* Pageant?"

Beauty contests require a panel to choose an individual to represent community standards of beauty and morality. During the 1920s and '30s, beauty contests consisted of swimsuit pageants and were mainly put on as tourist attractions. The contestants used these pageants as a platform to diverge from expected female social norms and advance their Hollywood careers.

It wasn't until World War II that these contests transformed into mainstream, respected communal events. During a period of decolonization and nationalist movements, these competitions became a means of expressing nationalist sentiments and pride, and they gathered momentum around the world. The pageants began to include other components—talent, evening gown, etc., and scholarships were offered as prizes. Beauty pageants evolved into representing what society viewed as the embodiment of an ideal American woman: well-mannered, intelligent, beautiful, and epitomizing moral excellence.

The Miss Universe Pageant, one of the three largest beauty

pageants in the world, features contestants from eighty to more than one hundred countries and attracts a global audience of millions. It represents the international ideal of beauty, and the pageant's logo—"the woman with stars"—represents the magnificence and responsibility of women around the world. It's a public forum available to women to showcase their physical attributes, talents, and social skills.

The pageants are often used as a political forum as well. In 2002, Miss Lebanon withdrew from the competition because she refused to compete with Miss Israel. Iran never participated in the pageant because of religious barriers. However, in 2003, Nazanin Afshin-Jam, an Iranian Canadian, represented Canada in the Miss World contest, which defied the conservative Iranian community and caused a stir.

Since the 1979 Revolution, Iranian women have been banned by the government from participating in pageants because they couldn't compete uncovered. Furthermore, the Islamic Republic views pageants as being counter to Islam. Still, I watched the Miss Universe Pageant on satellite TV every year in Iran with my friends and family growing up. Some of the most beautiful women in the world compete, and I always mourned the fact that Iranian women were not among them. They were just as beautiful, influential, and talented. Could it be possible to find a way to represent the striking beauty and intelligence of the women of my country through this organization?

Shortly after I told Erika that I wanted to make swimwear for the pageant, she received a phone call from an unknown number. The woman on the other end of the line was Kara, an executive from the Miss Universe Organization. She had called because a few days earlier, taking the subway on her way to the Miss Universe office, she'd come across my article in *Marie Claire*. She believed it was fate and said that if anyone should design swimwear for the Miss Universe Pageant it should be a woman whose mission is to empower other women through the message of "Fashion is Freedom." The Miss Universe Organization had been working to promote female empowerment for years, and this pairing would be a match made in heaven.

I patiently waited for Erika to finish the conversation, and the second she hung up, I jumped up from my seat and asked, "What's the catch? If this is a match made in heaven, then what are we waiting for?" The one thing I didn't understand was why, if the pageant was just two and a half months away, they still hadn't secured a swimwear sponsor. There *had* to be a catch!

Erika clarified that there was a hefty sponsorship fee and that fee wouldn't cover the costs of producing four hundred bikinis for the contestants and traveling with the organization to Las Vegas for nearly two months. The terms seemed to be impossible to meet. I couldn't think of how I could come up with such a hefty sum in such a short period of time. But I had to find a way to do it, because I didn't want to let this opportunity slip through my fingers. We decided to sleep on the idea and reconvene the next morning.

Later that evening, I couldn't stop thinking about the endless opportunities this pageant could produce for me. I phoned Eric and expressed fervently how much I wished to be involved with the Miss Universe Organization. This platform would mean so much to me. I wanted Iran to be represented in a pageant from which Iranian women were banned. My contribution could be a symbol for women who never had the opportunity or freedom to follow their dreams, and for those who wanted to participate in these pageants but didn't have the choice to. I couldn't think of a more fitting outlet to broad-cast my "Fashion is Freedom" message.

Eric listened intently as I spoke. And after I was done, he asked the same question I had when the sponsorship was proposed to me: "What's the catch?" I was kind of terrified to even tell Eric the terms, because I was convinced he would say they were just too absurd.

"We need $140,000, which includes $85,000 for the ten-second NBC segment that would air the night of the pageant announcing Dar Be Dar as the official swimwear sponsor, plus the cost to produce four hundred bikinis, travel costs, PR, and other expenses," I said timidly.

Eric laughed out loud. "Holy crap, that's just silly!"

Eric and I discussed my concerns about my full-time job and the fact that the pageant was only about two and a half months away. We agreed that there was no way I could handle such a huge under-taking. It was too expensive, and there was not enough lead time to fulfill the organization's expectations. I hung up the phone and con-templated my fate. I thought if the sky is the limit, then why doesn't someone just hand me some wings and allow me to fly through all these obstacles to my dreams?

The sudden ring of my phone pulled me from my thoughts. Eric's voice came confidently through the receiver: "Let's do it."

He told me that his company had just signed a substantial con-tract, giving him the capital to invest in such a huge opportunity. He saw the synergy between my company and the Miss Universe Organization and believed it could become a very lucrative pairing. Of course, as soon as he'd handed me those wings, I was immediately petrified, and I definitely didn't feel ready to fly the limitless skies.

"Are you crazy? How could I possibly do this on my own?"

"Tala, if anyone on this planet can do this, it's you," Eric replied.

As flattered as I was by his compliment and motivational speech, I still didn't think I could pull this off in such a limited amount of time—even if I sewed myself a Superwoman costume. I wasn't afraid to work hard; I had an excellent work ethic (or at least I would like to think I do). Even so, I couldn't do the impossible. I was a one-woman army running Dar Be Dar and working full time. When would I find the time?

Eric managed to remind me that it's important to take chances in business. I had just recently come to terms with the dissolution of my boutique, and Dar Be Dar was doing just fine. I knew if I put my mind to it I could handle the business aspect, but I was hesitant because I didn't want to suffer another personal collapse if this didn't work out. This time around, my audience wasn't just DC, it was the world. I had the physical endurance, but was my soul ready for such a big commitment, and such a risk?

The following morning, Eric and I had a thirty-minute conference call with the Miss Universe Organization. They made their sales pitch, and it felt like they tried to sell us on the facts that the pageant is watched by the entire world every year, their website receives billions of hits, and my company would benefit enormously from the exposure this opportunity would create. I had hoped to hear a more genuine pitch about female empowerment, freedom, and the synergy between our companies, but this felt more like I was buying a car at a dealership. It was all numbers. But, of course, at the end of the day this was all about business.

Then they gave us an ultimatum—either we sign the contract in the next few days or they would sign someone else on their long list of companies "dying for this opportunity." Obviously, I was extremely skeptical. My gut was telling me that the entire offer placed an unreasonable demand on our money, time, and energy. But I didn't follow that instinct because I craved an opportunity that would bring meaning and purpose to my life. I would receive the necessary funding from Eric and couldn't bring myself to pass up a chance to make a difference. There aren't many people in the world who can say, "I sponsored the Miss Universe Pageant." I snatched the opportunity while it was still within reach.

Eric negotiated for the payment to be split into four parts, which they agreed to. We also requested to use all the attending contestants for a high-end fashion show featuring my swimwear. Our proposal was verbally accepted, but we were told the fashion show couldn't be worked into the contract on such a short timeline.

And just like that, within a few days of the initial phone call, Dar Be Dar was the official swimwear sponsor for the 2010 Miss Universe Pageant. *Oh my God, this is huge*, I thought. So huge that I had no other choice but to leave my job at the cosmetics company. I was scared to do it because it was my only stream of steady income, but I believed the risk would be worth the reward.

I knew there was a chance that the Miss Universe Pageant wouldn't work out the way I predicted. The unknown is always intimidating, and it's human nature to focus on the possibility of catastrophe. It's a fact of life that many of the risks you take won't pay off the way you want them to.

But remember: beyond the risk lies the opportunity for wisdom and growth. Besides, how are we supposed to achieve greatness if we always play it safe? Don't let the possibility of failing stop you. Miss Universe was giving me the chance to grow, and that is exactly why I took the risk.

CHAPTER 27

LIVING THE DREAM

A few days after the sponsorship became official, I traveled to the *Marie Claire* headquarters in New York to give a speech about my journey and what it was like to be published in its magazine. After all that had happened, I felt like I was living my own fairy tale. I had never given a speech in that type of forum, but had always been comfortable speaking about messages I felt passionately about, no matter the setting. I finally felt like I was getting the hang of public speaking. Plus there wasn't the added pressure of cameras.

I arrived at their headquarters in the Hearst Tower, a high rise in Midtown Manhattan, wearing a sleek black-and-white dress with a blazer. I felt empowered just from standing there. That was the type of place I had always envisioned myself working in—or more like being the boss in!

That day I was a bit too eager and arrived an hour before my meeting was scheduled. As I walked through the corridors people introduced themselves and congratulated me on my success. Some even took photos with me. Who was I to them? I was very confused, but beyond humbled.

Abigail Pesta, the editor of my story, introduced herself. She had ivory skin and very short red hair that tapered neatly around

her face. She was very warm and made me feel welcome. I followed
Abigail for a tour of the huge, bright headquarters, which had many
cubicles filled with fascinating people. Everyone who worked there
oozed glamour and style. I was a bit intimidated. As we passed by
the offices, more employees stepped out and introduced themselves
or Abigail introduced them to me.

Then she took me to the *Marie Claire* fashion closet, where I got
to experience a small taste of heaven. A beautiful rainbow of colors
brightened my vision as I stared at all the haute couture garments.
This room contained all the clothing, accessories, shoes, bags, and
everything else that the hottest fashion designers in the world sent to
the fashion editors for photo shoots, editorials, and the like. I stood
there in awe for a few moments. I couldn't believe how many coveted
collections of clothing, not to mention Chanel and Birkin bags, were
in my presence. I wanted to feel, smell, and try on every single item.

Abigail finished the tour and took me to meet Joanna Coles,
the editor in chief of *Marie Claire* at the time. She began her career
in journalism in her native UK and has been aggressively making a
name for herself ever since.

I approached her office and saw her sitting there. She was striking. I was dying to take out my phone and snap a million selfies with
her. At the same time I was trying really hard to keep my cool and
pretend that fireworks weren't shooting from my head. The entire
scene was plucked out of *The Devil Wears Prada*. Joanna even resembled Meryl Streep. She was fabulous and very classy. Her hair was
styled to perfection; I almost didn't believe it was real.

She greeted me in her elegant British accent and invited Abigail
and me into her office. Joanna sat behind her spotless executive-style
desk, and we sat in the chairs facing her. I felt blessed to have the

opportunity to sit across from such a brilliant woman and honored that she had taken the time out of her busy schedule to converse with me. I also felt very badass just for having the chance to sit my butt in a seat at her office.

We chatted about my experiences, Dar Be Dar, and my personal life. She said if I ever became overwhelmed with running my own swimwear business, she could always put me in touch with a renowned designer I could work with. I was flattered and overjoyed by her trust in me. I felt she believed in me enough to recommend my talent to a respected industry professional. That in itself felt like an accomplishment that no money could buy.

As I walked out of her office, I asked what she thought about my sponsorship with the Miss Universe Pageant. Joanna said, "I think with your story and message, it could be a good pairing." She offered to write about my new partnership in the editor's comments section of the upcoming issue of *Marie Claire*. I was break dancing in my head.

Finally, Abigail led me to the enormous conference room where I would give my speech. It was filled with chairs facing a podium, and it had floor-to-ceiling windows overlooking a breathtaking view of the New York skyline—it oozed power, and I could feel it everywhere around me. As the room filled with people, I sat in the last row and admired everyone walking in. I couldn't believe these intelligent, stylish, and authoritative men and women had come to hear me speak.

Everyone clapped as I approached the podium, and I couldn't hide my exhilaration and the huge smile on my face. After I thanked the audience, I paused for what felt like sixty seconds. Then I told my story and cracked jokes about the stupid mistakes I had made in the fashion industry. It hit me as I was speaking that I had been so busy trying to be a huge success, that I had forgotten about the little accomplishments I'd achieved throughout my journey. That reminder gave me a fresh sense of strength about taking the risk with the Miss Universe Pageant.

Since time was of the essence, I wanted to squeeze as much as I could out of the Big Apple. So I set up a photo shoot for Dar Be Dar's 2010 resort collection. I used a stunning model from a Miami-based modeling agency and hired a French photographer, Pierre, and three of his assistants through a mutual friend. I had seen their work in *Vogue Paris*, the French edition of the magazine, and seren-dipitously, they were in town.

We had to shoot the entire collection in a six-hour time frame because the photographer's flight back to Paris was later that eve-ning. This was the first time I had worked with such a renowned photographer. Pierre and his team were typical Parisian artists—cocky, loud, and delightfully eccentric. They spoke in strong French accents, and I didn't think anyone could speak faster than I do, but they did. Pierre looked like he had just stuck his fingers into an elec-trical socket. His hair was out of control.

For the shoot, we transformed the streets of New York City into our very own studio. We decided to shoot in the heart of Chinatown because of its busy streets and bursting colors. Most importantly, we wanted to incorporate its glimmers of the exotic—the crisply roasted meats hanging in butcher-shop windows, lychee nuts and dried fruits decorating the produce markets, and bakery signs advertising one dollar for the best pork buns you've ever tasted. The never-ending rows of fake jewelry and the bands of colorful scarves and garments created a sparkling sight outside the storefronts, which added to the traditional Eastern flavor. One of the best things about art, and fashion in particular, is that the more peculiar the concept, the better. What isn't exotic about seeing a woman in a bikini stride through Chinatown? So let's blame the outrageousness of the shoot on art, not the lack of budget and time constraints.

When we arrived, Chinatown was bustling. It felt like a city within a city. Diverse crowds of people filled the streets, and vendors sold everything from knockoff handbags and leather goods to dried squid and fungi. As we walked through the streets, I heard the clangs of pots and pans from restaurant kitchens and smelled the enticing aromas of take-out food. We were offered fake Rolexes and Gucci bags every other block.

We encountered obstacles throughout the shoot but managed to overcome them. For example, where would the model change? Erika and I had stopped by the Garment District the day before and bought a few yards of black fabric to cover the windows of the rented minivan that we used to get around. It transformed the space into the model's very own fitting room. It was also a great way for people to mistake us for serial killers. Either way, the black fabric did the trick.

How would we glam up the photo shoot? We purchased an array of colorful feathers and accessories to add a Brazilian Carnival flare to Chinatown. And by "array of colorful feathers," I mean three plush feathers on three long, colorful sticks. There was a bright yellow one, a hot pink one, and a turquoise one. I would have loved to buy more, but who knew feathers were so expensive? Don't try to understand the fashion synergy between Brazil and China— there is none. The only commonality these two countries share is that they're both BRIC economies (i.e., at similar stages of newly advanced economic development). We also borrowed a mirror from the hair salon that did the model's hair to reflect the sun for optimal lighting, since natural lighting was all we had. Sounds just like any glitzy, high-end fashion shoot, doesn't it?

With all our supplies and enthusiasm we took over the streets of Chinatown in the middle of a hot, steamy June day. Crowds of people gathered around to take photos of the model. She was a gorgeous brunette with long legs and a perfectly toned figure. Her bronzed body looked amazing in my contemporary bikinis, and I was impressed with her modeling capability. This wasn't her first rodeo.

In the middle of the photo shoot, we were stopped by the NYPD. Just my luck! They requested a permit to show that we had approval to photograph in Chinatown. Since I assumed all the streets on this planet belonged to God, I didn't have a permit prepared. Erika and I made our pitch and became friends with the officers. They say if you can't convince them, confuse them. And that is exactly what I did by name-dropping the Miss Universe Organization and showcasing the beauty of my swimwear on the exquisite model.

It didn't take long for the officers to join in the fun. The difference between the police in Iran and the police in the United States was eye-opening. They took pictures of the scantily clad model and joked with us good-naturedly. They even called in some firefighters who came and joined us. We got some great shots of the model posing in front of the police cars and fire trucks. It was crazy to witness the power of a woman's physical beauty on the opposite sex.

In the 1970s *Vogue* magazine did a photo shoot in Iran. The images were full spreads of a stunning model wearing haute couture in some of the most historical destinations in the country. Doing something like that after the Revolution would obviously only be a dream. But here I was representing my country with a French photographer who had worked for *Vogue*, an American model, in the heart of Chinatown in New York City, creating my very own vision.

A few days after my trip to New York, I was off to Colombia to oversee the production of the newest Dar Be Dar and Miss Universe collections. I had the opportunity to examine the quality of other designers' swimsuits during Miami swim week, which helped me discover both production facilities that I ended up using.

The Miss Universe Organization requested that I produce two different styles of swimwear. The first was a "fun" style for the contestants to wear throughout their six-week stay in Las Vegas. And the second was a "pageant" style for the night of the event. We worked with styles from my already existing Dar Be Dar Spring/Summer 2010 collection. I would have preferred to design new bikinis, but I didn't have a choice. We were too short on time.

I was extremely disappointed with the organization's pick for the "fun" style. The team ultimately chose a plain black bikini with a triangular top. The only touch of gusto was the silver leather piece in the center of the back. I didn't think this was the wisest choice because it appeared to be a plain black bikini from the front. Next, they chose a purple bikini for the "pageant" style. The bottom had a cutout on one side and the top was a triangular shape. The tops and bottoms of each bikini were covered with more than one hundred silver studs. This would surely hurt my manufacturing budget, but I knew it would look fantastic onstage.

My first stop was in Bogotá to pick out new fabrics. Then I would venture to Medellín to manufacture the swimsuits out of those fabrics. The fabric manufacturer in Bogotá worked closely with the production facility I was going to work with. After spending two

days searching for fabrics, I traveled to Medellín to begin the manufacturing process.

Medellín reminded me of Tehran—a city built into the
mountains and filled with warm, welcoming people. As I drove
down the mountains from the airport, the fresh air brought back
so many memories of my childhood.

The small factory was located in an old, three-floor apartment
building. The husband and wife team, Miguel and Paola, lived on the
third floor, and their factory took up the second floor. A wall covered
in threads of every color and hue imaginable (including twenty shades
of blue from fully saturated teal to pale, nearly white) always caught my
eye when I first walked in. About a dozen Colombian women worked
behind small tables, concentrating intensely on their sewing machines.

At the end of the hallway was Miguel's office. A small wooden
desk supported a permanent mess that included what must have
been the first computer ever built (perhaps a very old Apple), which
I think served more as decoration than anything useful. While in
Medellín, I never spent fewer than ten hours a day at the factory. My
days were filled with approving patterns, cutting fabrics, sketching,
arguing over prices, and, much of the time, waiting for my translator to find the necessary words. Occasionally, I would take naps in
the storage area. Paola would wake me up with freshly cut mangoes
sprinkled with salt and fresh lemon juice.

Paola was a talented patternmaker and a swimwear expert.
She helped me create the patterns for the newest Dar Be Dar and
Miss Universe collections. We had to work within NBC's guidelines,
which were given to us by the Miss Universe staff and dictated that
the swimsuits couldn't expose side boob or butt cheeks. It's ironic
how Miley Cyrus could wear booty shorts to twerk on live television,

but the contestants couldn't wear Dar Be Dar's classy Brazilian and European-style bikinis. We ultimately had to create more conservative swimsuits than we were accustomed to.

After creating the patterns, the next step was to create samples. Miguel and Paola almost had heart attacks when I told them that we needed the samples to fit the body types of eighty-three different women. They were even more aghast when I gave them a six-week deadline. I ordered bikinis in each size (small, medium, large, and extra large) for the "fun" and "pageant" styles, for a total of four hundred bikinis. If the contestants didn't fit the standard sizes, I would have to alter them on location. I also designed eighty-three different styles of bikinis for the fashion show at the Mandalay Bay resort in Vegas that we had negotiated with the organization. I wanted every contestant to wear a different style. Warning: if you are reading this and you are a designer or aspiring designer, *don't ever* do this! The sampling and production costs will be outrageous.

The women in the factory were excited to be a part of the process. Pageants are very popular in South America, and winners frequently seemed to be from there. Their enthusiasm was awesome, which was great, because we couldn't afford mistakes. I refused to leave the factory until every single style was perfected.

Back in DC, following my productive trip to Colombia, I immediately began to meet with TV channels, radio stations, newspapers, magazines, and blogs. Interviews became routine, and I was comfortable talking to the media. Their questions and comments centered mainly on my excitement about being the newest Miss Universe sponsor. It was a big deal for me as an independent designer to get such a revered opportunity, and I was grateful and humbled to be a part of such an honorable organization that served as an inspiration to women around the world. I invited Joanna Coles along with other renowned editors, stylists, and fashion-industry gurus to my Dar Be Dar/Mandalay Bay fashion show and the Miss Universe Pageant. I also asked the people in my life who I needed to impress the most: my family! They were finally going to bear witness to one of my proudest moments.

In the midst of all the excitement, an executive from Miss Universe introduced me to Christopher Griffin, the president of the MAGIC Market Week fashion trade show. MAGIC is a biannual trade show based in Las Vegas, and it would be happening during my six-week stay there. Designers get the opportunity to showcase apparel, fashion accessories, swimwear, and footwear to buyers from across the globe. This was a chance to get my swimwear in stores worldwide. I was even able to persuade the Miss Universe Organization to let me have Stefanía Fernández, the 2009 titleholder, at my booth for an hour every day during MAGIC.

Erika and I sent out countless press releases, made personal phone calls, and wrote personal emails so we could reach as many buyers and attract as much press as we possibly could. We invited them to stop by my booth to meet the gorgeous Stefanía Fernández, get a chance to win free tickets to the Miss Universe Pageant, and, most importantly, view my swimwear line.

My friends and family were amazed by the Miss Universe opportunity, but they mistakenly believed that the work was all fun and glamorous. Trust me, my daily tasks were far from glamorous, but I knew that after this journey was over I would reap the rewards of all my hard work. Repeating this to myself is what got me through the hard days. This was my third company, and you know what they say: "The third time is a charm."

CHAPTER 28

FAKE REALITY

The fashion industry is one of the most competitive and expensive industries in the world, and although I love my job and wouldn't change it for anything, the details involved are challenging and far from mindless. Every day was a struggle, and we were constantly faced with obstacles that we had to overcome. I spent the majority of my time on tasks that had little to do with designing swimwear, such as finances, contract negotiations, corporate identity creation, marketing, and lots of other administrative work. It's not just about being involved in creative photo shoots or promoting the brand at exciting events and receptions. There is so much more that goes into every garment that you wear.

How cool would it be to do a reality show about the unglamorous sides of the most glamorous industry in the world? There aren't many inspiring and educational shows on TV these days, and this could truly showcase something different. Erika loved the idea and suggested we pitch the show while we were involved with the Miss Universe Pageant. We got in touch with a production company based out of LA that worked on some really popular television shows. We were incredibly pumped when the producers wanted to meet with us to discuss the idea. It was an opportunity for my company that I couldn't pass up, so we headed out to LA.

I dressed as I would for any fashion-related meeting—I wore a tank top tucked into a short, tight skirt, a blazer, and very high black Christian Louboutin heels. Erika and I met the production team at their LA office, which looked more like a run-down old house with gray concrete walls. The girl working at the front desk was dressed like a real-life rock star, with piercings covering her ears, nose, eyebrows, and lips. She was very welcoming and offered us beverages while we waited for our meeting. The walls were covered with posters and awards they had received, but it was certainly no polished *Marie Claire* headquarters.

Three gentlemen awaited us in a nondescript office. When I walked in, they gazed at me like I was a minted sports car at a car dealership. Erika and I exchanged looks of discomfort. When we sat down on their old musty couch, a cloud of dust encircled us. I couldn't help but ask the men confrontationally, "Do you like what you see?" It was the only way I knew how to break the awkwardness in the room.

The man sitting behind the desk, who was clearly in charge, finally said, "Sorry, Tala, we didn't mean to make you feel uncomfortable, but we look at you and this project as a business deal. We were observing you to see how you would look on camera. There were no bad intentions." Before I could respond, he immediately added, "Is this how you always dress?" I couldn't believe a man wearing baggy jeans and an old T-shirt made of dreadful cotton would judge my outfit.

I gazed silently at Erika as he continued, "Let me rephrase myself. Your outfit looks too classy, as if you were going to a job interview." The men all chuckled at his comment.

I looked at him defensively and replied, "I'm sorry, but I am a little confused. In what kind of job interview would someone wear a miniskirt that barely covers her ass?"

He responded, "I love the skirt, but the blazer is too conservative. Do you ever wear your own bikinis?"

I replied, "Of course I do."

"Frequently?"

"I wear them at the pool or on the beach," I answered.

"Would you ever consider wearing them around the office?" He tried to convince me how sexy it would be, especially if I wore one while fitting the models in my Dar Be Dar bikinis. In the meantime, I was having a mini seizure inside from his lack of class and vision. He said, "You see, Tala, people need to relate more to you than to the models, because you are the main character of the show."

I didn't quite understand how people could relate to me more if I wore a bikini instead of being properly clothed. The premise of the show was meant to capture the struggles of an independent designer trying to follow her dreams, not how sexy an independent designer looked in a swimsuit. I get it—sex and drama sells—but I didn't think being in a bikini on TV would excite viewers. At least, not in the empowering way that I envisioned.

Erika and I discussed our vision for the show and what we wanted viewers to take away from it. We didn't come to any sort of an agreement, since it was just an informal meeting, but they said they would be in touch. When the meeting came to a close, the man looked at me as I walked out of his office and said, "You have very nice legs. You would look great in a bikini."

I brushed off the comment with a forced smile. "I guess so."

I had never felt more objectified. These men didn't care about my story of change, the Miss Universe sponsorship, or my vision for the motivating premise of the show. And many people with similar interests as them wouldn't either. Most people watch reality TV for entertainment and to escape the gloomy moments of their own lives. The producers' sole focus was my marketability on television and a tacky vision. I didn't want to put a price tag on my appearance.

Studies have shown that successful people stay away from reading novels, tabloids, and entertainment magazines. They don't watch reality television unless it's educational and beneficial to their knowledge. However, about 66 percent of those *not* deemed successful spend several hours per day watching reality television. Successful people would rather be educated than entertained. I sought to develop a show that would benefit entrepreneurs like myself, who had to start from zero without having a famous name or money. But the production company wasn't interested in that.

We headed back to DC with only a week left before we were scheduled to leave for Miami and Vegas. Much to my dismay, there were major issues with production in Colombia. This is just a perk of manufacturing overseas. Deadlines and organizational systems don't exist. The bikinis were supposed to be delivered to Miss Universe's office in Las Vegas within the next few days, and they weren't ready.

A few nights before having to make a last-minute trip to Colombia to get the suits ready, I met up with a friend of mine, Jonathan, for dinner. I told him about the unsuccessful meeting with the production company in LA, which ultimately fell through.

Jonathan told me he knew the producer of *America's Most Wanted* very well, and he wanted to put me in touch with him. I giggled and said, "Maybe if he was the producer of *Iran's Most Wanted* he would be more interested in a partnership with me." Nevertheless, he gave me the producer's contact information and suggested that I send him my proposal. Only a few hours after sending the email, the producer responded that he wanted to meet me in person the next day. *Here we go again*, I thought, *maybe I should show up to the meeting in a bikini this time.*

The following evening, Erika and I met the producer at the Four Seasons hotel bar in Washington, DC. An older gentleman in his sixties, wearing Converse shoes, came to greet us. There is something really cool about an older man in Converse. He seemed very easygoing. He was accompanied by his son and two other colleagues.

As soon as we sat down, he asked me about my background, what I envisioned for the premise of the show, and what specifically would occur in my life over the next two months. We started our pitch, which I rattled off in one long-winded breath:

"Tomorrow, I am traveling to a Colombian factory to pick up the bikinis. Then I need to clear customs and have them overnighted from Miami to Las Vegas from the airport. The following morning, I am holding a model casting at a Miami-based modeling agency. The models I choose will be featured in a photo shoot. Then I fly back to DC the next morning to finish packing for my six-week trip to Vegas, where I have Miss Universe and MAGIC trade show events every day. I am also hosting a fashion show with all the contestants from Miss Universe at the Mandalay Bay resort. After that, only God knows what's next."

He listened attentively and asked whether his crew could have access behind the scenes of Miss Universe. The organization ended up providing media passes to the production crew and clearing them to film at the Miss Universe locations in Vegas. He also asked if two cameramen could travel with me everywhere I went. I told him that wouldn't be a problem and that we had ourselves a deal.

Erika and I walked out of the bar beaming. She looked at me and asked, "Do you realize what just happened in there?"

"Yes, I think I'm going to be traveling with a bunch of guys for the next two months," I replied.

It was hard to believe that the producer had been so quick to pounce on the opportunity to document my journey with Miss Universe. He sent me a boilerplate contract later that evening. Eric and I went over the contract, which I signed and sent back the following day. *Wait!* I thought, *Do I need to get plastic surgery now that I may be on TV?*

Soon after that, I was in Medellín ready to pick up my bikinis with the two-person camera crew. They were extremely friendly, and it felt surprisingly natural having them around all the time. Maman was relieved that I had men traveling with me, so that I wouldn't be alone, or even worse—kidnapped by the Colombian drug lords.

My production manager and translator, Evelyn, picked us up at the airport. When I got settled into her car, she turned to me and prefaced her greeting with, "Please don't be mad." At this point in life nothing surprised me anymore, so I was quite calm and ready for her to deliver yet another round of bad news.

Apparently, she had gone to the factory that morning and the bikinis still weren't ready. When I arrived at the factory everyone was running around frantically trying to sew the hundreds of bikinis and finish them as fast as they could. Not a single bikini was completed.

Miraculously, the factory workers managed to finish all the swimwear that I needed for Miss Universe and the new collection that I was going to showcase in two big fashion shows, *two hours* before my flight was scheduled to take off. I think I had about a hundred nearly missed heart failures that day as I paced back and forth the messy factory trying to finish everything. I didn't think I would make the flight, especially since I had to clear the swimsuits through customs, which is very strict in Colombia. I made sure to stand in the line for a male customs agent. This was one time I needed to put my professional flirting to good use.

The agent asked what I was carrying in my four large pieces of luggage. I replied, "It's filled with very cute bikinis to gift Miss Colombia at the Miss Universe Pageant." I went on to say how beautiful I found Medellín and how much I looked forward to meeting Miss Colombia. I didn't even let the poor guy get a word in. I must have sounded like such an airhead. I continued to ramble on anyway, dying of laughter inside. Luckily, it worked. He smiled and let me pass through without looking through any of my bags. One less thing I had to worry about.

I knew that this flirtatious tactic wouldn't work with U.S. Customs, especially as an Iranian traveling back to the United States on a one-day trip to Colombia. Before my trip, I had contacted a company that specialized in easing that process. They prepared the necessary paperwork before I landed just in case I got stuck.

When I arrived in Miami, I collected my army of suitcases and walked confidently through the customs line. The customs agent suspiciously asked me what I could possibly be carrying back from a one-day trip to Medellín, a city once known to be the world's drug capital. I answered that I was bringing back bikinis for the Miss Universe Pageant and they weren't for sale.

He shouted to his coworkers, "Guys, this is Miss Universe!"

"No, no. I am not Miss Universe! I designed bikinis for the contestants."

He sent me to a waiting room where I stared at a white wall for five hours. Maybe if I were Miss Universe he would've let me go on the spot. The cameramen had already cleared customs and left the airport. I had a feeling this would be one of my last opportunities to be alone for the next several weeks.

Each bikini was inside a ziplock bag, which was inside a Dar Be Dar bag. The customs agents opened every single one of them. Miami International Airport is the air transport gateway for drugs from South America, so it came as little surprise that they wanted to check every little crevice. Fortunately, I wasn't part of a drug trafficking cartel.

The customs authorities told me the entire process of clearance would take a few days, which I didn't have. I called the Miss Universe Organization and they faxed a letter to expedite the process. As we waited for the fax, I pleaded with the customs agent to let the bikinis through. I explained that if he didn't, my career would be shattered. The combination of my begging, the company I hired, and the organization's letter worked. They made an exception, and the bikinis were cleared.

Now that's what I call a close call. If the swimwear hadn't cleared customs by that day, I am not so sure the contestants would have had a swimwear portion that year. I went straight to a FedEx flagship store, sat on the floor exhausted, and rewrapped every single bikini. Four large boxes and a hefty fee later, the bikinis were on their way to Vegas. I ended my trip to Miami with a photo shoot showcasing the new collection to present at the MAGIC trade show in Vegas.

The behind the scenes of success in fashion truly doesn't look anything like the end results that people see. Sponsoring the Miss Universe Pageant didn't just mean that I would wear a beautiful gown and walk down a red carpet with the contestants. It didn't mean that I was going to be at fabulous parties schmoozing with industry moguls. I was a one-woman army, and this was the road I was traveling to get to that red-carpet fantasy. And there was nothing glamorous about it. But hey, God doesn't give you things you can't handle, so I engaged in every step of the process and made it work the best that I could.

CHAPTER 29

WOMEN IN POWER

F lashing neon lights illuminate the four-mile-long strip. Some of the world's most preeminent hotels, restaurants, and entertainment are in this city. People come from near and far to gamble all day and party all night. This city was developed for the express purpose of having fun around the clock, and it remains one of the most enticing and exciting places in the United States. Welcome to Las Vegas!

The temptation begins the second you step foot on Las Vegas soil. Upon landing at the McCarran International Airport, I was surprised to be greeted by the clinking of coins being thrust into slot machines—people couldn't even wait to get to the casinos before they started gambling. Row upon row of slot machines lined the airport—thirteen hundred to be exact—to entice visitors to try their luck. Huge banners draped the walls advertising the most mesmerizing shows, casinos, and nightclubs in the world—anything to lure you into Sin City. I had never been to Vegas before. Coming from a country where gambling is illegal, this was a whole new experience for me, but I was already enjoying all the glitz and glamour greeting me at the airport.

Erika and I stayed at a hotel, which was close to the Mandalay

Bay resort and casino. Most of the Miss Universe events were hosted at Mandalay Bay. Crammed into the hotel was an entire city packed with retailers, spas, and even a wedding chapel for those spontaneous enough to get married on a whim, or after a few too many drinks. It had almost five thousand rooms, and its walkways peered over to the casinos and theaters.

After we checked in, we took our many bags to what would be our new home (and office) for the next six weeks. We stood in silence as we looked around the tiny room, which was decorated with antique-looking furniture. It could barely accommodate all our suitcases. The color scheme was very dark, and the design was heavy. The comforters looked like my great grandparents' 1920s sofa covers. And the view from the balcony-less windows was of a seemingly never-ending, deserted parking lot. We were both thinking the same thing—how were we going to live here for the next six weeks? I guess it's true that you get what you pay for. I tried to reassure her (and myself) by saying, "We will never be in the room anyway."

We didn't waste any time. Together we moved all the furniture around to fit more comfortably in the room, then unpacked and organized the bikinis. After we'd rearranged everything, it was time to get to work. I had expected more extravagance from the renowned luxury hotel, but the lobby was dimly lit, dirty, and rather depressing. Little did I know, the vintage-themed hotel would be the site of many unfortunate events throughout my Miss Universe journey.

On our way down to the registration area, we saw portraits of Stefanía Fernández, Miss Universe 2009, and Rima Fakih, Miss USA 2010, hanging on the walls in almost every corner of the hotel. It felt like the city of Miss Universe. Despite my initial disappointment with the hotel, seeing the Miss Universe girls on posters along the way was fanning the flames inside me. With each step toward the registration area, I was getting more and more fired up.

Erika and I registered as the swimwear sponsor and received all-access passes, which allowed us into the restricted areas of the hotel reserved for Miss Universe personnel. I took my badge with pride. My stress and worry began to evaporate as I saw this portion of the path I was racing down on my journey to success. We ambled through a labyrinth of silent, massive hallways; we must have passed more than a hundred rooms. Suddenly I could hear the noise double as we approached the space set up specifically for pageant preparations. When I walked in, I didn't recognize anyone.

It was time to fit the contestants in their Dar Be Dar bikinis, and I was extremely eager to meet them. Miss Universe staff had set up changing and fitting rooms, and I have to admit, I was kind of happy to see that they had also used simple black fabric draped down from a few horizontal metal bars to create their fitting rooms. I guess Erika and I weren't the only ones with serial-killer tendencies!

We located the swimwear fitting area, which was adjacent to the area where the contestants were being fitted for dresses, shoes, accessories, and sashes. Seeing my swimwear placed on a table next to Miss Universe sashes and Sherri Hill gowns set my soul on fire. I thought it was so cool. Two gentlemen, Robert and Matt, were the only others handling fittings besides us. I could tell they were well seasoned in pageant preparations and had been doing this for many years. They confidently chose just the right size and color for each contestant.

One by one, the contestants filed in—most were coming directly from the airport. Even though they had traveled from distant countries, the women had big smiles on their faces and seemed genuinely happy to be a part of the experience. They were beautiful and very polite, each with an extraordinarily striking presence.

At one point, I stood back and just observed them. I watched women from eighty-three different countries with eighty-three different personalities interact. They were all competing against one another for the crown, yet they all tried to get to know each other and were extremely friendly to one another. It was like they were there representing the personality and demeanor of their country. The United Nations could learn a lesson or two from them.

The first contestant to be fitted was Anna Poslavska—Miss Ukraine. Her beauty and elegance blew Erika and me away. She resembled a real-life version of a delicate porcelain doll. Her light golden-brown hair flowed down to her shoulder blades. She was captivating. I couldn't divert my gaze.

Anna introduced herself and shook hands with everyone around her. I could sense her enthusiasm. She wanted everything to be flawless—like a bride on her wedding day. She asked the photographers to retake her beauty shots a few times and kept changing her swimsuit size to find the perfect fit for her body. But truly, her self-confidence was the most important outfit she was wearing, and she owned it. She set a very high standard for the rest of the women.

As I fitted the women and got to know them, I grew more and more inspired. Being in the presence of powerful and strong women motivated me. I was aware of the intense pressure they felt from their families, communities, and the world. I couldn't imagine the amount of preparation and dedication it took for them to be there. Participating in the pageant was no easy feat. It takes a very strong woman to be able to stand next to eighty-two or more other women on live national television knowing the odds of winning are against them.

The fitting process was far from easy. The women had such diverse body types. Athletic, pear-shaped, top heavy, bottom heavy— you name it, we saw it. It was obvious that beauty comes in all shapes and sizes. What made these women even more beautiful was their acceptance of their bodies. Australian supermodel Miranda Kerr once said, "A rose can never be a sunflower, and a sunflower can never be a rose... All flowers are beautiful in their own way, and that's like women too." I could see how each contestant was blossoming in her appearance. We mixed and matched the tops and bottoms of four hundred bikinis to find the perfect fit for each of them.

Some of the women had breast augmentations, which I was surprised to learn was not against Miss Universe rules. I felt old-fashioned for thinking that pageants still looked for natural beauty. One contestant in particular still had bloody stitches on her breasts from her very recent breast augmentation surgery. The sight of blood made me extremely nauseous, and I got very light-headed when she disrobed. She didn't seem to be in pain, so I proceeded with the fitting. If she was in pain, then she did a damn good job of concealing it. Poor girl. You know what they say, beauty hurts!

Erika and I ended up helping Robert and Matt fit the contestants not only in their swimwear, but also shoes, sashes, and dresses as well, even though it went beyond our duties. It was my pleasure to lend a helping hand because I wanted to be involved with the process as much as possible. For me, it meant much more than just fitting the contestants. I was the only woman there from Iran, and I felt compelled to represent my fellow countrywomen to the best of my ability.

As the day came to an end, we felt exhausted. We needed to prepare ourselves for three more days of fittings and photo shoots. A few hours later, a familiar face appeared—an executive from the

Miss Universe Organization. We had met a few times previously in their New York office, and I was thrilled to finally see someone I knew, even though I'd borne witness to her sharklike personality during the contract negotiations and when she picked out the bikinis for the pageant.

I jumped up from my chair and enthusiastically said, "Hi there." I can only assume she didn't hear me because she didn't acknowledge me at all. She turned around, looked at me, and walked away. I couldn't have been more embarrassed in front of the interns, cameramen, Miss Universe contestants, and everyone else in the room.

That was the first of many alarm bells that seemed to ring every waking hour that we spent in Las Vegas, the loudest of which was the unpleasantness of the people we were working with. Constantly confronting difficult and disempowering situations was causing me to lose sight of my goals and my mission. The entire atmosphere conflicted with what I had envisioned it would be. This became even more evident when I walked past the Miss Universe registration area and overheard two men on their staff asking contestants about their accomplishments and future plans. The two young, sleazy-looking men then proceeded to mock the contestants' answers. This seemed so cruel to me that I had to confront them.

"Why are you guys laughing?"

One of them answered, "These women say they want to be doctors, lawyers, and entrepreneurs while also running charities and helping save the world." He condescendingly continued, "These women will end up working as models or in some fashion-related career, becoming reality stars, or marrying rich men and turning into housewives."

Yes, the contestants' answers were ambitious, but wasn't that the point? There is nothing wrong with having big dreams. I wanted to build the next Victoria's Secret-style empire, be involved with many charities, get married, and have enough children to fill a soccer team. I related to them and their dreams, so I took the men's insults to heart.

I also noticed the Miss Universe staff mocking the physical appearances of some of the contestants. They would talk behind their backs and call girls who had more masculine features "mister," instead of "miss." It was their unpleasant inside joke. Erika and I would get very upset every time we heard them. It wasn't fair. These girls weren't here to defend themselves against ridicule; they were here to represent their countries for a good cause.

Nevertheless, I continued to go with the flow and just observe what was happening around me. So many things that we saw bothered us a lot, but unfortunately, I didn't do anything about it. I didn't think it would matter because I wasn't even respected enough as a paying sponsor to be greeted by the Miss Universe executive, so I figured my words would mean nothing to people who simply didn't seem to care.

That day Erika and I felt extremely irritated, perturbed, and drained. We were disappointed with the way we were treated, but also because we had no idea what our tasks were and when we were supposed to perform them. The schedule that was initially given to us was useless. The times and locations were constantly changed. And it didn't help that we were provided with conflicting or no information at all about the changes.

I was most worried when the organization never gave me a time and place for my NBC segment shoot. This was my one chance to promote my brand on national television. I needed to make sure it was perfect.

On our way out of Mandalay Bay, we ran into Steven, another executive at the organization. I always found him very charming. He was tall, with short brown hair and skin that was so light that it almost looked pink—like a typical Irishman with a ruddy complexion around his cheeks. He liked to give big hugs and always smothered us in them. Everyone needs a little TLC once in a while, and both of us desperately needed some then.

Steven welcomed us with his immense hug, but he knew immediately that something wasn't right. So he followed us as I candidly told him, "I can work hard and give the organization every ounce of my energy, but I won't stand to stay here for the next six weeks if we aren't given any direction." Steven listened attentively and accompanied us back to our hotel room. He sat on a chair, crammed between suitcases and bikinis, apologized profusely, and promised that we would have a detailed schedule of the swimwear events by the following day.

The next morning at the fitting, everyone was overly friendly to us. Kara apologized on behalf of the top executive and invited Erika and me out to dinner that evening to meet Andrew, the executive liaison to the chairman and CEO of one of the biggest hotels in Vegas. Andrew also managed all of the on-location activities for Miss Universe.

It was great to have the Miss Universe staff finally on our side, but I felt like my obligations were becoming a never-ending black hole that was sucking me in. Physically, I needed a break, but mentally, I had to prepare myself for a marathon. I had to stay strong and believe deep within myself that all this work would pay off and my involvement with Miss Universe was going to yield incredible rewards.

CHAPTER 30

MATCH MADE IN HELL

T hat night, Erika and I attended Kara's dinner. I lived an au naturel life in Vegas—quite unorthodox for that city—and we dressed very casually day-to-day. I had packed some of my most voguish attire but ended up recycling the same outfit over and over again. We had become very unmotivated by the events unfolding around us.

The hostess escorted us to a private room at a swanky restaurant in the hotel. We were the first to arrive, but Steven, Kara, Andrew, and another gentleman joined us soon after. Once we all sat down at the round table for six, the staff closed the curtains. Considering the improper dinner conversation that would take place throughout the night, I turned out to be glad it was private.

While hanging out with the staff of Miss Universe could have been amusing in another scenario, I was feeling completely shattered at that moment. I had raced a really tough road to get to this point and now that I was here, I was constantly being challenged by unacceptable engagements and complications. And all I craved was some resolution and reward, or at least a little recognition.

The dinner guests became increasingly drunk and more comfortable with one another. They shared what seemed to me like many intimate stories about the organization—rivalries, how outrageous their last sponsors were, drug usage, weight issues, and much more. I thought the trash-talking session was inappropriate, but who am I to say? And of course, as an outsider and newcomer to the group, I couldn't help but be fascinated by all the scandal. Andrew asked me to share my experiences in Iran with his colleague. It wasn't the right setting to go into detail, so I gave the CliffsNotes version. His all-American, preppy-looking colleague said, "That sucks, so now if your boyfriend wanted to lash you, you wouldn't like it?" The entire table fell silent. Everyone knew his comment was absurdly out of line.

I looked at him squarely in the eyes and replied, "It must be very unfortunate to be so uncultured." Steven and Kara quickly redirected this heated conversation to a new and just as awkward topic—everyone's favorite sexual positions. I excused myself from the dinner table to go outside and get some fresh air.

I paced back and forth outside the restaurant for a few minutes to collect my thoughts. *Why am I here?* I pulled out my phone and looked through all the missed calls from everyone who I had been avoiding because I didn't want to tell them how disappointed I was by this experience. I redialed Maman's phone number, wanting to feel a sense of comfort, but immediately hung up and called Eric instead.

"Hello Tala, what's up? I'm about to get on a plane," Eric responded in a rush.

I said, "Oh no worries, just wanted to see how you were doing."

Eric, who knew my voice very well, replied: "Are you overwhelmed? Anything I can do to help?"

I took a few seconds and then hesitantly said: "Is it too late to take all this back? This is not what I had expected. I don't—"

Eric instantly cut me off. "Do the best that you can, Tala, and that is all that you can do. I have to run, will give you a ring later."

Behind me was the entrance of the hotel. I wanted to run out, get in a cab, and head to the airport. I simply didn't trust that this was a match made in heaven anymore. Surely it wouldn't be this difficult if it were. But instead, I stepped forward and went back to the dinner table to "do the best that I could," because I couldn't let Eric down, or the contestants and those who still believed in my mission.

After the dreadful dinner finally came to an end, Erika and I walked back through the hallways to our decrepit room. We replayed the day and the dinner and were both stupefied. We couldn't understand how some of these people could be in charge of such remarkable women.

Over the next few days, we got shuffled from one event to another. We were forced to play our schedule by ear, since we didn't know which events we were invited to until a few hours, or even minutes, beforehand. We were supposed to use these events as opportunities to get press for Dar Be Dar, so when we found out that there were some swimwear gatherings we weren't invited to, we were understandably irritated. Why else would we have come to Vegas for so many weeks before the start of the pageant?

One night, I received a phone call from Steven asking whether we could join him, Andrew, and some of the contestants for the soft opening of a club. Upon our arrival, the contestants posed on the red carpet, displaying their sashes in short party dresses in front of the flashing lights of cameras. Erika, Steven, Andrew, and I stood back and watched. When we entered the club, cocktail waitresses escorted us to a table with empty Grey Goose bottles. The entire production was set up to shoot the women dancing and having a blast, and then the club would use the footage for advertising on the night of the pageant. Even though there was fake alcohol on the table for the shoot, the women were offered real alcoholic beverages.

A camera crew directed the women to dance on top of the tables, in the middle of the crowded dance floor, and on podiums. And this was empowering, how? It was especially disturbing because I thought some of the girls were under twenty-one and didn't speak a word of English. I have absolutely no problem with people dancing on tables in clubs. Perhaps I have done it myself, but not with a sash on. I did it because I wanted to, not because I was told to.

The following morning, there was a photo shoot set up with the contestants featuring Dar Be Dar bikinis. These images would be shared across a Miss Universe magazine, and Erika and I were eager to use them for promotional purposes and to create more momentum around the sponsorship. We arrived to the shoot bright and early. Shockingly, I was greeted by some contestants who were not in my swimwear. At my own photo shoot! Seeing other swim-wear brands felt outrageous.

Concrete walls covered the pool area so that any outsiders couldn't peer into the exclusive space. The contestants were photo-graphed covered in multicolored body paint. Makeup artists tediously painted the women's bodies in bright designs. Once they were ready, they posed around the beach club; some lay by the pool or on chaise lounges while others stood against palm trees or climbed the walls. It was enthralling to observe all the girls and see how far they were willing to push themselves.

In an unexpected twist, the Miss Universe Organization gave the girls the option of going topless. I think they were excited about the stir it would create in the media. Some contestants seemed tenser than others about the nudity, and I believe only a few women actually went topless, including Miss USA, Rima Fakih. This gorgeous girl was a Muslim originally from Lebanon—the first Muslim woman to be crowned Miss USA. I admired the fact that she could express herself freely and not hold back, even though she knew there could be a backlash from the Muslim community. She looked beautiful.

An hour into the shoot, I was interviewing with Access Hollywood when I felt the energy on the set suddenly shift. The staff tidied the pool area, and the contestants were asked to fix themselves up and line up along the wall. I thought either God or Donald Trump was about to walk in.

The Miss Universe staff told the contestants to scream, "We love you Farouk!" Farouk is the founder of Farouk Systems, the makers of the CHI ceramic hairstyling iron and the official haircare sponsor for the Miss Universe, Miss USA, and Miss Teen pageants. The company had paid millions to be the sponsor over the last seven years. Farouk entered the pool area, in the searing Nevada heat, wearing a black pinstripe suit paired with red cowboy boots and a red tie to match. Half-naked girls, from eighteen years old to their midtwenties, with paint all over their bodies, screamed, "We love you Farouk! We love CHI!" Erika and I couldn't peel ourselves away. The scene was absolutely ridiculous. He hugged some of the girls and posed with them for photos.

All of a sudden the world had stopped because a big sponsor with more money had arrived. I mean, I totally get it, money talks! But the interaction seemed completely staged, and quite frankly, I found it pretty disturbing. During this absurd spectacle, I told Erika, "I guess we are not cool anymore. Let's get out of here." And if you were wondering, no one even noticed that we left a shoot that was supposed to feature my line.

Around midnight that night, I was already tucked away in bed, depressed and cuddling my bikinis, when I received a phone call. It was one of the stylists working on the NBC TV segment. I was pleased and relieved to hear from him. This meant it was actually going to happen.

This segment would star Stefanía Fernández and was the most media exposure I would receive as the sponsor. Millions of people would see it—six million Americans and half a billion people world-wide, to be more exact. He told me that the shoot was scheduled to take place the following day at 8:00 a.m. at the Moorea Beach Club. Erika and I had been requesting the scheduling for this event for weeks on end, and now we were being told that it was happening in less than *eight hours*?

The next day, I went on set in a sour mood. The Moorea Beach Club was a private pool at the Mandalay Bay, with dipping pools, red-cushioned chaise lounges, relaxing beds, and a private pavilion. Stefanía was wearing a black-and-white pin-striped Dar Be Dar suit. She was a beautiful, tall, curvy girl with short brown hair. The hairstylists and makeup artists were already in the middle of prepar-ing her hair and makeup. We didn't have any say about the vision or direction of the shoot; all I was allowed to do was provide one of the stylists with a few different bikini styles for the star to wear on set. With nothing much to do, Erika and I sat back and watched the mayhem unfold. I couldn't help thinking what would've hap-pened—or not happened—if I hadn't answered my phone at mid-night the night before.

Suddenly a crowd of about twenty-five beefy men and very

tan women in their midtwenties appeared on set. The women were already in cheesy-looking swimsuits, which were not Dar Be Dar bikinis. They were asked to hang around the pool and make it look like Stefanía was at a pool party.

I felt like I was at an alcohol-fueled crazy pool rave on an episode of *Jersey Shore*. The entire scene was tasteless. I watched my vision get botched by a bunch of muscled, tacky men parading around my swimwear. They danced and fist-pumped behind the pool, or lay around in beach chairs flexing their muscles. Stefanía lay by the edge of the pool in front of them like a goddess. It wasn't the TV segment I had envisioned to represent my brand.

CHAPTER 31

LIFE AND LEMONS

After the shoot, Erika and I were scheduled to meet with Kara and Steven about my Mandalay Bay fashion show. This was a big deal because it was the only fashion show where all eighty-three contestants would participate. It was also the show for which I had created a massive collection and worked so hard to promote in the media. They told us that it was imperative that we meet.

I was curious to know what Kara and Steven wanted to discuss. Perhaps they were aware of how disappointed I was about the entire Miss Universe experience. I thought maybe they wanted to make things right. As Erika and I approached them in the lobby, Kara began to mumble under her breath.

"We have some really bad news," she said, "*but* we also have an amazing solution." Erika and I froze, but Kara continued in the same tone. "Unfortunately, we are having issues with the venue the night of your big Mandalay Bay fashion show. It's also too close to the night of the pageant, so the girls will be too tired to participate. This means that we can no longer honor your fashion show."

You could cut the tension with a knife. Erika, Steven, and Kara silently stared at me for a solid minute. They waited for my reaction, but I was numb, and I can't even tell you if it was from shock or anger. She hesitantly continued, "So the girls will be handing out lemonade at the mall tomorrow, and we can just have them wear your bikinis at the lemonade stand."

I had no words. I had designed an entire collection that would fit eighty-three women, and it had taken a vast amount of time, money, and dynamism to make that happen. I had spoken to media outlets about the incredible opportunity of showcasing my line on all the contestants at a high-end fashion show. I had invited well-known media personalities, friends, and family to sit front row. It had been advertised on the Mandalay Bay website, the Miss Universe website, and the Dar Be Dar website for two months. Now, someone was telling me that my bikinis would be worn by the contestants at a *lemonade stand* at a Nevada *mall* instead? No, thank you!

I stood there, mutely crying a river on the inside, as the whole casino spun around my head.

"What do you think?" Kara enthusiastically continued. I looked at Steven, who was speechless with guilt. Then I heard Erika desperately beginning to come up with solutions, but I quickly turned to Kara.

"I think you should go fuck yourself."

I walked away as fast as I could, bawling my eyes out. This Mandalay Bay fashion show meant a lot to my career, and to me personally. I felt exploited. Why was it so difficult for such a recognized, well-established organization to follow through with its promises?

All I wanted at that point was to have a drink. I spotted a bar as I walked through the casino back to my hotel room. I sat at a bar stool and told the bartender to keep the drinks coming. I didn't care that it was only 11:00 a.m. If you drink enough vodka it tastes like love, and that was all I needed at that point.

A few hours later I stumbled back to the lobby of the hotel in tears to meet my brother, Aria, and Kimberly, a stunning friend who was going to model at my booth during the MAGIC trade show. I felt absolutely helpless, and there was nothing I could do to change that. In my mind, all that I had worked toward meant nothing. Even the fashion show ended up being a flop. While I wasn't in the best state of mind to greet them, I managed to collect myself. I was very happy to see some familiar faces.

Erika, Kimberly, Aria, and I went to the convention center the following morning to set up for MAGIC. I was relieved to finally have some sane people other than Erika around to help. This time around, my booth looked much more glamorous than the one I had set up in Miami a year before. It was two times larger, with many more designs to showcase, and a full staff. It didn't matter that they were my friends and family.

I needed to figure out an alternative to the canceled Mandalay Bay fashion show, and time was running out. I took my fate into my own hands and made the best out of the situation. At the trade show, I looked for Christopher Griffin, the president of MAGIC, with whom I had spoken over the phone and emailed about the booth.

Chris was a tall, fit, middle-aged man with brown hair. When I finally found him, I told him about the cancellation and how important it was for me to find a solution. He suggested that I host a fashion show at the happy hour event in a hotel suite at the Palms Casino Resort on the last day of MAGIC. The only conditions were that it was up to me to plan the entire show and I only had three days to put the event together. It would be tough to execute while also participating in MAGIC, but I accepted. You need to understand what you can control and what you cannot control, and forget about the things that are out of your hands. I put the canceled fashion show behind me and took control of this new opportunity.

The organization agreed that I could choose twenty contestants to model in my fashion show at the Palms. They also promised to provide hair and makeup the day of the event. There was nothing I could do to get my time and money back, but I felt better about the situation. At least this was an alternative solution. They say when life gives you lemons, make lemonade. I had decided against the swimwear display at the lemonade stand and created a much better opportunity to make my own juice!

At the first day of MAGIC, I was thrilled that so many buyers, media, and people working in the industry visited the Dar Be Dar booth. Some even came to take photos with me. We took some orders and got a lot of positive feedback. Overall, we had a very successful day. It was refreshing to have something go right for a change.

Just when things seemed to be going smoothly, the Miss Universe titleholder, Stefanía Fernández, was a no-show. Based on Kara's assurances, she was supposed to stand in our booth for an hour per day, every day during the three-day event. Buyers, media, models, and staff came to the booth wanting to meet her, but I had to tell them she hadn't arrived. I called Kara frantically to ask why she wasn't there, but I was told the titleholder was too busy with other commitments to show up.

Worried that the visitors who stopped by our booth to see the Venezuelan beauty would think that we had falsely advertised Stefanía's appearance just to generate buzz, I explained pathetically that she was very ill and couldn't make it. People left the booth disenchanted. I could hear them whispering that we had probably lied to get them to come to the booth. Instead of creating solid business relationships with buyers and people working in the industry, we were stuck doing damage control. If there were a company that specialized in damage control, I would be its number-one employee; it felt like that's all I had been doing for years.

Before I knew it, it was the last day of MAGIC and time for the Palms fashion show. The enormous Hollywood Suite that the show was held in was the type of suite you see in rap videos: high ceilings, gray brick walls, modern decor, and spacious rooms. It even had a basketball court in the middle of the living room. It belonged to Adrienne Maloof from *The Real Housewives of Beverly Hills*, and when we arrived, it was already filled with many sleazy men drinking and waiting for the Miss Universe contestants.

Kimberly, Aria, and Erika mingled with the crowd while I prepped for the runway show. I realized that some of the contestants I had handpicked weren't there and had been swapped with other contestants I hadn't chosen. Steven, as usual, apologized on behalf of the organization. He said those contestants had already been booked for a dinner with one of the customers of the casino, who was predictably rich and spent an outrageous amount of money gambling. He had wished to dine with specific Miss Universe contestants, and that wish was granted.

Wow. We didn't even know what to say about that. These girls were so much better than being reduced to escorts.

Have you ever borne witness to a group of frat boys at a home football game? Imagine that scene, and then add twenty beautiful women in bikinis to the mix. When the fashion show got under way, so did a pathetic display of horny men yelling, "Go Miss USA!" as the women walked down the catwalk in Dar Be Dar's brand-new, cutting-edge collection. The men looked like dogs in heat. They were shouting, clapping, and making ridiculous "whoo whoo whoo" noises. They took countless photos of the women as they walked the runway. After all of my hard work and overcoming so many challenges over the last decade, this fashion show felt like my very first show at Pearl. But at least that one hadn't cost me thousands and thousands of dollars!

I was beyond embarrassed, especially in front of the media. The image of a high-end swimwear line headed by a powerful and independent woman was very far from what this fashion show portrayed. It felt like any other tasteless club promotion event. And with that, I wrapped up my involvement with MAGIC.

After the show, I dolefully tiptoed into my dark, claustrophobic room and crawled into bed. About forty-five minutes after I fell asleep, I was awakened by a phone call from the front desk. The gentleman on the phone sounded troubled.

"Ma'am, one of your employees is naked in the lobby."

He must have dialed the wrong number. I hung up the phone.

Moments later, he called back and said, "Does Kimberly model for Dar Be Dar?" When I replied sleepily in the affirmative, he said, "Get down here immediately, this is an emergency." I woke up Erika and we threw on whatever clothing we could find lying around a room that had been hit by a swimwear tornado. I could never have dreamt of what I witnessed next.

Kimberly was lying on the floor of the hotel lobby in the fetal position, shaking and crying hysterically. She was braless in a white tank top and pink boy shorts, and her mascara was smeared across her face from tears. The sight of her propelled me into a state of panic. People had gathered around to see what was going on, so my protective instincts kicked in. I sat on the floor next to Kimberly, shielding her from view and rubbing her shoulders and back in an effort to comfort her. How many more lemons was this life going to give me? Maybe I should just get into the lemonade business!

Kimberly explained that after the fashion show at the Palms, she went back to her room and went to bed. A few hours later, she awoke feeling a movement on the bed. When she opened her eyes, she saw a man pulling a chair close to the bed with a video recorder in his hand. They made eye contact, and he smiled at her. She freaked out, sprinted out of the room screaming, and went down the elevator straight to the lobby. As Kimberly was explaining what had happened to her, I had the fleeting thought that either I was hallucinating or she was insane.

I filed a complaint on her behalf. I also needed to find out what had truly happened in her room that night, because she was a Dar Be Dar employee and my company could be liable. I demanded to see the video footage from the hallways of our floor, but was told that there were no security cameras set up in the hallways on any floor.

I was pulled me aside and told, "Miss Raassi, I'm not sure how to explain this situation in a way for you to understand, but I don't think there was actually anyone in the room." I came to Kimberly's defense. There had to be an explanation as to why she saw someone in her room. Her state of panic and fear could not have been an act, and I believed her. He looked me straight in the eyes, dead serious, and said, "The hotel has been experiencing some odd situations involving the supernatural. I don't believe your employee actually saw a person, but it was most likely a ghost."

That's it, who is messing with me? I thought Aria was going to jump out of a closet and say this was a prank, like the ones he used to play at the Rose Garden. But when there was no sign of Aria, and the security guy kept the same facial expression, I realized that this was not a prank.

Erika and I stood there thunderstruck. I couldn't even form a reaction. He explained the hotel had history: a worker had died in the hotel, and years ago a young girl had committed suicide.

"Is it better to be watched by a serial killer or a ghost?" I responded in astonishment. "How do you expect me to explain this to this poor girl?" I walked away and called Eric but found myself stumped as to how to explain the situation to him. Eric was more baffled than I was.

"Have you gone mad?" It was just too unbelievable.

I went back to Kimberly's room and packed her possessions to bring over to our room. I couldn't leave her alone, and I felt guilty for the trauma she was experiencing. She was a total wreck and remained very quiet and withdrawn. In her state of shock, she had written an email to her friends and family saying she was almost murdered. I felt terribly about the entire ordeal, and our questions about that night were forever left unanswered. We later spent hours researching on the Internet about other people's experiences with ghosts at the hotel. It turned out, we were not alone!

Erika and I couldn't sleep that night. We were both scared by the thought of a ghost, not to mention the possibility of a serial killer or a sex offender, being on the loose. I didn't know whether I should cry or laugh. Is there a handbook out there somewhere that teaches you how to deal with situations like these? Perhaps a *Ghosts at Fashion Week for Dummies*?

The night of the preliminary competition, my entourage and I sat front row. I wore a short white dress, while my friends dressed more casually. Our energy was pretty low from dealing with the harassment of ghosts the night before. The preliminary competition was fairly uneventful, but I was still enthusiastic to watch the women because I had grown to really admire them and even became good friends with some of them. They seemed to have a blast onstage.

Right before the contestants walked out in their Dar Be Dar bikinis, the organization aired what they were so proud to gift to me for my sponsorship—a video called "Swimsuits for Empowerment." It spotlighted my story and explained why the organization had chosen me as the official swimwear sponsor: because my line represented fashion as a form of freedom to help empower women to follow their dreams. The top executive was shown in the clip saying wonderful things about my company and me. As I watched the film, I realized how much I needed that reminder to focus on why I was there to begin with. With all the unexpected and unfortunate events that had taken place, I had totally lost sight of my larger mission.

The next morning I was scheduled to give a speech to the eighty-three contestants about my experiences and why I started my swimwear line. I was nervous because I was more inspired by these women than they could ever be inspired by me. Throughout the weeks that I spent in Vegas, I had found myself learning a lot from these strong independent women who all had big dreams. Their passion and confidence taught me to focus more on my strengths and consistently reminded me of my goals. Their courage, dedication, and beauty were mind-blowing.

I had asked Erika to write my speech. I wore a sophisticated black dress and brought my superwoman mind-set. But as I stood up at the podium in front of some of the most stunning women from around the world, I suddenly felt alone. I couldn't speak.

My entire body was heavy and burning up. My mind went blank. I forgot the entire speech that Erika had prepared. I looked at her, and she smiled back at me and mouthed, "Go for it." I turned around and looked at Steven, who I could tell was waiting impatiently for me to start my speech. The silence stretched out for a solid sixty seconds as I stared vacantly at the perfectly groomed, glamorous women with pageant curls and fake lashes. They stared back at me, waiting enthusiastically for me to begin. All I wanted to do was cry and let my eyes speak instead, because my words couldn't explain how broken I felt.

It wasn't the women who made me feel this way, but the entire situation that had left me wordless. It suddenly hit home that I no longer believed in the Miss Universe Organization, and in that moment I was happy that Iranian women were banned from participating in such a pageant. It felt clear to me that they didn't take a strong and supportive view of women. That seemed obvious from how Erika and I were treated throughout the time we were there. True, we weren't wearing sashes or crowns, but we were still young women who could have used the support of such a powerful organization. We deserved to be treated with more respect. They had chosen me for my strength, but I didn't feel that they expected me to show any of it once I got there.

I gathered my thoughts and garnered the energy to give a rushed five-minute speech that briefly described the story behind my designs. Then I wished them the best of luck and quickly disappeared from the stage.

As I headed for the door, a few women followed me. Some asked for my business card while others said that they were very inspired by my accomplishments and were proud to wear my swimwear at the pageant. Miss Australia, Jesinta Campbell, a beautiful, tall woman with dirty-blond hair and a strong presence, came up to me and shook my hand. She said that she never realized how fortunate she was and that she would never forget my speech. That warmed my heart. Maybe I had made a small difference after all.

My two best friends, Lina and Mariana, were coming to Vegas, and I had to welcome them at the gates of Sin City. I hadn't talked to them, or anyone else back home for that matter, for the past five weeks. I knew they would be upset, but they would soon find out my reasons for having gone MIA. They stayed at a different luxury hotel that was connected to the Mandalay Bay, and I was anxious to escape the walls of my haunted hotel. Maybe this was my chance to infuse some new energy into my empty and exhausted body.

I knocked on their door and could hear them screaming my name behind it. When they opened the door, their faces dropped at the sight of me.

"Hey guys," I said miserably, despite trying my hardest to sound cheerful. After a long, much-needed hug, I excused myself to the restroom to douse cold water on my face. I looked at myself in the mirror for a few moments, and I realized why they had looked at me in astonishment. I had black circles under my eyes and my skin was pale from never being exposed to daylight. If this is what stress, anxiety, and disappointment combined with anger does to you, then don't sign me up for anything like this again. In the past, when I had overextended myself, I'd always found a way to turn things around. Not this time. I was afraid that I had reached a point of no return. That point when you are willing to push your dreams to the side and settle for an average life.

I walked into the room with tears in my eyes. Mariana sat me down apprehensively and asked me to provide details on what was going on. She said that in six years, we had never gone more than a day without speaking to each other, something I hadn't thought about. "Who are you?" she asked. "You even talk differently." Maybe I had picked up a Vegas accent or forgotten my English because of the number of foreigners who surrounded me on a daily basis.

I tried to explain as best as I could, but I needed much more time and I wasn't in the right state of mind. How could I even begin to explain everything that had happened to people who hadn't been there? Trust me, it was very difficult to write it all down in this book. You had to live through it to fully understand it.

I explained that living and working in a casino for weeks takes its toll. Most people escape Vegas after a quick weekend getaway. It took me weeks to understand the games casinos play with their malleable guests. They mesmerize you and then suck you in. You are at their mercy. Except that I wasn't mesmerized or sucked in by them; I just had nowhere else to go.

By the end of my time in Las Vegas, I could easily spot the big-shot gamblers, casino virgins, loners, social gamblers, problem gamblers—I witnessed it all. I spent much of my time in casinos. Days and nights merged together. I never knew what time it was. But I knew I had been there for far too long when I realized that I even knew some of the staff by name.

I was trapped there with drunks, married men cavorting with cocktail waitresses half their age, insomniac poker lovers, and people rushing to the Hangover Heaven bus for IVs to infuse themselves with hydration fluid. Not to mention dealing with the staff of the Miss Universe Organization in that setting. I can still see and hear the siren-like lights flashing, bells ringing, and digital sounds buzzing—it was exciting at first. It's meant to suck you in and keep you there. But eventually, every little sound irked me. Every time I heard a *ding*, I felt like I was being tortured and my body would tense up. I was happy to be nearing the finish line of the Miss Universe race. I just had to get through the night of the actual pageant and I could leave this journey behind me forever.

CHAPTER 32

THE FRAGILITY OF FAME

The time had finally arrived: the night of the Miss Universe Pageant. I was excited that my friends and family would get to see my swimwear on TV. At least they could see one good slice of this experience. I was impatient to find out which remarkable woman would win the crown. But more than anything, I was thrilled that in twenty-four hours I could get out of Las Vegas!

I had spent the night at Mariana and Lina's hotel because I didn't want to step foot in the haunted halls of my own lodging. A few other friends came into town that day to watch the pageant and enjoy the festivities. That morning I went to my messy room, showered, packed, and got ready alone. I needed to center myself. I was supposed to be happy, but I just felt waves of disillusionment.

Sherri Hill, the fashion designer who designed all the Miss Universe Pageant dresses, had given me a beautiful gown to wear. One day, while I fitted the contestants, I spotted a beautiful, long, one-sleeved black beaded gown on a rack. The fabric from the knee down was black and sheer, and the rest was an elastic, fitted fabric. It exuded class and elegance. And it was love at first sight. I pointed it out to Erika and said, "Oh my god! I want to try this on."

Sherri heard me and said, "I would love for you to wear it the night of the pageant." I was relieved because this meant I wouldn't have to fuss over an outfit for my big night.

That night, we made our way toward the red carpet. I was taken aback by the number of cameras—there must have been more than a hundred of them snapping and flashing away. Several celebrities were there, including Niki Taylor, Chazz Palminteri, Bret Michaels, Natalie Morales, John Legend, and others who I either missed or didn't recognize.

Erika and I entered a room where about forty VIP guests and celebrities mingled. The room was filled with alcohol, an assortment of finger foods, and many gift bags that contained T-shirts, CHI hair products, and other items. Why weren't we asked to gift swimwear? The organization had asked us to manufacture 400 bikinis, of which only 166 were used. That left us with 234 bikinis that we could easily have contributed to the gift bags instead of giving them away to the organization's staff.

We headed to the bar for a drink. A few minutes later, Donald Trump walked in with a big entourage of people, and the sea parted. He courteously shook our hands as one of Stefanía's bodyguards introduced Erika and me as the official swimwear sponsors. Erika wanted to take a picture of me with Trump on her phone. It took her a second to get her phone to work, so she apologized for the delay. Trump said, "No worries, I am just fine standing next to this young lady."

As Trump left, he turned to his friend and said, "That is our swimwear sponsor. She paid two million dollars to be here." They both chuckled. And Trump shot me a smile as he walked to the judging room.

I turned to Erika and asked, "Did he just make fun of how

much we paid to become a sponsor?" Maybe the thousands we paid wasn't much money to the organization or Donald Trump, but it was to us.

We were told that inside the judging room, Trump and the other judges picked their top choices. They chose from the fifteen contestants who had won the preliminary competition. Just a few days before, the Miss Universe staff had asked Erika and me to recommend judges for the night of the pageant. We were confused as to why they didn't have all the judges lined up just days before the event, but I asked Joanna Coles of *Marie Claire* anyway. Unfortunately, she wasn't available, and when Erika asked her father, Carlos Gutierrez, the former U.S. secretary of commerce, he regretfully declined.

I think the criteria for being a judge had to do with how rich, famous, or powerful you were. The telecast judges were Chazz Palminteri, Chynna Phillips, Criss Angel, Evan Lysacek, Jane Seymour, Niki Taylor, Sheila E., Tamron Hall, and William Baldwin. The preliminary competition judges were Basim Shami, B. J. Coleman, Carlos Bremer, Corinne Nicolas, Louis Burgdorf, Natalie Rotman, and Sadoux Kim. I haven't watched a Miss Universe Pageant since this one, but hearing the panels of judges they've had in recent years always makes me chuckle. For example: Scott Disick, the famous Kardashians reality star, judged the pageant in 2012. It was difficult for me to see the connection between the judges and the mission of the organization.

We were soon escorted from the VIP room to the massive, contemporary space where the pageant would take place. The venue usually functioned as a sports and entertainment space at the Mandalay Bay, and it could hold about twelve thousand people. It was quite empty at that point in the evening. The people who were there were dressed in anything from formal evening attire to shorts and sneakers. I felt pretty overdressed as the sparkles on my gown shined under the spotlights. In the distance I could see family members of the contestants proudly holding up their countries' flags in the air. Before we took our seats, someone on the Miss Universe staff said that I had to walk the red carpet since I was a sponsor.

I walked through the wooden doors of the arena onto the red carpet. I could barely open my eyes as the flashing lights came from every direction. I spotted Mr. Trump in front of me and felt sick to my stomach. I realized that I was furious about the comment he had made earlier. I suppose I probably would've thought it just as funny as he did if we'd had a pleasant experience with the organization. Instead, it was like salt in an open wound.

Someone with an earpiece told me to start walking. I turned around and gave Erika a "fuck-my-life" look then slowly made my way toward the red carpet. Somehow all the photographers knew my name. They kept screaming, "Tala! Look here!" "Tala! This way!" I had never been on a red carpet this extravagant before. It was overwhelming.

Interviewers brought their microphones close to my face and fired question after question—"Tell me about your story" and "Talk about the synergy between your line and Miss Universe" and "What has your experience been like with the contestants?"

I kept very calm, polite, and composed. I was politically correct and told them what they wanted to hear. Telemundo and other Spanish networks were more interested in discussing Dar Be Dar's manufacturing process, since the swimwear was made in Colombia. Some interviewers tried to get political. I ignored them.

As I was ushered along the red carpet, I answered as many

questions as I possibly could and posed for a million photos. I wish
I could have enjoyed it, but the only thing going through my head
during those few minutes was Mr. Trump. I could still see him up
ahead of me, looking like a natural on the red carpet. He wore a black
suit and flashed his signature toothy smile. The media was going ber-
serk at the sight of him and Stefanía Fernández walking side by side.

I wondered if Trump knew how we had been treated. I was dying
to go up to him and express what I was feeling. I wanted to know
what he thought, if he knew what had happened to us. I ultimately
decided that the king of real estate wouldn't care. As the flashbulbs
continued to go off around my face, I was told to go back to my seat.

As I headed to our designated VIP seats, I spotted Miss USA
titleholder Rima Fakih's family sitting in the first row. Their enthusiasm was awesome. They didn't stop screaming her name throughout
the entire competition. When she didn't make it to the top fifteen,
they left their seats in tears. It was heartbreaking to see Rima's
mother so sad. All that they had worked for was over in the blink of
an eye. I wished Maman was next to me then.

The pageant was pretty uneventful, and I couldn't wait for it to
be over. It was like watching paint dry. I'm sure it was more fun to
watch on TV, but it was painfully long in person. There was a lot of
waiting around, and throughout the competition, a host mentioned
my story frequently during commercial breaks. Every time he mentioned my name, he asked me to stand up. But I didn't want to. I
wanted to hide under the chair. Finally, he got frustrated and asked
for someone to point me out in the crowd. Erika screamed, "She's
here!" I raised my hand, and the crowd broke into applause.

"This is the moment we have all been waiting for," he said
into the microphone, "the swimsuit competition." I gave a little

wave—and no, not a pageant wave—and he continued on with the show. I have to admit that it was pretty cool to hear Natalie Morales and Bret Michaels announce my sponsorship to the crowd before the ten-second NBC segment showcasing my swimwear was projected on the big screen. I finally had a chance to see how the cheesy video had turned out. *Oh God!* In our humble opinion, it was so bad. Erika and I could only laugh. I would've felt better about it if Pauly D or Mike "The Situation" Sorrentino had starred in the video as well.

Moments before the judges picked the top five, I decided to wish the contestants luck and bid them farewell, since I probably wouldn't see them again. I went backstage and found the women standing strong with big smiles on their faces, even though most of them had just lost on international television. They were still so full of grace. It was beautiful to witness, and for a moment I felt like I was standing next to the pageant girls I'd once admired so much on TV.

I waited backstage with the girls until the top five contestants were announced, then hurried back to my seat for the question-and-answer segment. Despite all the glitz and glamour of the show, I found this to be the most fascinating portion. I empathized with the women. I couldn't imagine how difficult it must be to answer a random question flawlessly in front of billions of viewers. Most of the women did amazingly well, and I enjoyed the questions they were asked.

Judge William Baldwin: What is one big mistake that you have made in your life, and what did you do to make it right?

I wish I had been asked that question onstage. I had the perfect answer: "Good evening, world. Sponsoring the Miss Universe

Pageant was one of the biggest mistakes of my life, and there is nothing I can do to make it right. Thank you, Las Vegas!"

Then it was Miss Australia titleholder Jesinta Campbell's turn. She walked up to the podium in a dramatic, long golden gown.

Judge Niki Taylor: Mine is a tough one... Legislation banning certain kinds of religious clothing has caused controversy around the world. What role should the government play in determining such a personal preference?

Jesinta: One of the greatest things we have is the freedom of choice. And tonight, we wore our swimsuits, which were designed by Tala, who says that "Fashion is Freedom." I don't think the government should have any say in what we wear because we can all make our own personal choices.

I put my hand up to my cheek to find tears of joy streaming down my face. Jesinta had stood onstage, in front of the whole world, and said "Fashion is Freedom." The message I had been working so tirelessly to promote. She probably has no idea the impact that she made on my life at that very moment. All I could think about was the influence my journey had on such a striking young woman. With just two short sentences, she had fulfilled my entire mission.

Erika's mouth dropped. She took my hand, squeezed it very hard, and said, "Oh my God, oh my God, *you did it!*"

On my other side, my brother said proudly, "You are *my* Miss Universe, what a beautiful job you have done."

My friends were all ecstatic. Eric also texted me and said: "Job beautifully done." The feeling of hopelessness that I'd experienced the previous day was slowly fading away. I wouldn't give up. We create our own futures and pave our paths to success. And even though that road is always under construction and there may be obstacles and crashes, there are no limits. Jesinta's answer confirmed for me that I shouldn't pull to the side of the road, but continue at full speed. Every success story leaves a trail behind it, and if I left a mark on even one person, that is a victory on its own.

A few minutes later, Miss Mexico was crowned Miss Universe 2010, and the crowd went crazy. Her family members were crying and screaming, and the Mexican flag was thrown in the air. I was asked to go onstage to take photos with the new titleholder, and in the midst of the mayhem, I stood back and observed the new Miss Universe. She stood at a podium while people and media treated her like a Holy Grail.

It was compelling to see how much power she now had as the sparkly crown settled down onto her beautiful hair. It was like that crown had a mysterious and magical superpower to change her future overnight. I was witnessing the creation of someone who now had the ability to bring positive change to this world. It would give her an opening to make a difference and be a role model for young women everywhere, and that was an extraordinary scene to watch.

And just like that, it was over. The whole time the contestants had been in Vegas, they'd had bodyguards and security protecting them around the clock. But it seemed that as soon as the pageant ended, so did that protection. Aria and I ran into one of the contestants walking out of the venue alone. A stampede of people harassed her, begging to take pictures. She shouted my name loudly to help her. I went into the mob of people to find her, and she apprehensively asked, "Tala, can I please walk with you guys?"

"What happened to your security?" I asked.

"Oh, we are done," she said. "We are on our own now."

I could tell from my brother's face that he was more irate than I was. He held her hand closely and escorted her to the hotel elevator so that she could make her way to her room safely. While I waited for Aria, I saw this scene happen over and over with other contestants. They all had difficulty pushing through the crowd to make it back to their hotel rooms. From what I could see, they seemed incredibly overwhelmed and frightened by the rush of hundreds of people. The contestants were pushed in every direction. It was awful to witness. People even asked to take photos with me, and I wasn't even wearing a sash. It felt like all of a sudden, these women meant nothing anymore. They had been used for photo shoots, marketing, videos, events, and now they had been abandoned. The only person with any power was the one with the crown.

As delighted as I was that the Miss Universe voyage had finally come to an end, I knew that for me this just meant a whole new beginning. More than that, it wasn't the ending or the beginning that I had hoped for. I departed Vegas hoping never to return, but I also wasn't ready to face what was ahead of me in DC. Miss Universe didn't help Dar Be Dar achieve any financial stability, nor did it set me in a direction in terms of what to do next with my mission. I had absolutely no idea what I was going to do next. Everything that happens in your life is preparing you for a moment that is yet to come, but even after all that, I was still desperately searching for a moment of peace.

CHAPTER 33

AFTERMATH AND BREAKDOWN

N ot everyone who walks through darkness makes it out, and that was exactly how I was feeling after the Miss Universe Pageant. I was in desperate need of my mother and a home-cooked meal. Even though she didn't always know the right thing to say, my mother was the only person in the world who could comfort me just by being there. They say that the best kind of people in your life are the ones that you can sit next to, not say a word to, and walk away feeling like that was the best conversation you ever had.

On my way to my mother's, my mind was racing a million miles a minute. Everyone thought that I was the woman behind this successful, inspiring company. But behind that facade, I was crumbling, and it wasn't pretty. I had gone back to work full time at the cosmetics company in order to pay my bills and keep my company afloat. I was falling deeper into depression and was afraid I wouldn't be able to dig myself out.

I had become extremely insecure and hated my body, my hair, and everything about myself. It was hard to even look at myself in the mirror. Every day was a struggle, and I had to start promising myself that I wouldn't wake up every morning crying. I wanted to stay strong and not let down the few people who believed in me, but even the thought of trying to do that gave me more anxiety. I felt like I wasn't smart or talented enough to make my clothing line work. I felt like my dreams would always be just dreams and never become a reality.

Suddenly I found myself, in a daze, parked outside my family's house, staring blankly at the garage door. I don't even remember how I got there. As I walked in and threw my bag on the kitchen counter, *E! News* blared loudly in the background, and the aroma of delicious Persian food reminded me how hungry I was.

I headed straight to the refrigerator to find a quick snack before I fainted. Maman didn't waste any time taking jabs at me. She asked, "Why are you dressed like that? And why do you reek of cigarettes?" I took a deep breath before opening the fridge.

Could I never catch a break? My spirits were low and I wasn't in the mood to make an effort. And, yes, I had been chain smoking because my stress levels were through the roof. How was I not even good enough for my own mother?

I had gotten pretty good at masking my feelings, so she had no idea how low I'd been feeling lately. I never told anyone what really happened with Miss Universe or why I went back to work. I just couldn't bring myself to look anyone in the eyes and talk about failing, both personally and professionally. In Maman's mind, my life was moving in a positive and exciting direction. Little did she know that what appeared to be a career high had actually led to the lowest point in my life.

As she continued to talk about my unfortunate outfit choice, my blood started to boil. My head turned slowly toward her face, and my eyes met hers with so much anger. *Make it stop*, I thought. But I couldn't.

"*Leave me alone!*" I yelled at the top of my lungs. "I want to look like this! Look at *yourself*! I hate this life; I will never be good enough for anyone or anything!"

I said this to the woman who raised me and did everything in her power to give me a better life. How could I disrespect her like this? Tears filled her eyes. I had never seen her look at me that way before. She wasn't scared of me, but she was scared *for* me. I briskly grabbed my bag and continued to yell as I ran out of the house.

My body was convulsing. I could barely inhale a breath. I climbed into my car and sped away as fast as I could. Looking in my rearview mirror at the house, I realized I had forgotten to close the door, and Maman hadn't gone to close it. After driving a block, I slammed on the brakes and pulled over, put my hands over my face, and collapsed on the steering wheel.

What the fuck just happened in there?

I pulled out my cell phone from my purse and stared at it, praying that she would call. But she didn't.

I had poured my heart and soul into my businesses and my mission. And for what? Is there a point where you just have to give up and accept that your dreams are out of reach, or do you continue to push forward? I spent more time avoiding the pain of failure than confronting it. I felt like I was dodging bullets in the middle of a war zone, except it was a pointless battle. I kept getting hit no matter how hard I tried to maneuver around the speed of those damn bullets.

When you try to achieve anything in your life, it can create a mess. The best thing to do is to clean up that mess. Once you start picking up the shattered pieces, you will discover all the magical reasons that got you there. No matter how big or small your mess may be.

So I turned around and drove back to the house to clean my

mess with Maman. The door was still open. I slowly walked back inside the house, not knowing what to expect. Before I could say anything, Maman looked at me and said very calmly, "Your dinner is on the table." She looked relieved that I had returned.

"I'm so sorry. It's just that—"

She cut me off. "What do you want to drink?"

It's okay to fall apart once in a while. We are human, and there is only so much we can take. Maman and I are two completely different women who had taken very different paths in life. And I know that if I ever had a daughter, she would be completely different than me. Maman couldn't understand what I was going through, but I knew she could feel my pain. You don't always have to pretend you are strong, and there is no need to constantly prove that everything is going great when it's not.

I had been racing at the speed of a Ferrari, except that I was out of fuel. I was running on empty, damaging myself and everything I was working on in the process. Sometimes you need to stop, pull over, and refuel. Success is not achieved by speed or out of anger. You need to have a clear mind to see your vision through.

A few months later a friend of mine, James, got in touch with me regarding a pageant called Miss Sinergy that he and a few of his friends were putting together in DC. He didn't have to say another word. The second I heard the word "pageant," I stopped him. Another request for a pageant? I would be out of my mind to agree to attend. But when James asked whether I could donate bikinis toward breast cancer research and deliver a speech for the Miss Sinergy contest, I couldn't bring myself to reject him. How could I say no to people trying to raise money for a good cause?

The event was held at the Swedish embassy, an elegant venue

by the Georgetown Waterfront. I wore a semiformal dress to the black-tie event. There was an assortment of different auction items, including Dar Be Dar bikinis. The guest list was mostly comprised of college students, people working in PR, housewives, and local celebrities. There were also some past Miss Universe titleholders, and of course, Miss Maryland, Miss District of Columbia, and Miss Virginia.

I delivered my speech about women's limited freedom in some parts of the world and what inspired me to start my line. After I stepped down from the podium, a young woman approached me and said, "I just want to say that I am so impressed with everything you have done, and I find you very inspiring." I thanked her, and she continued, "This is the third year in a row that I'm competing to win the Miss Maryland Pageant."

Without thinking, I asked, "Why would you do that?"

She looked at me in shock and replied, "Because it represents world peace."

"No, sweetie," I said in a judgmental tone. "You know what represents world peace? The people who are fighting for their freedom every day. You waving your hand and getting your hair and makeup done so that you can say 'world peace' in front of a camera isn't—" Before I even finished my own sentence, I stopped. I shook my head and said shamefully, "I am *so* sorry. You should do what you want, and that's all that matters. Good luck."

As I walked away, my friend grabbed me and said, "Tala. That was so mean." I knew it was. But I couldn't help myself from lashing out with all my Miss Universe emotional debris.

By this point in my life, I was 100 percent ready to give up. And I did give up after the Miss Universe catastrophe. But when I went back to a nine-to-five life, I realized that it's better to be at the bottom of a staircase you want to climb than at the top of one you don't. Just because your dreams aren't happening to you right now, it doesn't mean they will never happen. Sometimes, things have to go really wrong before they can go right.

It took me some time and a little break to realize all this, but when I did I went back at it full force. Don't get sad, get mad! Get mad enough to find a way to achieve what you really want. I put all my energy into making what seemed so impossible at the time possible for myself. I started fighting for my dreams like I never had before, and now I am living them every day with no regrets. Because if fashion is a form of freedom, so are the choices you make to follow your dreams.

Stand strong, as if all you have is love for this world. Stand strong, as if the sky is the limit and you are going to learn to fly. Stand strong, as if no one is going to hold you back. There is always a chance that you will fall. But as long as there is a chance you will succeed, it's worth going for.

Become more than just successful—become fearless!

ACKNOWLEDGMENTS

I would like to take a moment to acknowledge those who assisted in making this book a reality. From my family and friends who supported me in every manner imaginable, to the investors who believed in my dream, and the partnerships that went wrong but made me stronger. Many are mentioned in great length in this book, but many are not. I thank you all for the unforgettable journey.

A special recognition to my extraordinary Iran for teaching me tradition, culture, and the true meaning of love. Cheers to America for the endless possibilities and opportunities.

To my business mentor, Harry R. Haury, for believing I could do it, and for continuing to support my dreams even at times when they seemed entirely out of reach. Without you I would never be where I am today.

To Michele Shapiro, Abigail Pesta, and Joanna Coles for giving me countless opportunities to give voice to my mission. Your influence and triumphs continue to inspire me every day.

To my remarkable agent, Jessica Regel from Foundry Media, for trusting in this book and enthusiastically helping me find a home for it. To my Sourcebooks family for hearing my voice in the manuscript and giving me a way to share my voyage. To my amazing editors, Grace Menary-Winefield and Shana Drehs, for directing me through this expedition and bringing out my best every day.

To my father for showing me what entrepreneurship looks like in the most effective way. Thank you, Baba, for giving me the most amazing childhood anyone could possibly experience. To my stunning aunt Soodie Maleki for all her support; thank you for showing me what a striking, strong, independent woman looks like in real life. To my brother for loving me unconditionally. Chelsey Orth, you managed to make me smile when my soul was crying. Pamela Woodfield, I could never navigate this path without your support.

And to my beautiful mother: For all the times that you have selflessly been there, for all the times that you taught me to believe, for all the times that you gave me strength, for all the times that you made me value the true definition of love and respect.

You are the strongest woman I will ever know. I thank you for the life you gave me, I thank you for being you, I thank you for putting up with me, I thank you for being my number-one fan, and I thank you for never giving up on me.

You truly are an angel, and I am so powerfully blessed and honored to call you my mother. I love you more than anything in this world. Thank you for believing I could write this book and encouraging me every day to follow my dreams.

My sincere appreciation to everyone who reads this book and all my amazing supporters who wear my designs. I hope to be able to inspire you as much as you inspire me every day.

Much love,

Tala

ABOUT THE AUTHOR

photo © ZVHPhotography.com

Tala Raassi, an Iranian American fashion designer, was born in the United States and raised in Tehran. Named one of the "Most Fearless Women in the World" by *Newsweek*, Raassi made her mark in the fashion world at an early age with her talent in exclusive swimwear. She is devoted to celebrating the beauty of women's bodies through her designs and to empowering women all around the world to follow their dreams. For Raassi, "Fashion is Freedom."

TALA RAASSI

www.talaraassi.com